# Pra
## Starting to Frame

" ' S tarting to frame' is the favourite expression Roger Gordon's father used for 'getting your act together'. It is a perfect title for this memoir, as Gordon, a scientist and retired academic, shows his story-telling skills and courage in starting to frame his memories of growing up in a troubled family in Sheffield in the 50s and 60s. The reader gains insights along with the author, as he recognizes that compassion and forgiveness are necessary for personal healing to occur, making Starting to Frame a riveting and unforgettable read."

—DIANNE HICKS MORROW,
PEI Poet Laureate,
author of *What Really Happened Is This*,
2012 PEI Book Award winner

" W hen a memoir author allows us into the intimacy of their memories, it is always a privilege. When they take us into a richly remembered world, it is a tender joy. In *Starting to Frame*, Roger Gordon brings to life the language and social mores of 1950s Sheffield and 1960s England through the eyes of a boy in a disordered family. He grows to be a man of appreciative wit, forthright narration, and probing insight into family dynamics, mental health, and how parents' choices and social norms can shape identity—positively, negatively, or forgivably."

—JANE LEDWELL,
author of *Last Tomato*

# STARTING TO FRAME

*—a memoir*

## ROGER GORDON

DogsBody Books

Edited by Christine Gordon Manley, Manley Mann Media,
with early editorial advice from Jane Ledwell.
Book design and layout by Valerie Bellamy.
www.dog-earbookdesign.com
Photo "Sheffield Tram's Last Day" © Sheffield Newspapers Limited,
used with permission.

To respect the privacy of individuals mentioned in this book and with due regard to their descendants, I have used pseudonyms for many of the characters. There are no fictional characters. All are or were real people and the storyline and themes have not been altered by adopting this measure. The details of events and dialogues accompanying them are "to the best of my recollection." Reconstructed dialogues are not meant to be taken as verbatim.

ISBN-10: 0993673207
ISBN-13: 978-0993673207

Published by DogsBody Books,
Stratford, Prince Edward Island, Canada
Printed in the USA

Library and Archives Canada Cataloguing in Publication

Gordon, Roger, 1943-, author
    Starting to frame : a memoir / Roger Gordon.

Issued in print and electronic formats.
ISBN 978-0-9936732-0-7 (pbk.).--ISBN 978-0-9936732-1-4 (epub)

    1. Gordon, Roger, 1943-. 2. Gordon, Roger, 1943- --Family.
3. Families--Mental health.  I. Title.

PS8613.O73275S72 2014          C818'.6          C2014-904724-X
                                                C2014-904725-8

# DEDICATION

*I dedicate this book to all those caught in the throes of
family discord and to those suffering from mental illness.*

*Specifically, I dedicate the book to family members,
past and present, in Sheffield, England, and to all three
generations of my family in Canada.*

*To my wife, Alison, thank you for all your understanding,
support, and love.*

"A family is a place where minds come in contact with one another. If these minds love one another the home will be as beautiful as a flower garden. But if these minds get out of harmony with one another it is like a storm that plays havoc with the garden."

—BUDDHA

# CONTENTS

*Prologue* ........................................................ *11*

## PART I: EARLY CHILDHOOD (1943–1954)

*Talbot Place* ................................................ *19*

*Manor Lane* .................................................. *50*

*The Stradbroke* ............................................. *63*

*Woodhouse West* ............................................ *79*

*Other Grandma* ............................................. *94*

*Unsettling Times* ......................................... *107*

*Some turbulence* .......................................... *115*

## PART II: ADOLESCENT YEARS (1954–1961)

*High Storrs* ................................................. *127*

*Stormy Weekends* .......................................... *140*

*Gas Meets Water* .......................................... *149*

*House Rules* ................................................ *161*

*Car Rides* ................................................... *173*

*School Rules* ................................................ *185*

*Recreation* .................................................. *202*

*Didn't Frame* ............................................... *210*

*Breaking Point* ............................................. *214*

*Taking Sides* ................................................ *223*

*Fallout* ................................................ *241*

*Transitions* ............................................. *251*

## PART III: UNIVERSITY YEARS (1961–1969)

*First Term* .............................................. *263*

*Fierce Gale* ............................................. *270*

*Adjustments* ............................................ *280*

*Tin Lizzie* .............................................. *287*

*Persona Non Grata* ...................................... *293*

*Flying The Coop* ........................................ *302*

*Coming Unhinged* ........................................ *315*

*Plodding Along* ......................................... *320*

*Heartbreaks* ............................................ *331*

*Nervous Breakdowns* ..................................... *337*

## PART IV: CANADA (1969–2011)

*Catching A Break* ....................................... *349*

*Cardboard Boxes* ........................................ *353*

*Epilogue* ............................................... *392*

*Glossary* ............................................... *395*

*Acknowledgements* ....................................... *399*

*About the Author* ....................................... *402*

# PROLOGUE

The evening air is still and damp, dull and overcast, the approaching sunset indiscernible. I stand outside the front door of this unremarkable-looking home. Brick, semi-detached, it is a carbon copy of every other home in the Stradbroke estate, straddling the once proud steel city of Sheffield, England. Mile upon mile of similar titled streets, roads, drives, avenues, crescents, closes, and places, each one sporting concrete pavements and asphalted roadways— monotony runs amok in the layout and design of a British corporation estate.[1] Yet, this home, 23 Smelter Wood Way, draws me near. I want to go inside. My heart racing, I ring the doorbell. A middle-aged man answers the door. A nondescript-looking kind of bloke, thin on top, with a paunch to fill in the space between the bottom of his T–shirt and the waistband of his jeans. A working man. "What's tha want?" he asks.

I tell the man that I grew up in this house many years ago; my family was its first occupant, and since then, I immigrated to Canada. I then ask him if he would allow me to come inside, have a look around.

"S'ppose that'll be oreight," he says, stroking the stubble on his chin, puzzled. "Come in ter t'kitchen an' 'ave a cup er tea."

The front porch has been enlarged. In fact, one whole side of the house has been expanded to allow for extra rooms upstairs. I walk into the kitchen and look around. It hasn't changed much at all. The man introduces me to his wife, who is the female counterpart of him. Her salt and pepper coloured hair is tied in a bun at the back of her head, an apron emblazoned with the Union Jack covers her pear–shaped frame. A busy housewife.

The three of us sit around the old, wooden kitchen table. The table of my childhood—legs and trim painted bright yellow, the result of one of my mother's frenzied episodes of creativity. The chairs are two-tone red and yellow. Glossy oil paint—it lasts forever. I start to tell the couple about the neighbourhood as it used to be back in the fifties—the "hollow" with the stream running through it where my brother and I used to play; "Smelter Wood," where we used to swing from the trees and hide from an imaginary gang called the "Wenlocks"; the "Green Hill" at the top of the street where, as a teenager, I sneaked my first cigarette. I leave out the bad times, the ones that have left wounds. They listen, but say nothing. The nodding of their heads is the only indication that I have their attention.

Then, I rise from my chair, walk toward the back door,

and run my hands over it, transfixed. I feel every square inch, every surface irregularity.

"What are tha doin' that for?" the man asks, breaking the silence.

I answer him in an evasive manner, not wanting to delve into the unsavoury details. In fact, I am looking for evidence of the four holes that the table fork left in the door when my mother hurled it at my father. It just missed Dad's head, but it stuck like a dart in the door, leaving four neatly spaced holes, mementos of my mother's unbridled outbursts.

I can just see where the holes have been filled in with wood putty. Scars like that never completely vanish.

I ask the couple if I could look around upstairs, aware that such a request must sound odd to them. "No, love. That'll be oreight," says the woman of the house. "Don't mind t'bedrooms bein' in a mess. Ampt 'ad time ter tidy 'em."

She and I walk up the stairs, pause on the landing, and then open the bathroom door. The old toilet is still there, complete with its pull chain hanging down from the overhead cistern. Pull that chain and the swishing of water down pipes hidden behind the walls can be heard all over the house. The bathtub and the sink, 1950s-style white porcelain set, look a little worse for wear, but they're still there. Globs of bright blue toothpaste are daubed on the sink; a cake of green soap sits on a mushy mess of sticky goo beside the taps.

I peer into the adjacent bedroom, which overlooks the back of the house. It's just as I remember it. The head of the single bed sits centrally positioned against the wall furthest from the doorway. Surely, the blue candlewick bedspread can't have survived all these years, but indeed it has. In one corner of the room, there's the bureau with the drop-down lid that Mum and Dad bought me for passing my eleven-plus exams. Its darkly stained wood polished to perfection, it looks a gem. In the other corner, there's the wardrobe where I used to hang my clothes. The memories come flooding back and I stand there for what must seem like an eternity to the lady in the apron. I can see myself sitting on that bed playing my trumpet, hunkering down over the bureau doing my homework, waking up on Christmas morning to see the pillowcase left by Father Christmas at the bottom of the bed. Then, I start to remember a darker side to that room.

"Are tha oreight, luv?" the woman asks. "Want ter see any other rooms?"

I tell her that I've seen quite enough, but I ask her about the extension that has been built on the side of the house. I can see a bright light coming from it.

Before she can answer, I awake. I lay there, as always, troubled and perplexed. I try and go back to sleep, but I can't. So, I climb out of bed and put on the coffee pot.

I am haunted by that same recurring dream. There may be different supporting actors involved, varying scenarios played out, but I always wind up going into my childhood home. I am being brought back to my past, the part of it that I have tried to set aside all these years.

---

1    or "public housing," as it is called in North America.

# Part I: Early Childhood (1943–1954)

# Talbot Place

My mother, Nellie Gordon (nee Bonsall), was hospitalized prior to my birth because she had miscarried a set of twins two years previously. The father of those twins, a topic of gossip, was probably not my father who was elsewhere, doing his bit to help the war effort on an RAF base. In any event, my father came to the rescue and married my mother when the mysterious and unwanted pregnancy came to light and my subsequent birth was entirely legitimate, to coin the vernacular of the day.

I was a war baby. The birth announcement in the local daily, the *Sheffield Star*, two days later was simple enough: *Gordon – On April 17th at the City General to Nellie (nee Bonsall) and John, Flt. Sgt. R.A.F., a son (Roger).* An uncomplicated delivery. Quite a contrast from the complicated and troubled world into which I was born.

The war was raging on all fronts. The R.A.F. had taken heavy losses in its bombing raids on armament factories in Czechoslovakia and the Rhineland. Allied forces were taking Tunisia, and the Russians were forcing the Germans to retreat on the Eastern Front in Kuban. Then, on the eve of my birth, in the very city where I was born, a gale with wind gusts of seventy miles an hour had caused chimney pots and slates to take to the air and windows to be blown in. Yes, like many other war babies, I was born into a world of chaos, strife, and hardship. Yet, I believe that like many other families, we defied the world at large and found peace, happiness, and a measure of fulfilment at the time of my birth and in the few post-war years that followed.

My father, John Patrick O'Callaghan Gordon, was given weekend leave from his base at Dishforth in the Yorkshire Dales, a distance of fifty miles or so away from Sheffield. In later life, he told me with pride that he had come home to see me. In wartime England, travel by rail would have been hectic and memorable. While Dad was stationed on base, Mum and I lived with Grandma and Granddad Bonsall, my mother's parents. We were a three-generational family of four, at 3 Talbot Place, a Victorian era, two-story semi that my grandparents rented. It sat in a grubby, working-class area of Sheffield incongruously titled the Park district, a fifteen-minute walk from the city centre. Like all the other homes on the street, it was of sandstone construction on the front and red brick on the sides and rear. As a baby, I spent many a night in the damp, cold cellar of my grandparents' home, wrapped in a shawl, hidden away from the bombs that rained down on the steel city. Underground tunnels to those of neighbouring homes linked that cellar and, when the bombs were falling, everyone would gather in my grandparents' cellar seeking strength from the camaraderie.

The war ended on September 2, 1945. Exactly four months later on January 2, 1946, Dad was de-mobbed and he came home to Talbot Place. Though the three of us had ample sleeping accommodations on the second storey, our daytime living quarters consisted of a mouse-infested downstairs room—the Gordon Quarters. A twelve by twelve room with hard, cracked linoleum flooring, a peephole-sized sash window that looked into the back yard, and barely any furniture. A drop-leaf table, four rickety table chairs, two easy chairs that had springs and stuffing protruding out of them, and a small table that may euphemistically be referred to as an "occasional" one, realistically described as thrift-store variety. However, on that table, sat the pièce de résistance of the furniture ensemble—a Sobell® radio, or wireless as we called it back then.

All downstairs rooms in that house had fireplaces. Ours was a fireplace without a fire, as coal was in short supply and the chimney hadn't been serviced for many years. Still, we would spend many evenings clustered around a small electric heater placed in the fireplace, listening to the BBC news, a hastily slapped together mystery play, or a corny comedy show. My favourite comedians were Arthur Askey, Ben Warriss, and Jimmy Jewel, and later on, a ventriloquist called Peter Brough, who appeared with his dummy, Archie Andrews, on a show called *Educating Archie*. Strange that a performer whose skills can only be appreciated by viewing should be so popular on radio.

At first, there was the three of us. Then, when I was nearing three, in January 1946, my brother Trevor was born. As toddlers and infants, we would sit on the small scatter rug in front of the fire, while Mum and Dad braved the discomfort of the inaptly named "easy chairs." Even the mice provided comic relief from our bare bones existence. One night, Dad came home with a neighbour's cat, one that had a reputation as a good mouser. We all stayed downstairs into the early hours of the morning, listening to him pounce on mouse after mouse, pissing in his litter tray in between catches, and Dad delivering the coup de grâce to each trembling little perisher that had become Mr. Moggie's play toy. "They're comin' from t'chimney," exclaimed Dad.

Eventually, the three of us left the ammonia-impregnated room to Dad and the cat and trooped upstairs to bed. In the morning, Dad proudly gave us the score—one that was in the double digits.

Considered rationally, that room did not have a lot going for it. It offered cramped, impoverished conditions, with rodents thrown in for good measure. To us, though, it was home.

But even a home can be confining, and there was one occasion when I wanted to escape from the room so desperately that I injured myself in the process. It was November 5, 1949–Bonfire Night.[2] I was six years old and, alas, confined to the house with chickenpox. The rest of the family, grandparents and aunts included, lit a bonfire in the backyard and began setting off fireworks. I became so excited watching the action from inside the room that I put my head through the window, shattering the glass pane and causing a huge gash in my chin. Luckily, on Bonfire Night in those days, general practitioners were ready to respond to whatever emergencies came their way. Dad hurried along to the end of the street to Dr. Alex Hart's medical clinic. The dependable Scotsman was back at our house in no time, his magic leather case in one hand, and a cigarette in the other. He laid me out on the drop leaf table and stitched up my bloody, shard-embedded chin right on the spot. The scar is still there.

As kids, we had the run of the house. We would spend a lot of time with Grandma and Granddad Bonsall, who used a room at the back of the house leading at one end to the cellar and at the other end to the kitchen and backyard. My Granddad, John Willie Bonsall, was a wonderful man. A colossus at 5 ft, 10 in and in the neighbourhood of 22 stone.[3] Stout. Rotund. A down-to-earth carter by trade, he used his horse and cart to transport materials around the steelworks. A man who, aside from the occasion expostulation (a "Gio'er," "Sithee," or "I'll go ter foot er our stairs"), only spoke when he had something useful to say.

"I'm thinkin' er gettin' some blue streaks put in me 'air," says Grandma.

"Gio'er. Don't be ser daft," retorts Granddad.

"It says in t'paper that Mrs. Frith's store's been broken into," says Mum.

"Sithee. Things 'ave gone ter t'dogs."

"Our Roger's doin' ever so well at t'school. 'E came top er t'class in 'rithmetic today," Mum proudly announces.

"Wey, I'll go ter foot er our stairs,[4]" adds the old man, with an astounded expression on his face.

With his bald pate at one end of his body and his ever present "braan boots" at the other end, he could have passed for a character right out of a Dickens novel. A less affluent, but no less jovial, Samuel Pickwick, or a loyal and dependable Bob Crachit without his accountant's pen. I spent hours sitting on his ample knees and paunch, while he amused me by jiggling his false teeth around. When I was sad or upset, he'd stick his fat thumb in front of my face and chortle: "Sithee. If tha can't find owt ter laugh abart, laugh at that."

It never failed. I would soon be in convulsions. Anyone else could have done that trick and it would have left me cold. But there was just something about Granddad that connected with those around him. Overall good nature, sense of humour, sincerity, and common sense—he had it all in spades, just like every member of the Bonsall stock before him. My great-grandfather, William Bonsall, was also a carter who made a living out of collecting and selling horse manure to farmers, but he always dressed to the nines when out in public. His better half, my great-grandmother Rosa, was by all accounts a fun loving woman, whose youthful exploits included an incident in which she laced the baptismal font at the local St. John's Church with Rickett's Blue Dye. She was the only family member of her generation who was literate, so filmgoers would crowd around her at the Norfolk Picture Palace while she read out the subtitles on the silent films.

My Grandma, Mary Anne Bonsall (nee Spotswood), was a different kettle of fish from her husband. A short, bespectacled, woman of middling appearance, she would not have stood out in a crowd. Her personality was more complex than that of my Granddad. Talkative, often gossipy, she would sometimes interrupt her speech with long periods of near silence when she would whistle through her teeth to make a hissing sound as she twiddled her thumbs. This was a sure sign that something or someone was upsetting her. She was prone to playing favourites. I was favoured over my brother, while my mother was favoured over everyone on the planet. But, she also had a kind and caring side to her. At a time when Mum and Dad were skint, not a penny to rub together, she bought us gifts, took us to the pictures, and arranged day trips to the seaside for us. I remember how, without warning, she would grab hold of me, lift me into her arms and prance around the room singing "You Are My Sunshine," or while I was sitting, appear in front of me, and kick up her legs as she sang "Knees Up Mother Brown."

The duality of her character probably stems from her parentage. Her mother, my great grandmother Rachael (nee Clancy), was a hard woman who did not spare the rod, or in her case the horsewhip, in bringing up young Mary Anne. She knew no different. When Rachael was a child, her mother, my great-great-grandmother, beat her so badly that she was blinded and disfigured in one eye and forced to wear a patch over it. My great-great-grandmother's name may have been Patsy, but I have been unable to confirm this. In any event, "Patsy" and daughter Rachael fled the unrest in County Cork, Ireland, where my great-great-grandfather had been killed in a skirmish. If, indeed, my grandmother inherited the darker side of her character from her mother, she must have acquired the warm, generous side of it from her father, my great-grandfather George Spotswood, who was an amiable, loveable linesman on the railway. He died in 1915 at the age of forty-eight. Rachael survived him by a further thirty years.

That back room where Grandma and Granddad spent their days was a gathering place for relatives, friends, and drop-ins. Granddad gave them all nicknames. His daughter Rose (Mum's sister) was titled "Buddy" after a rose bud, or "Flats," because she lived with her husband Carl in one of the flats in a block known as Embassy Court on nearby Duke Street. The Buddy nickname became so entrenched that Trevor and I always called her "Aunty Buddy." Enigmatically, Granddad's brother Bill, who was his spitting image and seemed to lead a very comfortable lifestyle, was called "Poor Bill." Then, there was my grandmother's brother, my great-Uncle Walter, who somehow or other earned the title "Clever Walter." My mother was referred to as "Mag," because when she was a child, she chatted a mile a minute; the old Sheffield term for chatting was "magging." Even Mrs. Paynter from along the street who stopped by to do some house cleaning was given an alias— "Paint Pot." Of course, since most of these nicknames could be taken as uncomplimentary or mildly condescending, they were rarely used in front of the person concerned. With one exception—my Grandma, whom he would endearingly refer to as "Gus," again a puzzle, or "t'old en," meaning the old hen.

Only my Granddad could get away with this kind of razzing. His overall good nature allowed him to carry it off. Two of his offspring escaped this banter. His eldest daughter Rachel, my Aunt Ray, was "Our Ray." Likewise his son Johnny was "Our Johnny." In Sheffield, the possessive adjective preceded the name of everybody and everything remotely connected to the family, so even the family dog was "Our" Topsy.

There wasn't a day went by when one or more relatives or friends of my grandparents didn't drop in for a visit, the most frequent being my two aunts, Buddy and Ray. Sometimes, my grandparents' old chums would drop in and I would be encouraged to refer to them as "Aunty" or "Uncle" so and so. Even the milkman stopped in for a cooked breakfast every morning and Mr. George Gamble, an unfortunate surname for an insurance man, stopped by for a cooked tea on Friday nights. Providing for those meals must have been difficult in those early post-war years of food rationing. The eggs were no problem because Granddad reared hens, a practice that was then allowed. I have no idea how he managed to come up with the bacon and bread though.

My Granddad was a cook in a prisoner-of-war camp in WW 1 and knew a thing or two about cooking. Plain, simple, but delicious cooking. Eggs, bacon, and black pudding. Roast beef and Yorkshire pudding. Meat and potato pie. Rabbit stew. Nothing fancy. Always tasty. We would sometimes have to look the other way though as his own palate was a little too earthy for the rest of us. While we would be munching away on pork pie, ham slices, and salad, he would tuck into a plate of pickled pigs' trotters, chitterling bag,[5] or a bowl of tripe[6] and onions.

The back room, the gathering place, was dominated by a dining table that consumed most of its area. Though the room was ample-sized, so was the table, so one had to squeeze by the sofa and chairs that surrounded it. It was the only room in the house with a fireplace that was functional day in and day out. How my grandparents managed to work their way around the coal rationing and shortages caused by the ever-present miners' strikes is as puzzling to me as the better-than-average food they were able to lay on the table. In any event, they took that old World War I song "Keep the Home Fires

Burning" literally, and even on hot summer days, that old cast iron, black-leaded fireplace was stoked with brightly burning nutty slack. The fire had a hypnotic effect. Looking into the red, orange, and yellow crevices between the burning coal nuggets, I could see dragons' dens intermingled with places of warm serenity. Alarm and calm.

The back room was connected by a small set of descending stairs to the kitchen, which at ground level had a stone floor. Considering its multipurpose function, it was a narrow and congested room. It was where non-perishable food was kept, cooking was done, and laundry was washed using an old-fashioned washing tub, dolly posher, rubbing board, and mangle. The kitchen door led into the backyard. Now, there was an interesting place. Separated from the houses on either side by towering brick walls, it was a narrow strip of terrain with little actual garden that led through a large back gate to the narrow, cobbled street behind called Talbot Gardens. Yet, it contained a chicken coop, a coal shed, an outdoor toilet, and a large barn-like structure with multi-pane, old-style glass windows at either end of it. I later learned that this building in its heyday used to be the Registry Office for Births, Marriages, and Deaths for the Park District of Sheffield. The previous occupant of 3 Talbot Place was Mr. Frank Fulford, the district Registrar. As kids, we used the "barn" as a den, a gathering place for our friends. The outdoor toilet was never used, as there was a flush toilet indoors. The chicken coop contained a dozen or so hens, which provided us with all the eggs that we needed.

~~~

One day, when I was a youngster of six or seven, Granddad sauntered into the Gordon Quarters and plonked a cardboard crate on the floor. "Sithee, look at t'little chickens. Tha'll be able ter watch 'em grow inter big 'ens," he said to my brother and me.

Chirp. Chirp. Chirp. The box was full of fluffy little chirpers, which we excitedly touched, stroked, and picked up. Granddad has just come back from Ogley's, the animal barn at the old rag and tag market, where he believed he had got a bargain. Two dozen more egg layers in four or five month's time. We watched them grow, shed their down feathers, grow necks and legs and beaks and all the paraphernalia that goes with the beaks. But not a single egg was ever laid. "Abart time them 'ens started layin' some eggs," grumbled Granddad.

Then, one morning, the chorus started. "Cock a doodle doo." Two dozen cock a doodle doos, out of synchrony, so it sounded like one continuous cock a doodle doo. The whole neighbourhood was awakened. As we gathered around the chicken coop in our pyjamas and nightgowns, Granddad let out a big guffaw. "They sold me two dozen chuffin' roosters. Look at them big red combs on top er their 'eads. I should 'ave realized before now. They'll not be laying any eggs."

But they did provide relatives and neighbours with chicken

for the oven, as Granddad fed them up, then slaughtered and plucked them. "They really do run around when yer chop off their 'eads," he announced after the deadly deed was done.

The coop was a two-room affair. There was a six by six strutting and scratching area, bare earth surrounded by a chicken mesh fence. This led into an equally small brick room, with shelving for roosting hens to perch upon. The entire floor, as well as the shelves, was covered with straw. Trevor and I thought those hens looked so comfortable on those shelves.

"Let's join t'ens on t'shelves an' make it our den," I say to my brother Trevor one day.

So, we perch for a while on one of the shelves, rudely displacing the hens that cluck their disapproval.

When we return to the house, Mum takes one look at us and shrieks, "What's all that straw doin' all o'er yer both?"

"Just been in t'en 'ouse Mum. Smashin' place for a den."

"Let me take a closer look at yer. I can see summat movin' in yer 'air."

As she starts to poke through our hair, her shrieks grow louder. "Yer bloody 'air's full er lice an' nits. I can see 'em jumpin'. Yer stupid buggers. Yer've caught 'em from t'ens. Yer shun't er been in theree."

After the usual spanking of the bottoms, a ritual in those days, we were both marched to Frith's corner store at the end of the street and told to wait outside. "No use spreadin' 'em," announces Mum.

We can hear some of the banter going on inside between Mrs. Frith and Mum.

"Chuffin' den. Covered in straw an' bloody nits. Ooo. Little buggers."

"I'll get thee some carbolic soap, Nell. That should work."

Armed with bottles of vinegar, a large block of pungent carbolic soap, and a menacing looking metal comb with fine teeth, Mum marches us to the bathtub. "Bend o'er t' tub, both er yer." First the vinegar. Then the carbolic soap. Scrub. Scour. Comb. Over and over. Mum's knuckles chafing away at our scalps. Then, after an hour or so of this, she announces the treatment to be over. "Can't see any moore er t'buggers."

But, just to be sure, we have to endure this ordeal nightly for two or three days afterwards. "That'll teach yer."

It did.

During those early post-war years, Dad worked as an electrician. Mum had given up her office job at Wheatley and Bates, a downtown brewery, to look after Trevor and me.

In the summer of 1947, when I was a four-year-old toddler and Trevor a baby barely six months old, Dad contracted polio. The four of us were on holiday at Cayton Bay near Scarborough when Dad came down with a fever, started vomiting, and complained of soreness in his back and shoulders. We left the cabin behind and headed back to Sheffield on the train.

I vividly remember waiting with Mum by the gates of Lodge Moor Hospital on the outskirts of the city. Dad is walking down the long driveway from the hospital toward us, his arm in a sling and enclosed in a wire cage. The three of us walk down Lodge Moor Road past the Italian Prisoner of War Camp and then turn off into a picturesque valley, threaded by a meandering stream known as Wyming Brook. We walk along Wyming Brook through the woodland, eventually finding ourselves at the Rivelin Dams—major water sources for the city of Sheffield. On we walk along Manchester Road until, finally, we arrive at a fork in the road. Mum kisses Dad goodbye as he heads up Rivelin Valley Road to King Edward Hospital, where he is to continue his treatment. Mum and I catch the bus into town from the bus stop by the old post office on Manchester Road. That bus stop and post office is still there, as are the buildings for the two hospitals—now apartment complexes. My wife and I took that same walk in 2009. It took us two hours. In 1947, two adults and a toddler thought nothing of it.

"When's Dad comin' 'ome?" I remember asking Mum.

"Soon."

Dad was one of the luckier polio victims. The illness left him with a slight slump in his left shoulder. It could have been much worse.

There was general acknowledgement that Dad had contracted polio while he was wiring a home in which unsanitary conditions prevailed. In any event, his illness behind him, he decided to take up a white-collar job as a sales representative for an electrical parts company, Hallamshire Electric. He exchanged the boiler suit for a briefcase—an improvement in working conditions, if not in wages. Six or seven pounds a week, at a rough guess. In March 1949, the Ministry of Labour boasted, "the average industrial workman is earning exactly twice as much as he did ten years ago."[7] The average weekly wage had risen to 6 pounds 17 shillings and 11 pence.[8] Even accounting for inflation, that was a paltry sum by today's standards. Still, we were a happy, contented family unit back then, meagre resources and all.

When both Trevor and I were at Manor Lane School, Mum took a part-time day job as a housemaid at the estate of a doctor who lived nearby. Mum and Dad's combined wages, together with the obligatory government-issued ration book, added up to slim pickings though. At Christmas time, simple gifts met the needs of simple times: a snakes and ladders set; a roll the dice, move the plastic cars around the track board game; blow football; a Meccano® kit; a model farmyard with tiny Plaster of Paris farm animals; a Beano comic annual; crayons. For amusement, we played simple outdoor games with friends from the neighbourhood: piggy in the middle or games of tag and hide and seek, making full use of the Alms Houses, an early nineteenth-century senior-citizens complex at the end of Talbot Place. Built originally for retired poor people, the community consisted of several acres of sandstone Gothic-style houses with copious flowerbeds that were filled with rhododendron bushes—lots of great hiding places. We would often stray from the Alms Houses across Norfolk Road into the nearby cholera grounds, a landscaped area that contained a monument in remembrance of the victims of the Sheffield cholera epidemic of 1832. It, too, contained many bushes to hide in. We were frequently chased out of these areas by the maintenance staff, but that all added to the fun. Marbles and conkers[9] on the street or in the schoolyard. Cricket, makeshift games of football, roundabouts, slides and swings in Norfolk Park— one of my favourite play areas, consisting of a vast expanse of rolling grasslands, shrubs, woodlands, and tree-lined avenues. It used to be the country estate of the Duke of Norfolk who donated it to the city back in the mid–nineteenth century.

Once a year, during the last week of July, there was a fair. The four of us would march along together, a fifteen-minute walk from Talbot Place to the tent city that had sprung up on a piece of land known as the Farm Grounds, near the bottom of Granville Road. Coconut stands, games of chance, carousels, bumper cars, a haunted house, a miniature railway, pony rides, rides designed to turn your stomach inside out—perfect entertainment for young families such as ours. There was a boxing ring where those who thought they could strut their stuff could try their luck against the fair champion. On the milder side, there were dancing displays put on by Sheffield's dancing schools, as well as tents that contained a fat man, a fat woman, a woman with a beard, and a man with breasts. Ice cream, candyfloss, toffee apples, and a smell of burning sugar permeated the air. Courting couples walked arm-in-arm, many of the men in military uniform as national service was still in effect. One year, an aerial fly-by of spitfires was featured.

The hawkers were always in full throttle, as we would amble by the various concessions.

"Eyup luv. Best coconut shy tha'll ever see. Would tha like ter see me coconuts? Tha can 'ave a go at 'em if tha likes. Thrupence a try. Oh, I got a luvely bunch er coconuts. There they are all sittin'..."

"Now then mister. Would tha like ter tek thee missis in t'aunted 'ouse? No tellin' what goes on in there. I can see a twinkle in 'er eye. What's tha say? Tha't too old for owt like that? Come 'ere me luv, I'll tek thee in misen."

"Look at all these lasses 'oldin' prizes, Pat," Mum would say. "Big teddy bears, dolls, stuffed animals, balloons on ribbons. 'Ow come tha never wins me owt?"

Poor Dad, who was always referred to as "Pat," after his middle name, Patrick, would try his best, but he had the worst luck. He'd always get the consolation prize for those who failed to knock over a coconut, pierce a playing card with a dart, or shoot down a cardboard duck with a pellet gun. A plastic ring like you'd find in a Christmas cracker, a colouring pencil, a paper hat, and a horn with a bulb on the end of it that made a honking noise when it was squeezed. Maybe a goldfish, which Mum promptly declined. We all went home to number 3 as happy as bugs in a rug.

Mum and Dad didn't have enough money to be able to take us places on a regular basis, although Dad took me once to Hillsboro to watch a Sheffield Wednesday game. It was April 1950. Sheffield Wednesday, "the Owls," were playing Coventry City, "the Sky Blues." It was a key game because our lads were in the running for promotion from Division 2 to the First Division. It was a packed stadium of over 44,000 people and the tension was high. Dad and I stood alongside one another, pinned by a crash barrier behind one of the goals on the Spion Kop. Exposed to the elements, it was open-air standing in that part of the stadium. Men stood shoulder-to-shoulder and I was cramped in among them. Dad told me that an acquaintance of his had once had his coat pocket filled with piss, courtesy of the man who was standing next to him. I kept looking around, making sure nobody like that was near me. At my height, it wasn't my pockets that would be vulnerable. Now and again, Dad would lift me up so I could see over the many silhouettes that were blocking my view. Several times during the game, I was able to see the same scene unfolding—the play had stopped as a player lay on the pitch injured, clutching his legs or groin. No such things as substitute players back then. A man ran out onto the pitch with a wet sponge and gave him the once over with it. The supposedly crippled player then stood up and got back into the game. A miracle.

"Is 'e 'urt, Dad?"

"No. Magic sponge, that," replied Dad, smirking broadly.

For the entire first half, groans from the crowd permeated the air as Wednesday had the jitters. Then, just before half time, a chorus of "Oh, shit," "Bloody 'ell," and "What are tha playin' at, Gannon" rang out as the Coventry defence man George Allen put one in the net by Wednesday goalkeeper Dave McIntosh.

At half time, a brass band was the featured entertainment. I remember having to use the communal urinal and finding it strange that a bunch of men would line up against a wall and piss in unison. I felt a bit intimidated. Just after half time, the mood suddenly changed when Wednesday forward, Hugh McJarrow, headed one in from a well-judged corner kick. I knew Wednesday had scored when the roar went up from the crowd and people started twirling their blue and white wooden rattles, an accessory no longer used by today's more raucous spectators. The jeering suddenly changed to cheering. "Come on lads!" "Tha't playin' a blinder[10], Marriott." The game, what I could see of it, ended in a 1-1 draw and after the whistle blew, I was carried along out of the stadium, my feet not touching the ground, by the phalanx of spectators. Wednesday went on that season to gain promotion at the expense of their arch rivals Sheffield United, "the Blades," on the basis of a 0.008 better goal average. Although it turned out to be a squeaker, the Owls were certainly determined to do the job that season as they even tried to sign Sheffield United's brilliant forward and team captain Jimmy Hagan. Had that deal gone through, civil war between the fans of the two teams would surely have erupted.

~~~

Both aunts, Ray and Buddy, had childless marriages, so they showered their generousity upon Trevor and myself, taking us to places that Mum and Dad couldn't afford. For me, it was those memorable evenings at the speedway at Owlerton stadium, cheering on the Sheffield Tigers. Stan and Len Williams, Tommy Allott, and all the other greats. Dragging their legs on the track as they rounded the corners. The smell of burning rubber and oil, like incense, Aunt Bud and Uncle Carl chain smoking next to me. To top off the night, sitting around the table in our room at number 3, the gang of us, eating fish and chips, Aunt Bud and Uncle Carl filling Mum, Dad, and Trevor in on the night's events.

Aunt Bud once took me to watch a cricket game at Bramall Lane. From where we were sitting, I could see matchstick-sized men decked in white throwing a ball, occasionally hitting it, less often shouting, "Howzat."

"Who won t'game?" I asked Aunt Bud on the way home.

"Don't know love. There's three more days left to play."

A game that spans several days. You don't know who's won after watching it all day? Not much of a spectator sport, I think. But I did enjoy those fresh fried donuts.

Aunt Ray or Grandma and Granddad often put on Sunday day trips to the seaside at short notice. We'd line up on Snig Hill in the city centre for a Sheffield United bus company "charra," short for charabanc or coach. Skegness ("Skeggie"), Bridlington ("Brid"), or Cleethorpes ("Clee on a Donk") were the most popular destinations. My Granddad, supreme composer of nicknames, came up with the Clee on a Donk moniker to capture the common experience of riding on a donkey on the beach.

The day at the beach was standard fare. Rain or shine, deck chairs facing the sea, which in Cleethorpe's case could be a long way off as it is estuarine and at low tide there are miles of beach to cross just to get to the sea. Grandma and Granddad, like everyone in those days, dressed up for the beach. Granddad would loosen the laces on his brown boots, slip his raincoat and suit jacket over the back of the candy-striped deck chair, and roll up his shirt sleeves—small concessions to informality. His wide-brimmed Homburg would stay atop his crown, his waistcoat hugging his stiff collared shirt. If he felt really adventurous, he might detach the stiff collar and let some air in. Except for taking off the raincoat, Grandma would stay in formal attire—bonnet, cameo brooch around her neck (with earrings to match), woollen top and long skirt, heavy-duty nylon stockings, and black polished

shoes. Even Trevor and I would start off with collars and ties.
After the customary building of sand pies and sandcastles, bury-
ing of bare feet, and riding on a donk, Grandma would bring
out the flask of stewed tea and bag of boiled ham sandwiches—
a futile exercise at best. In next to no time, the sandwiches lived
up to their name and became flavoured with gritty, hard, salty
sand. Inevitably, we would give up on the sandwiches, stroll
past the Punch and Judy show[11] up onto the promenade, and
buy some fish and chips. This was what Trevor and I had hoped
for all along.

The ride home on the charra was always memorable. There
would be the ubiquitous stop at a pub. All the adults, including
the bus driver, would pile out of the charra and race to the pub,
leaving the kids behind. Soon, Granddad would appear with
a bag of crisps and a bottle of lemonade for each of us. Then,
half an hour later, several pints to the good, the adults would
pile back into the charra and the ride home would resume.
Now, for much of the year Granddad was under a strict teeto-
tal regime. Grandma's experience growing up with her mother
who was a heavy drinker imbued her with an abolitionist perspective. A drink or two at Christmas, that's all...except on
these trips to the seaside. Granddad, his system unaccustomed
to alcohol, would come out of the pub ruddy faced and grinning
from cheek to cheek. Then, as the bus took off, the man of few
words would break into song. A loud resonant voice that filled
the air in the bus from side-to-side, top-to-bottom, end-to-end.

*Be my love*

*For no one else can end this yearning...*

Raucous applause from the passengers, then on to the next song. "I'll Take You Home Again, Kathleen," Granddad's favourite song, would always be included in his repertoire.

As we neared Sheffield, Granddad would rise from his seat, take off his big hat, and go around the passengers shoving it under their faces, occasionally jiggling it at someone who took too long to put his hand in his pocket, prodding him into action. He knew how to shake 'em down. He would then place the hat alongside the driver and present its contents (shillings and half crowns) to him as we all left the bus.

There was also the nights at the pictures, Grandma opting to take us to the Norfolk Picture Palace (a misnomer if ever there was one). The Norfolk Picture Palace dated back to the time of the silent films. Its exterior facade consisted of yellow and black tiles, its entrance controlled by large concertina-like, folding metal gates. It resembled a public lavatory more than a cinema. Inside, its balcony section, nicknamed the Jury Box, was just a couple of feet higher than the remainder of the seating known as the stalls. A black curtain hanging on a rail separated the two sections. Like all picture houses in those days, the screen was hidden behind a fog of cigarette smoke. Every so often during the film, a shout would ring out from a scruffy group of teenagers:

"Fyffe's bananas."

"Kilroy's 'ere."

Nothing vulgar. Just disruptive enough to bring an usher to them armed with a flashlight.

"Who was shoutin'?"

Then, without waiting for the answer, he or she would hustle the yobs out through the main entrance on to the street. Five minutes later, they would creep back in, one-by-one through the side door. It was a game and the management either didn't clue in to it and fix the side door, or they enjoyed playing their part. Perhaps that side door had to be always open during performances for safety reasons.

The aroma at the Norfolk was not just confined to cigarette smoke and body sweat. It would be quite common during the film for patrons to start sniffing and muttering indignantly as the smell of rotten eggs wafted through the air. The give-away snickering that went along with this, coming as it did from a confined area of the cinema, meant that someone had dropped a stink bomb on the floor. Time to bring on a re-enactment of the irate usher—out on the street—back in the side entrance routine.

We would sit with Grandma near the front of the stalls, away from the stink bombers and shouters who tended to hide toward the middle. This had the additional advantage of positioning us far away from the peashooter brigade, who pinged the back of people's necks from the Jury Box.

We'd crack open our monkey nuts, peanuts in the shell, as we took in John Wayne in *Red River* or Robert Taylor in *Quo Vadis*. Midway through the film, the projectionist would have to change reels and the theatre was plunged into blackness. That was the signal for everyone to start stomping their feet and begin the slow hand clapping. An evening at the Norfolk provided an all-inclusive medley of entertainment. Our aunts Ray and Buddy had higher-class tastes than the Norfolk, preferring the more salubrious cinemas in the city centre. For them, it was the Picture House or the Gaumont in Barker's Pool. Thy took us to see some great films—*King Solomon's Mines* with Stewart Granger, *The Robe* starring the legendary Richard Burton, along with Walt Disney classics such as *Bambi* and *Treasure Island*.

Family and extended family life bounced along in a more or less happy-go-lucky fashion. At Christmas time, as aunts and uncles gathered around the fireplace in the front room of number 3, the one and only time that the room with its remarkable, antique-but-undervalued furniture was used, it could have been a scene from the iconic Bob Cratchit's house. Card games, gift exchanges, beer and sherry, and chatting until the early hours of the morning.

But, even back then in the days of contentedness and harmony, the glue that held our close-knit family together was showing early signs of breaking down. I never understood why, but Uncle Johnny, my mother's one and only brother, and his wife Flo were always on the periphery of the family circle. Perhaps on my mother's part, there might have been more than a tinge of jealousy, as her brother and sister-in-law seemed to be prospering running their own fruit and vegetable store in the Darnall area of the city, not far from the city centre.

I well remember when they showed up at Grandma's house clutching their new baby, my cousin Jennifer, in their arms. I waltzed into the back room where they were sitting with Grandma and Granddad, fascinated by my new cousin. I was made welcome. When I went back into Mum and Dad's room to tell them, however, the news was not welcomed. "What the blood 'ell 'as tha gone in there for?"

"It's a nice baby, Mum. Don't yer want to see 'er?"

"Bloody don't. They've got nowt I want ter see. Thee keep out. I don't want ter tell thee no moore."

But, as far as Uncle Johnny and Aunt Flo were concerned, Mum's feelings remained below the surface. They were still part of the gathering at Christmas time and Uncle Johnny took Trevor and me on fishing trips. He would show up at the door, no forewarning. He once appeared on a Friday night to announce that we could go with his family on holiday for two weeks in Torquay and Bournemouth. We just got ready and went. Seven of us packed in a two-tone Zephyr Zodiac—uncle and aunt, their two kids Jennifer and baby Jonathan, a middle-aged friend of the family called "Auntie," and the two of us. No seat belts in those days.

Unlike the cryptic nature of Mum's feelings about her brother and his wife, the rift that occurred between Aunt Ray's husband, Uncle George, and the rest of the family was out in the open, deep and permanent. It all resulted from a relatively innocuous incident that occurred while Trevor and I were young. Once in a while, we would be dropped off at Aunt Ray's to have our tea in the back room of her fish and chip shop. A delicious plate of fish, fish cake, and chips like none other. Uncle George, who was a scrap metal merchant, would drop by and exchange banter with us, mostly about football. He was a diehard Sheffield United fan, whereas we were true Sheffield Wednesday-ites. But, it was all in good fun. He even once took me to Bramall Lane to see United play, holding me on his strong shoulders so I could see over the crowd. He was a physically strong man who before the war, used to be an amateur boxer.

One Friday night, Uncle George walked in to the back room and saw Trevor and me tucking into our fish and chips, Aunt Ray chipping potatoes in the sink.

"Bloody 'ell. Can't I come 'ome an' 'ave me tea wi'out them two 'ere?" he railed at Aunt Ray.

"I invited 'em. They're not doin' any 'arm. Don't listen to yer Uncle George lads. 'E's just 'ad a bad day. 'E dun't mean it."

"I bloody do mean it. They're allus around. Don't bother wi' any tea for me."

After he had gone out slamming the door, Aunt Ray gamely tried to hide her tears. She put her arms around each of us saying how sorry she was and tried to make light of it.

And we should have made light of it. But we were kids, and when Grandma came to pick us up, we told her what had happened on the walk home. Grandma, who had no fondness for Uncle George anyway, was hopping mad. "Nell, tha wouldn't believe what George Adams 'as said to these lads," she spouts at Mum.

Mum, of course, also goes up one wall and down the other. "Right, we'll go and see abart this," she defiantly declares.

So, off we all go marching down to Broad Street—Mum, Grandma, the two of us—a posse. Wisely, Granddad stayed out of it. Once we reach the back door of Aunt Ray's fish and chip shop, which is also where she and Uncle George live, the inevitable scene unfolds. Thankfully, Uncle George still has not returned. Aunt Ray stands there crying her heart out, tears splashing down her cheeks, as Grandma and Mum rant and rave.

"Who the chuffin 'ell does 'e think 'e is? 'E can sit on 'is pile er scrap iron an' rot. If these kids aren't welcome 'ere, they won't be comin' no moore."

At that, Aunt Ray starts to plead with Mum to let us come back. "I know George is difficult. I'll work summat out. But please let them lads come back. I care so much for 'em."

And she was telling the truth. Aunt Ray did care for us. Alongside Granddad, she was the most genuine and loving of all my relatives. Mum and Grandma recognized this, which is why we did continue to visit Aunt Ray's and partake of her fish and chips by pre-arrangement. The rest of the family, except for Uncle Johnny and Aunt Flo, never spoke to Uncle George after that incident until almost twenty years later—in 1967, at Aunt Ray's funeral. Trevor and I were told never to have anything to do with him again and the indoctrination stayed with us.

Many years after the incident, while we were living on the Stradbroke Estate, there was a period when on Sunday afternoons, Trevor and I would often take the bus to the junction of Broad and Duke Streets and head up to Grandma and Granddad's for tea. On one occasion, Aunt Ray was waiting for us as we stepped off the bus. "Pop up ter t'ouse for a few minutes. Summat I want ter show yer."

When we got up to her house, which by now was separate and across the road from her fish and chip shop, Uncle George was waiting for us in his shiny, leather-seated Rover 90. "Want a ride in t'car, lads? Come in."

We looked to Aunt Ray for assurance. "Be a nice ride for yer," she nodded approvingly.

So, we set off up Duke Street, the four of us, awkward sentence fragments flowing between front and back seats.

"Oreight, lads? Comfortable, are tha? Not too cold is it?"

We just stared ahead at the mahogany dashboard, mouthing "Yes," or "No," as appropriate.

Uncle George pulled up beside Clarke's barber's shop opposite the end of Talbot Place. "Want ter come for a longer ride?" he asked.

"No, thanks," we said awkwardly and in unison.

That was the extent of it. George was excommunicated, sentenced to indefinite ostracism, for having a bad day.

---

2    Bonfire Night is celebrated annually in the U.K to mark the occasion when, on November 5, 1605, Guy Fawkes was arrested while guarding explosives that had been stored underneath the House of Lords. Fawkes was a member of a group who were plotting to assassinate King James I. Typically, celebrations on Bonfire Night involve gathering around numerous neighbourhood bonfires, where stuffed effigies of Guy Fawkes are burned, fireworks are set off, and molasses-laden toffee, roasted chestnuts, and other delicacies are eaten.

3    Around 300 lbs.

4    Slang expression meaning "Fancy that!"

5    The stomach and intestines of a pig.

6    The lining of a pig's stomach.

7    *The Sheffield Telegraph.* March 31, 1949.

8    Approximately 20 dollars US at the time.

9    A simple game in which horse chestnuts are hardened in the oven and/or by soaking them in vinegar, then each one tied on to the end of a length of string. Two people take turns striking one another's chestnut with their own one until one of the chestnuts is demolished.

10    Slang expression meaning playing a good game.

11    A traditional puppet show featuring Mr. Punch and his wife Judy held on the beach. Dates back to the 17th century in England.

# MANOR LANE

September 1947. The bombs may have stopped falling on British cities, but chaos reigned supreme.
Internationally, it was one of Britain's least "finest hours" as
its troops forced civilians, many of them concentration camp
survivors, to disembark from three naval ships in Hamburg.
The navy had intercepted their original ship, *Exodus 1947*,
as it tried to bring immigrants illegally into Palestine. In the
Sheffield area, the coal miners were on a wildcat strike. Even
officials within the miners' union called for the strikers to be
arrested. Cafés and restaurants were bracing for a cut in their
meat rations and a water shortage loomed after a summer
of continuous drought. School children prepared to go back
to school in the middle of a polio outbreak. The Director of
Education, Mr. Stanley Moffett, justified the re-opening of the
schools with the amazingly insensitive observation that "there
are 70,000 schoolchildren in Sheffield. We could not deprive
69,944 of education because of 56 cases of infantile paralysis."[12]

It was against this unpromising backdrop that, at the age
of four, I started my first day of school at Manor Lane County
School in a grade that was then referred to as nursery school,

the year preceding first-year elementary. Manor Lane was a short five-minute tram ride up Duke Street and City Road from where we lived. A Victorian–era stone edifice, built in 1876, it had a very institutional look about it. Except for the large playground surrounded by high walls that stretched out from the back of it, it could have been an orphanage, a government office building, or even a large Manse. Heavy on brickwork and stingy on windows and lighting. The only toilets were outdoors, at the bottom of the schoolyard. If you were lucky, you might find a roll of newspaper tucked behind the plumbing, this being easier on the bum than the waxy, non-porous toilet paper bearing the brand name Izal® that was sometimes on hand. Just behind the schoolyard wall was a pig farm. There was a muddy pen right beside the school on City Road where people could stop and admire two or three of the farmers' snorting Wessex Saddlebacks.

The Headmistress was Miss Gertrude Horner, a stout, grey-haired, matronly woman who was respected and well liked by the staff and children. She had been Headmistress of that school since the mid-1920s. The classrooms were dark and old style—desks faced the teacher who was fully in charge. After I had been at the school a couple of years, a new building was erected across the playground, and we moved there, the original building continuing to serve as a gathering place for lunches. The new building had lots of windows.

The daily routine was in keeping with the times—

unimaginative but effective. The teacher wielded her stick of chalk, scrolled a question on the blackboard, and then called for hands up from those who knew the answer. The eager beavers would compete to be recognized, waving their arms in the air and straining as though they had hernias. Lunch and break times would be spent outdoors unless it rained, when we were allowed inside and one of the teachers would read us a story. The tedium of rote learning was broken occasionally when we were allowed to play organized indoor games, the most common of which were musical chairs, Ring around the Roses, and London Bridge is Falling Down. Nowadays, that may sound boring, but back then we loved it. One odd activity that stands out in my mind was that of maypole dancing. Every May, a dozen kids at a time would each hold on to a coloured ribbon attached to a vertical pole and prance around in a circle, allowing their ribbons to become intertwined, then backwardly deconstructing their moves so as to unwind them. This took practice and skill. Especially in the early going, many of the youngsters would become so entwined in ribbons that they looked like steers that had been lassoed in a Wild West rodeo. The more graceful students were selected to put on a performance for the benefit of the parents.

Growing up in those early years, my family circle revolved entirely around the Bonsalls—my aunts, uncles, and cousins.

I had one set of grandparents and they were my mother's parents. It rarely occurred to me that Dad might have a family.

Some time during 1949—only four years after the end of the war—I was a six-year-old at Manor Lane Elementary School. It was lunchtime one overcast day. Kids racing around the schoolyard, yelling and bawling at one another, some playing marbles, others leapfrog. Girls performed handstands against the walls of the yard, their skirts down around their heads, skipping, playing hopscotch, twirling wooden tops. One unfortunate little boy had shit his pants, the other kids walking past him in a wide arc holding their noses. It was a lively and varied scene all right. Not being the gregarious type, or one to form close friendships, I moved around from group to group. A passer by, a little boy on the fringes of whatever was going on.

I joined a group of boys who were arguing about the two local football teams, Sheffield Wednesday and Sheffield United, when a boy and a girl came running up to me. "Are you Roger Gordon?" they screamed out excitedly. "There's a woman by t'gate who wants to speak ter yer."

I walked up to the wrought iron gate. She stood there on the other side of the bars, like a visitor to an inmate. A short woman with greying hair, wearing a navy blue raincoat. Holding sweets in her tiny hands. She was smiling as she spoke in a soft voice. "Hello, Roger. I'm your Grandma. Why don't you let me open the gate and you can pop outside so we can spend some time together?"

I shook my head. Said nothing.

She tried hard to persuade me, but I stood my ground, a little afraid and embarrassed. A small group of kids had started to gather around me. Who is this strange woman? My Grandma lives in the same house as me. And what are all the other boys and girls thinking about me?

"Just five minutes. There's nothing to be afraid of," she said.

"Don't want to," I finally said.

With that she thrust a hand through one of the gaps between the bars of the school gate. "Let me give you these then," she said, placing the sweets in my hand. "I'll come and see you again soon."

I raced back into the yard, anxious to blend into the crowd.

When Mum picked me up from school, I quickly told her what happened. "Mum, a strange lady came ter see me at lunch time. She says she's me Grandma."

"She is yer Grandma," says Mum. "She lives near your school. She's yer Dad's mummy. You 'ave two Grandmas. She's yer other Grandma. She won't harm yer. Do yer want 'er to come an' see yer again?"

"No," I say, afraid of the unknown.

"I'll 'ave a word wi' yer Dad then."

Just in time for tea, Dad walks into the small room we occupied in Grandma's house, our home. His day as a sales representative done.

"Pat, thee mother were round to see our Roger at school today. She frightened 'im. Tell 'er not to do it any moore."

"She's 'is grandmother. She only wants to see 'im, ter get ter know 'im," Dad says.

"I don't care. I don't want 'er upsettin' t'lad."

That was the first time I remember seeing my grandmother Gordon. My brother and I grew up to recognize that we had one set of real grandparents—my mother's parents, Mary and Johnny Bonsall, to whom we were encouraged to show affection. Grandma and Granddad. Then, there existed my father's mother, Teresa, and my father's stepfather, Arnold Lawson. We called them "other Grandma and other Granddad." Mother discouraged us from forming a bond with them. While her feelings were neutral toward Arnold, an affable sort of fellow, she disliked the other Grandma with a passion that was riddled with prejudices. Following her family tradition, she gave her a nickname, Teetee, which she always used in a derisory fashion.

School trips were not common, but during my last year at Manor Lane, when I was seven years old, our class was taken for a tour of the ruins of Manor Castle, a sixteenth-century ruin that was located just a couple of hundred yards up the road. It was one of several castles and estates where Mary Queen of Scots had been imprisoned.

Under the guidance of an old lady, the custodian of the

place, we clambered among the rubble-strewn landscape, and then climbed the narrow, spiral stairway inside the turret building, the only one that was still intact. As we gazed at the incredibly high ceilings of the various rooms, we learned that the ghost of Mary Queen of Scots had been seen roaming around the place, quite at home no doubt within its cold, damp brick walls. Once back in school, we were asked to write about our experience. Naturally, the ghost story dominated our recollections.

The teachers were all female, a little stern by today's standards, but one among them stood out. Her name was Miss Kathleen Carnall, a brunette in her early twenties. She was my favourite and she had a soft spot for me. After classes had closed each day, she would sit me on her knee until Mum came to pick me up. Then, she would gush over me to Mum, telling her that she wished she could take me home with her. I adored her. What seven year old wouldn't have?

What sticks out most in my mind about the journeys to and from school was the habitual presence of smog during the autumn months. Well before the infamous London smog outbreak of 1952 caught the attention of the public and government, Sheffield's steel factories and home coal fires were spewing out their toxic fumes into the atmosphere. We used to call it fog before we learned about such things as pollutants and temperature inversions. Mum would guide me to school on those mornings, like a Labrador retriever, plodding her way through the pea soup, occasionally encountering a neighbour or passing stranger, on the alert for hidden dangers.

"Watch out for t'tram comin'. Cover thee mouth an' nose wi' thee scarf."

Why cover one's respiratory passages with anything if it were only water vapour? That thought never occurred to me or anyone else for that matter. Mum often used to pick me up at school and take me for a walk through Norfolk Park before catching the tram down City Road to Talbot Place.

One afternoon during my last year at Manor Lane, while Trevor was in nursery school, Granddad turned up instead of Mum to escort the two of us home. The bell signalled a mass exodus of kids down the outside steps of the school and into the schoolyard. I joined the happy throng running and skipping in a disorderly procession toward the tall, wrought iron gates that had contained us within the school precincts. Then, I noticed one of my schoolmates pushing and shoving his way against the flow, seemingly going in the wrong direction. He ran up to meet me face-to-face. "Eyup, there's a man at t'school gates, says 'e's yer Granddad, wants to tek yer 'ome," he spluttered. "Tha's got a big, fat Granddad."

His reporting mission accomplished, the little tyke then began to spread the joyful news to all and sundry with much hilarity. My brother and I became the recipient of much chuckling, knee slapping, taunting, and finger pointing.

That did it. All of a sudden my dear old Granddad,

wonderful kind old man that he was, suddenly became an embarrassment to us. We kept our distance from him the entire journey home. I can still remember the two of us running on ahead of him along Talbot Place, as he plodded along a hundred yards or so behind us, his walking stick steadily hitting the pavement. "Come back 'ere," Granddad shouted at us.

"We just want ter see 'ow fast we can run," we shouted back.

We arrived back home several minutes ahead of Granddad. As he walked through the kitchen door, Grandma sitting by the fire darning socks, Mum listening to the radio, he pointed his walking stick at us, and then let out a loud guffaw. "Sithee. Little buggers din't want ter walk wi' their big fat Granddad. Ashamed they were."

Good old Granddad could see the funny side of it. I felt ashamed for what I had done and wasn't long climbing on his knee. Even now, I wish it hadn't happened.

 ⁓⌣⌣⌢

I was a bit of a slow starter at school and struggled at first with the rudiments of the three R's. I was half-way through my first full year post-nursery school when Miss Horner, the Headmistress, asked to see my mother to express her concern. Then, one day, to use one of Dad's favourite expressions, I started to frame—got my act together, in today's vernacular. I went from dimwit to quick-wit in record time to join the brainy kids at the top of the class. In those days, that often meant a physical re-location as the order of seating in the classroom was either determined alphabetically or by order of merit. In any event, the newfound respect that suddenly came my way from the teachers and some of the kids boosted my self-confidence. I was still shy though, introverted, easily embarrassed, in contrast to my younger brother Trevor who was extroverted, full of beans, and unflustered by what was going on around him. During the last year of my attendance at Manor lane, Trevor had started in nursery school, so we were both in the new building. One day, after morning assembly rituals had ended, Miss Horner told everyone to sit down. We knew she had something important to tell us and it was not likely to be good.

"Children, we have two naughty boys sitting with us this morning. I know the name of one of the naughty boys and it won't be long before I find out who the other one is."

Then incredibly, hands on hip she blurts, "Would Roger Gordon please stand up?"

White as chalk, unsteady as a teetering toddler, I slowly rise to my feet. My pallor changes from ashen to crimson. What on earth am I supposed to have done?

"Listen to me everyone. Miss Shepherd's nursery class is doing a project to discover how frogs develop from tadpoles. So, for the past week there has been an aquarium tank in her classroom containing pond water and one dozen tadpoles. But yesterday, we ran into a little problem. You see, instead of twelve tadpoles, there were only two of them. Ten little tadpoles were missing. Where had they gone, you may ask? Let me tell you where they have gone. They have been taken, stolen, from the tank by one or more naughty children. And one of those naughty children is standing right now. Isn't he Roger Gordon? You were one of the children who took those tadpoles weren't you, Roger Gordon?"

"No, miss." I stutter almost inaudibly.

"I beg your pardon. What was that you said?" booms Miss Horner.

"No, miss. Weren't me," I declare, a little more confidently.

"Telling lies in front of all the children in the school, are you? We'll see about that. After assembly is over, I want to see you in my office and you will tell me who your partners-in-crime were."

The whole school is looking at me. Nobody believes me. After assembly, head bowed, I trundle into Miss Horner's office. Miss Shepherd is with her.

"Roger, Miss Shepherd says you have a younger brother in her class and that I may have picked out the wrong Gordon in this morning's assembly. I'm going to look into this possibility. What do you have to say to that?"

"I don't know whether me brother Trevor did it, but it weren't me." I respond.

Trevor did own up to it. He and his friend Horace Ogden were the culprits. The tadpoles had died in the jam jar that they had used to collect them in. Horace was a little lad from Haig Lane in a slum housing area not very far from Talbot Place. Mum strongly disapproved of Trevor's friendship with a boy from such a home, so when she found out what had happened, it did not sit well with her. "'Ow many moore times do I 'ave ter tell thee not ter mix wi' that 'Orace Ogden," she railed at Trevor.

Miss Horner never did correct the mistake she had made in assembly and despite my protestations, many of my classmates continued to believe that I was the tadpole taker.

⁓⁓⁓

Mum took a keen interest in my schooling and would ask me each day what I had learned.

"We learned about Marco Polo today, Mum. 'E discovered China."

"Learnin' abart explorers. That must er been interestin'. Yer'll soon be learnin' abart Christopher Columbus. 'E discovered America."

One day, I came home from school to announce to Mum: "Miss Carnall was tellin' us all abart Germany today, Mum. She says people there are just like us an' we should be friends wi' 'em. What's wrong wi' t'Germans anyroad?"

This did not sit well with Mum who blamed Germany for the war and its harsh after-effects. "Germans. Warmongers. Rotten ter t'core. If it weren't for them, all them lives, young soldiers, smashin' lads, women and children, wun't er been lost. An we wun't be on t'rations—ten pence a week for meat, 'avin' ter use tea leaves o'er an o'er again, not enough coal to warm a sparrer. Germans. They've a lot ter answer for."

Well, maybe, but much of the coal problem was caused by the striking miners. Mum wasn't big on details.

"Wait till I see Miss Carnell. I'll tell 'er I don't want owt ter be taught abart t'Germans. That's all."

"That's all" was my mother's favourite expression. She used it as an exclamation mark after she had made a point. The alpha and the omega, it said, and nobody better disagree with her.

Mum's thoughts about Germany were misguided, shaped by the times through which she had come. But, in her own way, she did care about my schooling and about her small family, the four of us, nestled as we were in that little room where Granddad and Grandma Bonsall lived.

My four years at Manor Lane coincided with those happy-go-lucky years at Talbot Place. Living hand-to-mouth in decrepit, confined, mouse-infested quarters, our neighbourhood was our entire world and the four of us fitted comfortably within that world. My parents' marriage was not in peril; not even in question. The four of us were strongly connected with our grandparents and aunts. Without a doubt, they were our happiest years as a family.

---

12    *The Sheffield Telegraph* September 3, 1947.

# THE STRADBROKE

An overcast Friday afternoon in early July 1951. I'm sitting in Miss Carnell's class at Manor Lane Elementary School. As an eight year old, I would have been largely oblivious to the details of the topsy-turvy times in which I was living. Strikes by the London and Merseyside Dockers, working to rule by the railway workers, and it goes without saying, shortages of coal. One of Sheffield's leading steel factories, Steel Peech and Tozer, was forced to close one of its steel melting furnaces because of a shortage of pig iron. On the brighter side, six years after the ending of hostilities in the Second World War, the British government was about to announce an official end to its state of war with Germany. Better late than never.

As a counterpoint to all the doom and gloom arising from labour unrest and commodity shortages, the south side of the River Thames in London had been converted into a gigantic exposition, titled the Festival of Britain. Domes, halls, pavilions, theatres, and towers extolled the greatness of British industry and culture. Back in Sheffield, several of the rubble-strewn lots in the city centre resulting from the blitz had been cleared and prefabricated stores were sprouting up. German bombs left a huge portion of the city's residents homeless. Initially, asbestos-constructed prefabricated homes were cobbled together to cater to immediate needs. But, at the start of the 1950s, new council estates, containing real brick and mortar homes, were taking root outside of the city core. A record 1700 homes had been approved for construction during 1951.[13]

On this particular day, I sit at my desk daydreaming. What will it be like to live away from Grandma and Granddad, in a new neighbourhood I've never even heard of, let alone seen? Will I be able to make new friends? Will anyone else other than us even live there?

I am shaken out of my reverie by the sight of Miss Horner, accompanied by Mum, entering the classroom. I wasn't aware that my departure from the school would occur in quite so public a way.

"Now, children," says Miss Horner, "Roger is leaving us now. He's going to live with his Mum and Dad in a new house that is a long way from Manor Lane. So, he'll need to go to a new school. Say goodbye to him."

"Where is 'e goin'?" asks one of the little girls.

"To the brand new Stradbroke Estate on the outskirts of the city," Miss Horner replies.

And that's where we went the next morning, a sunny Saturday. Mum, Trevor and I took the bus to the terminus on the Woodthorpe housing estate, a 1930s council

development, then walked for about half an hour through
the posher Richmond Road area, finally downhill through a
gigantic construction site. Clay and mud-surfaced roadways,
pavements roughly shaped out or non existent, construction
rubble strewn everywhere, labourers climbing ladders, hods
filled with bricks precariously perched on their shoulders, car-
penters framing out concrete foundations, roofers prostrate on
all fours like mountain goats laying down tiles one at a time,
the sounds of hammers clanging, trowels scraping, concrete
mixers churning, pneumatic drills buzzing, and every so often,
a wolf whistle from one of the labourers directed at Mum—
at twenty eight, she was not hard to look at.

"Eyup luv, what tha doin' tonight?"

"I'm the man er yer dreams."

"Me an thee. Somewhere out er t'way. 'Ow abart it?"

"Don't listen ter 'em," says Mum, eyes straight ahead,
inwardly pleased.

Eventually, we arrived at the top of another short hill,
a road called Smelter Wood Way according to the white
and black metal plate affixed to the wall of the first house.
Some of the houses on this street had roofs and windows and
looked ready to occupy. Concrete-block pavements and kerbs
had been installed on both sides of the road, which was still
unpaved–dirty and dusty. We walked on the pavement along
the left-hand side to the bottom of the street. Mum stopped,
then started to move toward the front door of the end house,

number 23. Like every other house on the estate, it was two-storey, brick construction, semi-detached, and like every other house on the same side of the street, the front door was painted bottle green. Front doors of houses on the other side of the street were painted chocolate brown, throwing the bilateral symmetry a little askew.

She pulled a key out of her pocket and we entered our new house. The smell of new wood and plaster was a novel sensation to us as we were only used to old houses. We stomped around excitedly over the bare floorboards through the hallway and around the two rooms downstairs, an eat-in kitchen and a living room.

"Mum, what's this little room off t'kitchen?"

"That's a pantry."

"What's that?"

"It's where yer keep yer food."

"There's a back porch wi' two more little rooms off it."

"Aye, one's downstairs t'lavatory, other's t'coal shed."

And so the chatter went.

"Let's go upstairs," says Mum.

Three bedrooms and a bathroom, with a bath and another lavatory.

"Now, this lav is only for using at t'nightime or when yer indoors on account er t'weather. Unless t'weather's bad, yer play outdoors durin' t'day an' yer use t'downstairs one. No runnin' in an out." Mum's first rules set in stone.

"That bedroom is yours," she says, looking me in the eye and pointing to the room at the back of the house. "And that's yours," she says to Trevor, pointing to the smaller room at the front of the house. "Me and Dad get t'biggest one at t'front."

Soon Dad arrived with the movers. Not that we had much to move in. A kitchen table, four wooden chairs, one bed, three mattresses; no appliances. In those days, only the rich had fridges. Clothes washers were at a primitive stage of development and beyond the means of the working classes. Dishwashers hadn't been invented. A range and oven? We used a countertop toasting and grilling device for regular fare and for more elaborate meals, an oven that was built into a kitchen wall that backed onto the chimney and relied for heat on what came from the fire in the living room. After a few years, we bought a natural gas oven and range.

But that day, we sat around on the wooden chairs eating sandwiches that had been prepared earlier at Grandma's house and drinking tea from a thermos that Mum had brought with her. Trevor and I spent the rest of the day exploring around the house—the garden, and a structure attached to the house that was termed an outhouse (a storage and tool shed, not an outhouse in the North American usage of that term; no latrines in there).

That night, we sat around the fireplace in the living room—bums and feet on the bare floorboards. Dad had gone rummaging around the building sites, picking up scrap pieces of wood. We lit a fire. The electricity to the house had been switched on, but we just sat there through the dusk of the late evening and into the darkness of the night, watching the bright yellow flames leap up the chimney, then slowly die down, flickering, hissing occasionally, absorbed into a red mass of embers, which glowed brightly at first, then faded as their short life left them. For a while, there was just enough light in the room for us to play a game of hand shadows, each of us taking turns contorting our hands into different shapes, while the others guessed what images were being represented by the shadows cast on the opposite wall. Dad had rigged up our old Sobell wireless. We listened to a mystery play, occasionally throwing out one-liners that spoke to the excitement tinged with apprehension that we were all feeling.

"Smashin' innit?"

"Nice to be living in t'country?"

"Will Grandma an' Granddad be able to come an' see us?"

"Any snakes out 'ere?"

"Any kids our age live round 'ere?"

It was a happy time, that night. We were a tight family, on our own and no longer an appendage to Grandma and Granddad.

Trevor and I wasted no time in exploring the neighbourhood. Instead of grimy streets, old flagstone pavements, randomly scattered dog turds, and wall-to-wall soot-covered old houses, there were farmers' fields, natural ravines, streams, trees, wild flowers, and wildlife. Behind our house was a gully with a narrow brook running through it. It became generally known as the hollow, or to be phonetically precise, "t'oller." The bottom end of it, where the brook took a dive underground, was used as a landfill site, so it was scruffy and a bit of an eyesore. But, upstream from this was about two hundred yards of unspoiled terrain. Scattered bushes sprouted from the grass covered steep slopes on either side of the brook. The brook at the bottom of the gulch was lined on either side with willow trees—home for nesting birds, large coloured spiders, and devilish looking bright green caterpillars.

Across the road from t'oller at its bottom end was a field of wheat. One day, Trevor and I charged into this field, playing hide and seek among the stems. Butterflies of various colours and sizes took to the wing as we disturbed them—red admirals, common blues, small tortoiseshells, and meadow browns. Squawking crows and chirping sparrows joined the airborne throng. We slogged our way through the field to arrive at the terminus of a band of woodland that stretched as far as we could see toward the adjacent suburb of Handsworth.

The terrain of Smelter Wood, as we would later learn it was named, formed a gorge. A stream bubbled along the bottom of it. We descended part-way down the bank toward the stream. As we meandered among the oak, sycamore, and elm trees, we stumbled across a variety of shrubs—hawthorn, holly, hazel, and others. We followed the course of the brook upstream and came across a thick rope tied to a branch of a tree, evidence, likely, of other kids in the area.

Smelter Wood became one of my favourite haunts. Rambling through it with friends with no particular purpose in mind. Upstream, a wire fence traversed the gorge. We always climbed over it. Word travelled around that a gang called the "Wenlockers" used this part of the woodland. It was their turf and woe betides anyone caught there. So, it became a game of dare. Who could go in the farthest, stay in the longest? The Wenlockers were supposed to live on Wenlock Street in Handsworth. If such a gang existed at all, it must have been a small one because that street consisted of half a dozen or so row houses. Maybe they had large families? We never saw any sign of them.

Chopping down trees in Smelter Wood to provide fire-wood for Bonfire Night was commonly practiced and, to my discredit, I joined the party. Kids with axes and saws, chop-ping and sawing at tree trunks, then the cracking sounds of trunks on their way down along with shouts of "Timber" from the prepubescent lumberjacks. Trailing the spoils behind us, we'd head back home to place what had been a living tree on the pile of wood in our back garden. Back then, no one said it was wrong. "Oh, that's nice. But don't yer think yer've got enough already?" was as far as it got.

One afternoon, when I was nine or ten years old, I was walking with a couple of friends across the little makeshift bridge over the brook to go over to the Handsworth side of the woods. There was a large clump of bamboo shoots or similar-sized shrubs on the other side. We could hear sounds coming from inside the copse. As we threaded our way toward the source of the hubbub, the voices became clearer.

"Tha't next."

"Show me thine an' I'll show thee mine."

"Only if tha stands o'er there. Tha better not touch me."

"Oreight."

"Lift thee legs up a bit moore so I can see better."

"Will it start to get 'airy?"

"Few more years."

"Let me see thine now."

"'Ow come it's not got a skin o'er t'end er it like other boys?"

"'Cus it were circumscribed, that's why."

"It's not as big as t'lad before thee. Thee balls are like marbles. 'Is were like birds' eggs."

"It's growin' all time. Be big as a broomstick soon."

As we neared the scene, we saw a line-up of kids waiting to enter a tramped down area, a secluded spot.

I looked in to see young Jenny Leadbeater with her knickers down, skirt hauled up to her midriff, showing off all she had. Across from her was a young boy showing off his limp little jack-in-the-box. A game of show and tell. Harmless, but not for me that day.

"Wanna join t' queue an' 'ave a look?" one of the kids quizzed me.

"Na. Seen it before."

Off I walked, feeling very pleased with myself.

At the top of the street where we lived, was a mound of grassland perched at one end of a bulldozed and flattened piece of land. The dozer had left about an acre in its original condition. It became known as the Green Hill, a place where youngsters would play that politically incorrect but imaginative game called Cowboys and Indians. Sometimes, teenage couples would be seen snogging in the depressions that scoured the top of the hill. As a young lad of thirteen, I laid down in one of those depressions and smoked my first cigarette. I mean really smoked it—inhaled it, the whole bit. I felt dizzy, but exhilarated. (That first cigarette addicted me to nicotine. From then on, I'd smoke whenever I could sneak away. At home, it was the Green Hill; at school, the boys' lavatories. It would be another twenty-two years before I was able to kick the habit for good.)

The Stradbroke estate developed in leaps and bounds during those first three years while I was at Woodhouse West. Naturally, a pub was the first public amenity to be built. This was followed by a row of shops—a confectionary and newsagent, greengrocer, fish and chip shop, home-delivery grocery, butcher, and barber. The barber knew only one style of haircut—the short back and sides colliers' cut that looked like he'd placed a pudding bowl over the customer's head, cut around it so that it left a line all the way around the back of the neck, then hacked away at the top so the strands of hair were uniformly short and prickly. A bit like a long crew cut defined by the abrupt bareness of the neck. I only once had my hair cut there. That was enough for mother.

One day, while I was sitting in that little shop, waiting for a friend to have his hair cut, "Butcher Bill," as he was unflatteringly titled, abruptly stopped his piece of artistry, pointed at me, then shouted out to one of the other customers, presumably someone he knew. "Eyup. Look at 'im. 'Air almost down ter t'shoulders. Next thing 'e'll be wantin' a perm. 'E'll be wantin' me ter put rollers in it."

Chuckles all round the shop, except for me, who thought it was a stupid comment from someone who didn't know how to cut hair anyway.

"Maybe 'e needs a violin ter play. 'E looks like an out-er-work musician," continued the barber.

"I'm just waitin' for me friend," I finally said. "Yer won't be cuttin' me 'air." My red face and glum expression told it all.

"Oh are tha? Tekin' up space. Bein' mardy abart a bit a leg pullin'? Maybe tha should wait outside then."

"Don't worry. Wun't be seen dead in 'ere. Turrah, Cliff. See yer later on."

As I stormed out, there was a background of laughing, interspersed with one-liners. "Bloody musician." "Mardy bugger." "Better off wi'out likes er 'im."

The fish and chip shop was run by a middle-aged woman

who dyed her shoulder-length hair a vivid shade of yellow. Blonde would be too flattering a descriptor. Her bright red lipstick, often extending beyond the boundaries of her lips, complemented the hair-do. Her other half, a slight, mild mannered, nondescript-looking man, with Brylcreem®-plastered grey hair, scurried around the shop, silently obeying her commands with robotic precision.

"We're out er batter, Albert. Mix some moore up."

Albert nods.

"Albert, cut up some moore chips from t'peeled pertaters at back er t'store."

"Comin' up."

The sheets of greaseproof paper and newspaper for wrapping the entrées were stacked on her side of the counter. To separate one sheet from the other, Blondie would lick her index finger and use it to peel off the top sheet. Then, onto the paper went the fish and chips. Once mother noticed her doing this, she put Blondie and Albert's shop off limits.

"Filthy bugger. I'm not goin' theere anymoore. An' you two keep away. Puttin' 'er rotten spit on t'wrappin' paper. Ampt seen owt like it."

But, Trevor and I would sometimes sneak an order for ourselves on the sly. Sanitation was not of uppermost consideration to us.

By today's standards, Hamer's grocery store was a strange place. It was strictly behind-the-counter service, before the word supermarket even existed in Britain. Whenever I went in there, it would be devoid of customers—one or two at most. That's because most people would drop by the store once a week with their handwritten grocery lists, pass them to Mr. Hamer, then wait for them to be delivered. Door-to-door service; no need to hang around the premises. At our house, the cardboard box full of groceries was delivered to the outside toilet. Great location in amongst the spiders and the *E.coli*.

A bright red GPO telephone booth, glass-paned on all sides, soon appeared within spitting distance of the shops. One coin-operated, three-pence-a-call telephone for the entire estate— working-class folk could not afford private telephones. Needless to say, it was heavily patronized. There would often be a line-up of people outside the booth waiting for a caller to finish. More often than not, this caller fit the stereotype of an elderly woman wearing a headscarf and carrying a shopping bag. A wait of thirty minutes or so was not unusual. On occasions when a single person was waiting to use the phone, he, she, or I would play a peek-a-boo game with the caller inside the booth. The caller would turn her back to the person outside, who in turn would walk around to the other side of the booth, glare at the caller, who would respond by turning her back. And on it went, replete with hand gestures and profanities, one to the other.

Family life at number 23 during the early 1950s was, for the most part, harmonious. It was not Paradise, but neither was it

Hell on Earth. Mum played the traditional role expected of a stay-at-home mother. She baked cakes (delicious chocolate layer ones) and cleaned house scrupulously, did the laundry like clockwork, and knitted clothes expertly. Dad wore that long-sleeved, maroon cardigan, zippered down the front for years. We would all sit around listening to the radio in the evening, mother with her legs stretched out over Dad on the sofa, Dad rubbing her feet. Listening to a BBC drama, the quality variable. Some would be classics—for example, Evelyn William's *The Corn is Green* or Somerset Maugham's *The Sacred Flame*. Others would be lesser known and forgettable renditions. Following the adventures of the Archer family on Wimberton Farm , listening to Wilfred "Give 'im the money Mabel" Pickles on *Have a Go*, chuckling to Harry Secombe on *The Goon Show* were staples that we relished together.

We acquired a television in the spring of 1954. Made by Ekco®, it had a fourteen-inch black and white screen with rounded corners. It arrived just in time for us to take in the award-winning documentary series about WW 2, *War in the Air*. Everyone at school and in the town used to talk about the television programs that had been screened the previous night. It was a popular conversation topic on the buses. This was hardly surprising because television was a novelty and there was only one channel anyway, the BBC, so everyone who had a TV watched the same programs.

During those halcyon years, Mum and Dad often took us

to the Rex cinema, a thirty-minute plus journey that involved walking through a recreational expanse known as Richmond Park one or both ways in the dark. We saw the original *Christmas Carol* starring Alistair Sims, along with quintessentially British comedies such as *Down Among the Z men*, *Doctor in the House,* and *Genevieve.* Who could forget such luminaries as Peter Sellars, Kenneth Moore, Dirk Bogard, and John Gregson?

Gardening became a family pastime. We'd never had a real garden to cultivate, so it was a novelty for all of us. Upon occupancy, bare earth and weeds surrounded all the houses on the estate. Landscaping was strictly DIY. When Dad started to dig into the ground, he realized it would be a major undertaking. Yellow clay, blue clay, yellow clay streaked with blue, blue clay streaked with yellow. No soil. Dad and Bill Withers, our next door neighbour, dug up and transferred by wheelbarrow a foot or so of clay into the landfill area of t'oller, just to get to the soil. Then, digging, raking, hoeing...we all had a go at that. All plants were grown from seed, which we each took a turn at planting in the ground. At the end of it all, the garden looked wonderful. A front lawn surrounded by annuals, a rockery with assorted perennials sloping up to the pavement, all framed by a privet hedge. Hollyhocks and climbing roses on either side of the front door. A side garden that was terraced using natural rock walls to break up the downhill slope. We all helped to find these flat rocks from around the building sites and ferry them back to the house. More lawns, flowers, roses. Then, a back garden in which vegetable seeds were planted in rows. Green beans, peas, lettuce, radishes, beetroot. Rhubarb and strawberry patches. A compost heap.

Listening to the radio, watching the telly, and gardening became our family's communal activities.

---

13   *The Star*. Sheffield. January 17, 1951.

# WOODHOUSE WEST

The summer of '51 was a settling-in time for us all—Mum and Dad getting to know the Withers's next door, but few others. Our parents would watch families move in, exchange names and handshakes on the street, and then all concerned would retreat into their brick boxes. The house opposite to ours must have been under a curse. It was home to two sets of occupants, each a thorn in my mother's side.

"Thank God them Bagshaws, that bunch across t'street, are movin' out," says Mum one morning. She's looking out of the window at the moving van parked outside the house. "I'm 'opin' a quieter family 'll be movin' in. She's nowt but ignorant."

Not long after this, the same scene. This time, mother has the living room window open, head sticking out, yelling to the woman across the street, the successor to the one she couldn't get on with. "Now then," yells mother, "Tha'd better tell thee kids ter roller skate in front er thee own 'ouse. Seven a clock in t'bloody morning. Does tha think that's fair? 'Cus I don't."

"They can't skate in front er our 'ouse 'cus t'pavement is

broken up," retorts the woman with the as-yet unknown name, the one mother hasn't even met.

"Well that's not my bloody fault. I don't want wakin' up wi' thy noisy brats no moore."

"Family that lived 'ere warned us abart thee. Tha'rt 'ard ter gerron wi'."

"That's all," as mother has the last word and slams the window.

Last word it was. Not a word was exchanged between the new lady across the street, Mrs. Drinkwater, and Mum from thereon. And yes, the early morning roller-skating stopped. Then one afternoon, out of the blue, Mrs. Drinkwater's daughter came waltzing across the street dressed in her full bridal dress. She waltzed right into our kitchen. "Mrs. Gordon, Mum wanted me to let yer see me wedding dress. I'm gerrin married this Sat'day."

"Oo luv, it does look smashin'. Beautiful. 'E must be a lucky young man ter 'ave such a beautiful bride like thee."

I remember feeling respect for the woman across the street and pride for mother. At least for that brief moment in time, they'd buried their hatchets for a greater cause.

Trevor and I rounded up a small circle of friends who, during those first few years on the Stradbroke estate, were welcome companions outdoors, but never indoors. Another House Rule—no playing with friends indoors. When it rained, Trevor and I had to amuse ourselves. If it didn't rain, we were turfed outside to play.

One issue that became controversial during the summer of '51 was schooling. It wasn't worth our while to resume schooling before the summer break because there was only a week or so left of term after we moved. But which school should we attend in September? The Stradbroke estate had no school. The two closest schools were Woodthorpe and Woodhouse West. Woodthorpe was located in a pre-war council estate, while Woodhouse West was situated in a farming and coalmining village, with roots that dated back to the fifteenth century. From Mum's perspective, it embodied a historic character; most importantly, it was not a council estate—unlike Woodthorpe, or Stradbroke, ironically. The Education authority notified the residents of our street that according to the zoning that had been done, we were assigned to Woodthorpe. "Not bloody likely," screams mother, as she opens and reads the letter.

"Yer not goin' ter t'Woodthorpe. It'll be full er kids from that Woodthorpe Estate. It were used ter 'ouse people livin' in t'slums just before t'war. No, yer not goin' in wi' that common lot. I'll go an' see t'bloody school board. Speak ter t'man who's responsible. That's all."

So she did. And she came bouncing into the house afterwards pleased to the hilt. "I sorted 'em out. Yer'll both be goin' ter t'Woodhouse West. I'll go o'er an speak ter t'eadmaster tomorrer."

September rolled around. Trevor and I trundled along with

mother on that first morning of school. Through the streets of the estate, still a construction zone, across a field, down the unpaved extension of Richmond Road, across the playing fields of the Woodhouse Recreational Centre, into Woodhouse village itself. It was a twenty-minute brisk walk. After that first day, Trevor and I hoofed it there and back unassisted, including during the one-hour lunch break. No time for dilly–dallying.

Woodhouse West was of the same vintage as Manor Lane—stone building, late nineteenth century. The difference was that the schoolyards were segregated along gender lines. I recall that first day in the boys' yard feeling intimidated by the older boys, who gathered together in groups. One older boy decided to show off to the gallery and climbed the entire height of the three-storey building by scaling one of the drainpipes. Eventually, a teacher appeared and rung a hand bell. Start of classes.

A strict protocol was followed. After the first day, a student who had earned the honour did bell rings. Classes lined up in the yard, year by year. A teacher walked up and down between the rows making sure nobody spoiled the pattern, and then blew a whistle. At this command, we marched into the assembly area—formed by moving back the partition between two classrooms. Then, a religious service, closing remarks by the Headmaster, after which students headed off to their classrooms. Except for the service, this same ritual followed all breaks.

Woodhouse West was an old–fashioned village school even by standards of that era. Students sat in rows, side-by-side in double desks that were well worn and etched with initials of students from bygone days. Although the staff never admitted it, there was a design to the seating arrangement. School performance and family background went hand-in-hand. The higher achievers were placed on one side of the classroom, the dunderheads on the opposite side. There was a transition from clean clocks, groomed hair, white teeth, and tidy clothes to mucky mugs, colliers' cuts, rotting teeth, and rags. Jacket or pullover sleeves substituted for handkerchiefs among the less fortunate, resulting in slimy, snotty messes. One poor lad was so repellent that he was assigned a seat to himself. He was avoided and made fun of by the other kids. I was at the brainy end of the classroom sharing a double–seater with Graham Bamford, who became my best friend.

$\sim\!\!\smile\,\smile\!\!\!\curvearrowright$

It's a typical day in the fourth form of the elementary stream. Morning assembly is over. Mr. Isaac Thorpe, a middle-aged, short, sandy-haired man bearing a moustache, walks into the classroom carrying his briefcase. As always, Mr. Thorpe is impeccably decked out in a three-piece suit. He pulls out the class register from his case and begins to read from it.

"David Adams."

"Here, sir. Check.

"Christine Armitage."

Silence. Cross.

And so it goes on—a meticulous alphabetical recording of day-by-day attendance.

"We'll now go through our times tables."

He waves his arms like an orchestra conductor and in monotone unison, the class sings out: "One times one is one… six times five…" By the time it gets to eleven by eleven, not everyone is singing the same tune. Some are not singing at all.

"Now, open your exercise books, take out your pens, and solve the problems that I'm about to write on the blackboard."

The school supplied the pens to which he was referring— short sticks of wood, about the size of a pencil, each with a metal nib at one end. To write, you had to keep dipping the nib in an inkwell fitted into the desk containing a murky blue/black suspension. No fountain pens were allowed and absolutely no ball point pens. It was an art to be able to keep the ink flowing gracefully on the paper without splodges, smudges, or scratchy spots.

"Roger, would you come out to the front so I can have a word with you?" asks Mr. Thorpe, as he notices that I have finished the blackboard exercise.

As I stand by his desk, he slips a half crown into my hand and whispers in my ear.

"Would you go up to the corner store and get me a packet of twenty Senior Service® cigarettes? I don't have any for break time. Tell the storekeeper that Mr. Thorpe sent you." Not a bad way for a ten–year–old lad to spend some school time.

Yes, this was an old fashioned school with old fashioned teaching methods. Rote memorization, concentration on the three R's, and respect for authority were paramount. But it worked for me. I was among the top handful of students in my classes. Despite my introverted personality, I acquired a circle of friends. The teachers were approachable and capable. I loved Woodhouse West.

Our strict classroom-learning regime made way for some imaginative, fun activities from time to time. The Woodhouse recreational centre, a grassed ten acres or so, was just up the road from the school, so our phys. ed. classes were often held there. We played a game called rounders, which historically is the forerunner of the professional game of baseball. One afternoon a year, the school held its own version of an athletics contest, a "sports day," to which parents were invited. The events included races between pairs of students—a three-legged race, in which the students of each pair stood alongside one another and had adjacent legs tied together, and a wheelbarrow race, in which one member of a student pair walked upside down on his or her hands while the other person held on to the walker's legs. Individual races included egg and spoon races, in which contestants tried to balance an egg on a spoon as they raced to the finish line (imitation eggs were substituted for real ones in light of the food shortages of the times) and sack races, where each student climbed into a burlap potato sack, then bunny jumped down the makeshift track.

When we were in our fourth and final year, every couple of weeks the boys would walk across the village to an old shed where they would be taught carpentry by a teacher whose pedagogy included picking on someone and asking him to say the last word that the teacher had uttered. If the student got it wrong, he would be made to stand on a stool. Standing on stools, as I often was required to do, was not my favourite way to spend a morning, so I switched activities and went with the girls on the bus to the Park district swimming baths, where I did something useful—learned to swim.

Mr. Thorpe taught the fourth-year class and he was my favourite teacher in that school. He was able to let down his guard from time to time, deviate from his no–nonsense, slap-on-the-arse routine, and allow a measure of relaxation into the classroom. On a foggy November afternoon in 1953, he brought his portable radio into the classroom so that we could listen to the England versus Hungary football game, played at Wembley stadium. It had been hyped by the press as "The Match of the Century." The England team, trounced 6-3 by the brilliance of Ferenc Puskas and Nandor Hidegkuti, would just as soon forget it ever happened. We listened in disbelief in our little schoolroom.

While the football game was mostly of interest to the boys in the class, a couple of school trips were organized that appealed to everybody. During that last year at the West, we were herded on to buses to see Chipperfield's circus that had set up its big tents in the city. A man who was fired out of a cannon crowned the assembly of lions, tigers, elephants, performing clowns, and trapeze artists. On another occasion, we were bussed to the local Rex cinema to see a film about the scaling of Mount Everest by Edmund Hillary and Tenzing Norgay.

"Remember, class," pronounced Mr. Thorpe on a windy morning in May of 1954, "nothing is impossible if you set your minds to it. A while ago, we all saw a film about Mount Everest being conquered. Many people thought that was impossible. Just yesterday, a student at Oxford University ran a mile in under four minutes. That, too, was thought to be impossible. You can set your own targets in life and strive to achieve them."

The entire staff at Woodhouse West was excellent. Mr. Rees Vaughan, a larger-than-life elderly Welshman, was the epitome of a headmaster. He commanded respect because he cared, not because he was feared. At a time when political correctness had not yet been invented, when people didn't think to look for lechery and sexual deviancy in well-intended expressions, he was able to call the children under his wing "darlings" and everyone knew he meant it in the best possible way.

One morning I rolled up late for school. I joined half a dozen other miscreants, all boys, in the cloakroom. As per the custom, we were locked out of the main part of the school. Like a bunch of feral tomcats caught in a trap. Once assembly was over, Mr. Vaughan appeared, unlocked the door, and told us to line up. He was holding a cane. Sympathetically, he listened to each boy's tale of woe:

"Me Mum din't wake me up in time, sir."

"'Ad ter go back ter t'ouse 'cus I forgot me sick note, sir."

"Lost track er time, sir."

Looking straight at us, Mr. V delivered a message that seemed out of step with the gentle, lilting, musical Welsh voice that he used to deliver it.

"I know you darlings can do better. Try harder next time, will you. I don't like doing it, but I'm going to have to cane each of you. Hold out your left arms."

Caning? I'd never been caned. *If he doesn't like doing it, I wouldn't mind if he gave it a miss,* I remember thinking.

Whack. Whack. Whack. Three swipes on the palms of the hand. But when he got to me, I caught the gleam in his eye. He liked me because he had taught my Aunt Buddy when she was young. I knew I was going to be spared the fullness of the rod. Whhhhaaack. Whhhhhaaacck. Whhhhhaaaacckk. Each down stroke lost momentum just before impact, so that it felt more like a heavy tap than a whack. Thankfully, the other boys didn't seem to notice and I went through the façade of rubbing my hand, pretending that I had been hurt.

"There darlings. It'll soon stop hurting. Just make you think a bit won't it, Jimmie," as he tousles the lad's hair. "Now, Billie and Freddie, I want you to stay behind. I'm going to show you how to polish your shoes. Looks like you don't know how to do that. It's not hard. I have a kit in my office."

Back then, corporal punishment was the norm, but Mr. V was able to administer it without malice, even apologetically, and for good measure, throw in a practical act of kindness, a lesson in personal appearance. He really believed that the caning had to be done for our own good, and I could tell that it hurt him just as much as it did us.

The walks to and from school could be eventful—like the time that I decided to take a short cut across a farmer's field. When I attempted to crawl under the fence to exit the field, I surfaced too early, gave my head an almighty bump on the lower rail. I don't know how long I was unconscious, but I wasn't late for school.

Then, there was the memorable time that David Adams and I were walking home during a phase we were going through when we thought it cool to play with matches. We spied a hedgerow that separated a farmer's field from a narrow, dirt pathway known by local children as the Fairy Dell. Fairies and gnomes who spoke a strange language were supposed to inhabit this mystical place—the conspiring together of children's imaginations, inventions, and rumours.

"I bet that 'edge would catch fire reight quick," says Dave, "Let's see. We can allus put it out," says I.

Scratch and flick. I send a lighted match into the hedge. Whoosh. The hedge becomes an inferno in no time.

"Bloody 'ell. Din't think that'd 'appen," I'm screaming.

Both of us take off our jackets and beat at the flames with little effect. The flames spread along the hedgerow, leaving blackened skeletons of bushes in their wake.

Along comes a young lad on a bicycle. He stops.

"Eyup, 'as tha done that? Farmer's just up theere in t'field," as he points up the road. "'E'll be reight mad. Wun't wanna be thee."

Then, a flash of brilliance comes to me.

"Eyup, Dave, if we find t'farmer an' tell 'im abart fire, 'e'll never suspect we did it. 'E'll just think we're doin' 'im a good turn." Dave concurred.

So, running like a pair of foxes with hounds on their tails, we race up the road and find a farmer with his wellies on standing in the field.

"Mister," I yell, "Yer 'edge is on fire back theere, " as I point to the scene of the crime.

"What the bloody 'ell 'ave yer been up to?" he snarls back at us, "Yer varmints."

"Weren't us, sir. 'Onest," I say.

"No it weren't. Yer should be thankful ter us," offers Dave. But, shovel in hand, he continues to berate us as we lead him to the burning bushes.

"I'll be in touch wi' yer school," he says. "Yer go ter t'Woodhouse West. Yer can't fool me."

He starts to shovel up dirt from around the hedge and

throws it on the burning flames. "Bugger off, yer rotten sods," he says and needing no persuasion, we take his advice.

Arriving home, smoke-steeped jacket over my arm, mother sniffs me from the other side of the kitchen and she's not fooled either. "Gimme thee jacket." Sniffs again. "What's tha been up to? Settin' bloody fires—by t'smell er thee jacket."

Then, without waiting for feedback, she smacks me hard on the back of my bare legs. "Gerrup them bloody stairs an' go to thee room."

Later, I was forced to give her the details. I was careful to stress that the fire was almost out after we left it.

True to his word, the farmer did contact the school. Next day, at morning assembly, Mr. V recounted the incident and gave everyone a lecture on the dangers of playing with matches. We were never discovered as being the culprits.

～～～

The dinnertime lunches at home were comforting. Mum was always ready with a tasty offering, usually leftovers— meat and potato pie, cold beef from the Sunday dinner with fried up mashed potatoes, soup with sliced bread. The three of us, Mum, Trevor and I, would sit around the table listening to BBC Radio.

*Ladies and Gentlemen. Workers' Playtime.*

Whistles, cheers, pounding piano.

*We have particular pleasure in welcoming back two famous*

*stars of radio—Elsie and Doris Waters, otherwise known as Gert and Daisy...*[14]

Trevor and I would scoff down our morsels. We were on a tight time schedule. "Please may I leave the table, Mum?" each of us would say. Then, permission granted, we'd head out the door.

One lunchtime, October 1951, just a few weeks after we had started school at the West, Trevor and I arrived home to find Aunt Ray and Mum deep in conversation.

"Thank God folk 'ave come ter their senses. Good old Winston Churchill's back runnin' t'country," says Aunt Ray.

"Aye. Labour got us inter a reight mess," agrees Mum, as she gives the pan of Lancashire hotpot another stir. "National Health Service were a wonderful idea but people took advantage er it. All them people gettin' free glasses, 'avin their teeth took out. Walkin' around wi' their free sets er false teeth. Where's t'money comin' from ter pay for all that?"

Mum and her two sisters, my aunts Ray and Buddy, were politically out of step with their working-class lifestyles. They were staunch Conservatives, monarchists to the core. Aunt Ray had a photo of Winston Churchill decorating the wall of her tiny kitchen at the back of her fish and chip shop, while the walls and furniture in Aunt Bud's flat paid tribute to the King and Queen. It was drilled into me from an early age that folk who supported Labour were layabouts who wanted something for nothing. This always puzzled me because Grandma and Granddad Bonsall voted Labour and they were decent, hardworking folk.

---

14    http://www.turnipnet.com/whirligig/radio/workersplaytime.htm

# OTHER GRANDMA

Every October, during the early to mid-fifties, Dad's employer, Hallamshire Electric Company, paid for its entire staff to go for a social weekend in London together. Trevor was routinely billeted at Grandma and Granddad's while I was shipped to other Grandma's house. Mum thought that the two of us would have been too much for either grandparent to handle.

My first weekend stay over at other Grandma's was in 1953. I hadn't seen her for three years—since her impromptu visit to the gates of Manor Lane School.

It was a rainy, mid-week summer evening. The four of us were sitting around the kitchen table having polished off our bangers and mash. Dad proceeded to announce the company trip.

"Oh, nice 'otel again," said mother, "Bit er sighteseein', dinner an' dance. That'll be oreight."

"I'll be staying at Grandma and Granddad's, won't I?" asked Trevor.

"Aye, an' 'e'll be goin' ter yer other Grandma's," she said, jerking her thumb in my direction.

"Why can't I go ter Grandma's as well?" I cried plaintively.

"Because," said mother.

"But why, Mum?" I persisted.

"Because I said so," she elaborated.

"It's not fair. 'E gets ter stay at Grandma and Granddads. I get stuck wi' t' other Grandma."

"Listen 'ere. Tha'll go where tha told. That's all."

The dreaded weekend in October rolled around. Friday evening. Carrier bag in hand, Dad escorted me up the steps and through the gate leading into other Grandma's back garden. Along the concrete pathway we walked, past the greenhouse and the neatly manicured lawn and flowerbeds that other Granddad, an avid gardener, had carefully nurtured. The tablecloth-sized back garden struck me as tidy, cared for, fit to be looked at but not played in—this being in sharp contrast to Grandma and Granddad Bonsall's yard, where annuals were hard to find and unruly patches of grass and barren earth were allowed to flourish, none the worse for being played upon.

"Mother, we're 'ere," shouted Dad, as he opened the back door and entered other Grandma's kitchen. "I've brought our Roger."

A diminutive, grey-haired woman, whom I recognized from our meeting at the school gates several years earlier, emerged from the front room. She was preceded by Terry, a brindle coloured Heinz 57 terrier mix, who greeted me by leaping up and depositing a stream of saliva on my legs. My mother was right. He really was a "mangy looking, foul smelling thing." But, he was friendly enough and I loved dogs.

"Put t'dog outside, mother," said Dad.

After she had done so, she turned around to face me, extending an arm to clasp hold of my hand. "Well, Roger, aren't you growing up? My, look at you. You're so handsome." Her voice was soft, neutral in texture, lacking the harshness of the Sheffield twang that I had grown accustomed to using and hearing.

*She's posh, stuck up, doesn't speak like my real Grandma,* I thought. Wonder if this is why Mum doesn't like her?

Then I noticed that her face had a kind look about it as she smiled from cheek to cheek. She did have a slightly pointed nose, but it was not a "beak" as mother would often claim. Her eyes were a little "beady," but they sparkled. A white apron, a cotton dress, a silver chain, a crucifix around her neck, woollen house slippers, cleanliness, tidiness, everything in its place.

Dad hung around the kitchen for a few minutes, chatting while he finished smoking his Woodbine® cigarette. Then, he looked at his watch. "'Ave ter go now, mother. Our Roger's change er clothes and 'is pyjamas are in that carrier bag." With that, he left.

Having seen so little of me, other Grandma was just as much on edge as I was. She was anxious to please me, whereas I was pre-occupied cross checking a mental list of her reputed flaws. That's how it was all weekend when she and I were alone:

fidgeting and awkward moments of silence, broken by other Grandma periodically leaping up from her chair and fussing over me. Would I like a glass of pop? A chocolate biscuit? How about some toast? "No thank you Grandma." I remember her holding out the palms of her hands to touch mine, then with childlike delight acting out finger rhymes:

*Here's the church, and here's the steeple*
*Open the door and see all the people.*
*Here's the parson going upstairs,*
*And here he is saying his prayers.*

What I remember most about that weekend, all weekends that I spent at other Grandma's house, is a pervasive sense of quietness, even isolation. Nobody ever stopped by like at Grandma Bonsall's home. No neighbours—who were they anyway? No friends, extended family. No relatives. Were there any? It was just the three of us.

But, it wasn't all sitting around. Friday night, other Granddad took me down to the *Sheffield Star and Telegraph* building and showed me around the printing shop where he worked. Gigantic drums of paper, rollers, conveyor belts, metal sheets embossed with type print, the smell of oil and molten metal. Saturday morning, he escorted me around the Sheffield Museum on Western Bank. Statues, swords, jewellery recovered from archaeological digs, bats, butterflies, and spiders. Then, on Saturday afternoon, we caught the tram down to the bottom of Duke Street. In those days, Duke Street, a major artery leading into the centre of Sheffield, was a hive of activity, especially on Saturdays. It was lined with an eclectic variety of shops: butcher, baker, fishmonger, greengrocer, shoe store, wallpaper shop, chemist, newsagent, fish and chip shop, a barber, and it goes without saying, numerous pubs. There were even shops that sold tripe and horsemeat. To add a touch of sobriety to the mix, there was a church and a funeral director. As we stepped off the tram onto the sidewalk, we positioned ourselves adroitly among the hustle and bustle of the throng of shoppers. Old people. Young people. Those in-between. Kids racing around. Women with shopping bags, swinging them back and forth like missiles. People walking. Looking in shop windows. Women stood in pairs gossiping. "Yer wun't believe what I 'eard Minnie whats-er-name did t'other day…" "Gio'er. She din't, did she? Blimey."

Navigating one's way among the human traffic was taken for granted. We could smell the mouth-watering aroma wafting up the street from Gunstone's bakery, to be replaced temporarily, as we trudged up the street, by emanations of a more pungent variety from Rosie Wilde's fresh fish store. Then, other Granddad stopped.

"Let's go in 'ere," he says.

I look at the sign above the shop window—T. Sandler & Sons Clothiers.

"That's a men and boys' clothing store, Granddad. Do yer need ter buy some new clothes?"

"No. We're goin' ter buy yer a new suit."

"No Granddad. I can't. That's too much."

"It's yer Grandma and my surprise."

The store was shoulder-to-shoulder customers, milling around the racks of suits placed close together in a room so lacking in space that I expected someone to announce "Everyone breathe in together." A cacophony of voices, the young and the old. A musky, unpleasant aroma of underarm sweat. Thanks to the services of someone who wore a tape measure around his neck. I wound up leaving the store in possession of a nondescript looking suit, wondering whether this would sit well on the home front.

I had a nagging feeling that mother would not approve of the suit. I didn't know why, but for the rest of the weekend, I wondered what lay ahead.

"Your Mum and Dad are going to get a lovely surprise, aren't they?" asked other Grandma.

"How shall we break the news to Mum?" I responded.

"Well, let's see. How about if we say, GuesswhatMumigot-anewsuit. Drrrrrr. Just like that. So quickly, she'll never guess?"

"We'll do that," I laughed.

Sunday evening. Along came the witching hour. The cuckoo clock on the mantel struck eight. Almost as if by appointment, Mum, Dad, and Trevor walked into the front room where I was sitting with other Grandma and Granddad—Trevor had already been picked up from the custody of my real grandparents.

"'Ello. 'Ow tha gerrin on? Tha looks well. Thanks ever so much for lookin' after our Roger." The usual exchange of greetings, invitations to sit down, Dad lighting a fag, other Grandma bringing him an ashtray, getting up to empty it every time Dad tapped an ash or two into it.

"Will tha stop fussin', Teresa? Sit thee'sen darn. Leave t'ashtray alone," said Arnold exasperatedly. Unlike other Grandma, he spoke the Sheffield brogue.

All sitting around in a circle. Dad took the lead. "Lovely time in London. Smashin' 'otel. Crackin' food an' t'lavatories were spotless."

I could never figure out why, but wherever he went, Dad made a special point of inspecting and rating the latrines. A few drops of piss on the floor, snot on the walls, turds that had not been flushed, all came under Dad's watchful eye. It made or broke a place for him.

The adults chatting amiably about this and that, events of the day, shifting awkwardly from topic to topic.

"Lovely Coronation, weren't it?" asks Mum, referring to Queen Elizabeth II's installation ceremony back in June. "We watched it on one er them tellys. Me mother's boss let us all watch it at t'otel 'e owns."

"Yes, it was," agrees other Grandma. "We just had the radio to listen to it."

"Have you been in that new Walsh's department store they've opened up in town?" asks other Grandma. "They've even got moving staircases called escalators to get you from floor to floor."

"Aye. Been in it. Lovely place. Nice stuff. Bit dear though," says Mum.

"Terrible thing abart that Sheffield Wednesday player, Derek Dooley, breakin 'is leg," offers Dad, referring to the young footballer whose career had been stopped in its tracks when he collided with Preston North End's goalkeeper in a game at Preston.

"Aye, 'is leg 'ad ter be amputated," other Granddad responds.

"They say t'meat prices are goin' ter go through t'roof next year when rationin' ends."

"Aye, there's summat ter be said for limitin' what folk can buy," nods other Granddad thoughtfully.

"And how are you liking it now on that housing estate where you're living?" asks other Grandma.

"Well, it's alright, it were fine at first, but now they've let some families in near us, musta come from slum housin' or summat, but they're draggin' t'neighborhood darn. Not botherin' wi' their gardens. Drinking an' shoutin' till late at night," offers Mum.

"There were summat in t'paper t'other day. Some bloke were sayin' that sterilizin' these people might be t'answer." Other Granddad was referring to controversial remarks made by the Medical Officer of the nearby town of Chesterfield.[15]

"Anyroad, we're not goin' ter solve problems er t'world,

are we?" interjects Dad mildly. "'Ow were our Roger this weekend? Were 'e any trouble?"

"No trouble at all," says other Grandma. "We got along famously."

I look over at other Grandma. She winks and smiles at me. I return the gestures. It's time to spill the beans.

"GuesswhatMumigotanewsuit," I blurt out at breakneck speed, all words merged into one.

Silence, broken only by a faint chortling sound coming from other Grandma. She alone saw the humour in it. Nobody else.

Mother looks me square in the face. She has probably caught a whiff of what I was trying to say and is clearly not amused. "I can't understand what you're saying. Speak more slowly," says she in her Sunday-best accent, the swanky one that she puts on for special occasions.

"Guess what. Mum. Igotanewsuit," I reply, a little more slowly but keeping the critical words unseparated.

"I still can't understand you. What's going on? Speak more slowly."

"Guess what. I got. A new suit," I finally enunciate, so as not to prolong the agony.

An awkward pause, then a three-word sentence from mother so loaded with insincerity that it fooled nobody. "Oh, that's nice." No tone of excitement or change of posture. Doesn't even ask to see it. She just holds eye contact with me, her expression of the "I'll speak to you later" type.

"Would yer like to see it?" asks other Granddad eventually.

"Yes. But you shouldn't have. It's too much."

Other Granddad disappears, then comes back holding up the suit for all to see. Mother stays rooted in the chair, uninterested, nodding politely.

A one-word sentence. "Lovely." Then, she elaborates. "You know, we're not short of anything now. Pat's doing ever so well at work. He makes eleven pounds a week now."

"That's wonderful, smashing," sing out the other grandparents in union, somewhat impressed by a wage that in hindsight seems pitiful, but was still fifty percent more than that of a labourer.

As we prepare to leave the house, Grandma places half a crown in Trevor's hands and in mine. Inevitably, this was followed by protestations from Mum and Dad. "No. They don't need money. Give it back, you two." The custom of the time among the working class was for adults to give money to children of family or friends who visited the home, and half a crown was a lot of money to kids like Trevor and me. At least to our parents, it was considered good manners to refuse such gifts. As kids, we were even expected to join in the charade, so we half-heartedly held out the coins for other Grandma. She took them and while mother wasn't looking, slipped them in our pockets with a nod and a wink. Dad didn't care.

The four of us trudge up the street toward the Manor Park Estate, a council housing development of mixed pre- and post-war vintage, to catch the bus home. Dad carries the new suit. Nobody speaks until we are well out of earshot of other Grandma's house. Then, mother explodes as she turns on me. "What the bloody 'ell were tha doin' lettin' thee other Granddad buy thee that bloody suit? Only common kids wear suits. Does tha think we come from t'Wybourn estate or Attercliffe Common?"

Those districts of Sheffield were at or near the bottom of the social ladder. Slum or poorly maintained housing. Disproportionate numbers of people on social assistance, higher crime rates, the usual afflictions of the bottom rung of the British lower working-class back then. So that's the problem, I think. It has nothing to do with other Granddad spending his money. It's all about mother's strange version of snobbery, her idea of a suitable wardrobe for our esteemed station in life. A station that includes living on a corporation estate, but a newer one than the Wybourn, living week-to-week on eleven pounds, and without a car, having to rely like ninety percent of the other residents of Sheffield on public transport. Lots of people were far worse off, but we were hardly in a position to be high-and-mighty.

"Tha't not even old enough to be wearin' long trousers anyroad. Nowt looks better than a navy blue blazer an' charcoal grey short trousers for a lad er your age."

"Mum, I din't know there were owt wrong wi' t'suit. An' other Granddad wanted ter buy it me," I respond.

"Tha won't be wearin' it. That's all."

So that was the end of the suit as far as I was concerned. I never saw it again. A few weeks after that weekend at other Grandma's, it cropped up in conversation around the dinner table at Grandma and Granddad Bonsall's place. Mother had apparently shown the suit to Granddad.

"Nowt wrong wi' t'bloody suit," says Granddad. "Lad should be wearin' it."

"Well 'e won't be," says mother. "It makes 'im look common."

Granddad shakes his head. "I don't know what gets inter their bloody minds, nowadays. Never 'eard such cock and bull."

Once Dad moved from Hallamshire Electric and the annual weekend trips to London became a thing of the past, I rarely saw my other Grandma. She had served her purpose.

Who was this woman who was just as much a part of my DNA as my maternal grandparents?

And, who was my real other Granddad? Other Grandma married Arnold Lawson in the mid 1930s, when Dad was a teenager. We were always told that this was her second marriage, her first husband (my biological other Granddad) having died shortly before or after Dad's birth in 1920. This is almost certainly untrue, a story concocted and perpetuated to hide the fact that Dad was the result of what was then called an illegitimate birth. A badge of shame in an unenlightened era. I shall probably never know who my real other Granddad was.

I have traced the Gordon lineage back to my great great great grandfather Alexander Gordon, who was born in Portsmouth in 1806 and living in Liverpool in the mid-nineteenth century. My great grandmother Caroline May Ryan (nee Gordon) named her daughter Teresa Gordon Ryan—other Grandma. Gordon was other Grandma's middle name. Her maiden surname was Ryan.

So, I do know that other Grandma was concealing part of her past. She was a single parent, born in Liverpool, plying her trade as a confectionary assistant in Nottingham where Dad was born, then in Sheffield where her mother Caroline May operated a confectionary store.

Notwithstanding mother's verbiage to the contrary, the only connection to the green sod of Ireland that I can find in Dad's ancestry lies in the fact that my great grandfather, Robert Ryan, the only record of whom is on my other Grandma's birth certificate, hailed from county Cork. Mother herself has just as strong or weak a connection to the Emerald Isle.

I have absolutely no idea how mother got the idea that other Grandma was promiscuous. Because Dad was a bastard? I don't think so. Even mother believed the family story. I'm content to leave that one unanswered. To be honest, I don't care.

---

15   *The Star.* September 26, 1953.

# UNSETTLING TIMES

We went on a family holiday in the summer of 1953, when I was ten years old. Aunt Bud and Uncle Carl came along with us to Prestatyn Holiday Camp in North Wales. Holiday Camps are a uniquely British creation. Some of them were military bases during WW 2, then used as vacation resorts afterwards; others evolved in the opposite direction, from leisure to military training usage. Regardless, they all looked like military bases and embodied a lifestyle that would do the armed forces proud. The loudspeaker blaring at seven o'clock in the morning—"Good morning and wakey wakey, campers. Report for breakfast in thirty minutes." The breakfast hall with row after row of long wooden tables, sixteen seaters, the two campers at one end of the table dishing out the nosh. The patrolling of the campsite by men in blue blazers, weaving themselves in among row after row of unimaginative prefabricated cabins—four walls and a roof. At 9:30 a.m., there was rambling, in other words, a walk around the neighbouring countryside; a swimming contest at 3 p.m.; children's races to follow at 4 p.m. Then, later in the week, at precisely-set times, the men's knobbly knee contest and the inevitable Miss Prestatyn pageant. Nightly drinking and dancing for the adults, which Mum and Dad and my aunt and uncle usually partook of. By all accounts, it was a cheap holiday and as kids, we considered the regimental style to be part of the fun.

What was not fun was finding out that Trevor and I had been provided with only a miniscule amount of the savings that we had carefully stashed away in our moneybox over the preceding year. The moneybox was the torso of a stereotypical black man, Joe Crow with only one arm, made out of metal. When you put a coin into his hand and pressed a lever, it fed the coin into his mouth. Every time we visited a relative, we'd be handed a coin, a shilling or a half crown, so that we could have lots of treats. An unlimited supply of those ice cream sundaes called Knickerbocker Glories that the Holiday Camp sold, so we were led to believe. One afternoon, Aunt Ray arrived with a stash of pre-war silver three-penny bits. We polished them one by one, all seven pounds of them, bringing our total holiday savings to nine pounds. Then, the moneybox, which had stood on the mantelpiece all year, disappeared just before the holiday. It was in the safe keeping of Mum and Dad, we were told. Late in the holiday, Trevor and I realized that we had only savoured the much-ballyhooed Knickers once during the entire week. Where did all the rest of the money go? We asked Mum and Dad.

"These 'olidays cost a lot er money. Who do yer think pays for t'cabin an' t'meals an' t'train fare?" asks Mum.

We challenge her. "But our aunts and uncles and Grandma and Granddad gave us that money for treats, not for you to use for them expenses".

"Ungrateful buggers. Go back ter t'cabin an' stay there till yer Dad an' me get back."

Trevor and I shuffled back to the cabin in tears. If we had been told all along that times being hard, the donations to Joe Crow were for the communal good and that we were likely to receive only a crumb or two from it, we could have accepted that. But, to lead us to believe otherwise left us feeling robbed. Afterwards, we mentioned what had happened to Aunt Ray, probably the chief contributor. She half-heartedly defended our parents—cost of living, blah, blah, blah. But her facial expressions told a different story—the surprised look then the grimace, clenched teeth. She was not amused, but was afraid to be seen supporting us lest she incur mother's wrath.

～～～

"Gio'er doin' that. Tha'll kill thee'sen," Dad yells at me. I pick myself up from the front lawn. I had scaled the drain-pipe to climb up on to the roof of the outhouse then jumped on to the lawn, a drop of about ten feet.

"Anyroad," continues Dad, "Tha'll be pleased ter know that thee tortoise 'as turned up. It's inside t'outhouse. A man found it up at Woodthorpe bus terminus. 'Ow it got there, all that way, God only knows."

"Blimey. 'Ow did 'e know it were mine, Dad?"

"'E asked around. Someone said 'e knew tha 'ad a tortoise so 'e brought it ter t'ouse. Tek care er it now."

Pets consisted largely of a succession of tortoises because they could be kept in the outhouse and taken for an occasional stroll in the garden. Mum would have no pets indoors. Dogs were strictly off limits, as they would patrol the very innards of the home, walk on the rugs, the linoleum, maybe leave their offensive trademarks behind them. So, tortoise after tortoise left the confines of Ogley's pet barn at the old Rag and Tag Sheaf market to take up residence in our outhouse and amble around our front lawn. The trouble was that Trevor and I would forget about them and they would wander off. One Christmas, Mum relaxed the house pet rule and allowed us to have a bird in a cage as an indoor pet, a green and yellow budgie, which we named Billy. Sometimes, when Mum was in a good mood (or out of the room), we would set Billy free to fly around the kitchen, settle on our heads, and peck away at our hair. But the pet that endeared herself to me the most was a calico cat that Aunt Ray gave us. She was found hanging around her fish and chip shop—a stray in a busy area of town. Without a four-legged family, she was in need of the next best thing—a human family. We called her Tibbles. Her home was the outhouse and the great outdoors. Each day I'd feed her, change her litter, play with her, and make sure she was bedded down in the outhouse for the night. Then, one day, she didn't return home. I scouted the neighbourhood, but there was no sign of her.

"Mum, I can't find Tibbles. Yer ampt seen 'er 'ave yer?"

"No. I don't know where she is. She might 'ave just run off."

Dad was equally non-informative. She never did return. I would keep asking my parents from time to time where they thought she might be.

"She'll be oreight. She'll 'ave found another 'ome chances are. Stop thinking abart 'er." That was the stock in trade answer from mother. Dad just said he didn't know.

I remember the Christmas after she disappeared. I had convinced myself that she would turn up on Christmas day. I kept opening the door, looking out of the window.

"She's not comin 'ome. All these presents we bought thee an' tha't lookin' for t'cat. Lerrit drop." says mother.

I cried that night.

Years later, Dad revealed the ugly truth.

Tibbles, an unspayed female who was allowed to roam, had become pregnant. Mother had told Dad she wanted no kittens at number 23.

"I did what she told me. I put t'cat in a bag, carried 'er ter Smelter Wood an' drowned 'er in that stream that runs through there. It weren't easy. 'Ad nightmares for months afterwards." I didn't pass judgement. Dad knew the consequences of disobeying mother. So, he had to live with the nightmares.

Speaking of nightmares, it was about the same time as the Tibbles episode, toward the end of my elementary schooling at Woodhouse West, that I started to have sleeping problems. I became afraid of the dark, of what could be happening to me in the real world while I slept. Better to stay awake—to be on guard. My childhood imagination navigated a world of blackness, where heinousness and fear reigned supreme. It was a world in which I, the victim, was surrounded by forces and beings that were out to harm me—but only at nighttimes while I slept. I hated being this way, but my parents could not understand this and even chastised me for it.

Around midnight. I'm pretending to be asleep. My parents, en route to their own bed, decide to take a diversion. On goes the ceiling light in my room. Better not react. Keep up the façade. Then, they both hover over me.

"'E's not asleep. Only play actin'," snarls mother.

"I can see 'is eyes movin under 'is lids," offers Dad, the smell of cigarette breath letting me know that he's only a few inches from my face.

"I'm bloody fed up wi' this racket. 'E'd just better be asleep," warns dear old Mum.

How long are they going to stay here? What will happen if they do find out I'm still awake? How long can I keep it up?

Then, I hear their footsteps moving away from me. I can

sense the light being switched off. I keep my eyes closed, which is a good thing because a few seconds later it suddenly goes on again, then off for good. I knew they'd try to catch me out.

Mum and Dad got into the habit of spending Friday evenings at the Witherses. I hated those evenings.

"Why don't yer ask t'Witherses up ter our 'ouse," I'd say.

"None er yer business." was the standard reply.

Trevor and I would be in bed when they left—around eight o'clock. As soon as they left, I'd crawl out of bed and spend the next two hours sitting on the stairs, occasionally daring to go down to the kitchen, just to check things out. How could I sleep? Who knows what might happen when no one's around downstairs? Might as well invite all the criminals in Sheffield into the home. It was a long wait, but I stayed at my post. Thankfully, when Mum and Dad left the Witherses to come back home, Mum's loud "turrahs" carried. So, I was able to sneak back into bed, close my eyes, and act the part.

I'll always remember one night in particular—one of the few occasions when a semblance of understanding came from my parents. It was the early hours of the morning on the night in question. I was terrified. Shadows on the bedroom walls became faces, hands, or feet of intruders, silhouettes taking on three-dimensional forms. The yapping of a neighbourhood dog, left out for the night, became a pack of Dobermans snarling and baring their teeth at me. I got up out of bed and gently closed my bedroom door—as always, it was left ajar so that

I could see the upstairs landing. I switched on the light and walked around my bedroom to make sure that it harboured no interlopers, two- or four-legged, and then started toward the light switch. The door opened and in walked Dad. "'Ow come tha't not asleep? What's goin' on?"

"I'm scared. I keep seein' people in t'room an 'earing packs er dogs barking." My voice quivers.

"Packs er dogs?" asks Dad incredulously. Maybe that tipped him off that I needed some kind of help. He turns off the light and asks me to point out the wall images. One by one he identifies its source. The leg is a piece of curtain, the face a jug, and so it goes on. Back to bed. But not resting, not at peace, still tightly wound.

She's standing there. Facing me. A ghostly figure of white light. Shimmering around her silhouette. Her hands behind her back. Holding something. A knife. I know it's a knife. And she's walking toward me. The expression on her face— grim, determined, uncompromising. I am terrified and I cry out. "Nooooo."

Then she vanishes and my mother comes running into my bedroom. "What on earth is goin' on?"

"A ghost, a white woman 'oldin a knife came inter me room," I sob.

"I know yer imaginin' it, but who was she?" asks mother.

"I don't know."

A lie. That apparition was my mother.

# SOME TURBULENCE

My parents sought medical help for me, so they did appreciate that I had a nervous disorder. It's just that their patience and compassion were in short supply inside the home. Once a month, I took a morning away from school so that Mum could take me across the city to see a child psychiatrist employed by the School Board, the eminent Dr. Bartholomew Winterbottom, M.R.CC.L.R.C.P., D.P.M. Two double-decker bus rides each way. His clinic was located in an old Victorian home that sported a brass nameplate on one of the pillars of its gateway—"Sheffield Education Committee. Child Guidance Clinic." It was located in one of the more desired, established areas of the city—directly opposite King Edward VII Grammar School for Boys.

In retrospect, I wonder who was the patient on these visits. The man of many letters spent most of his time talking to Mum behind closed doors. I hardly ever saw him. His secretary would give me a drawing pad and pencil, and I would be asked to depict the theme of the month: Peace and Contentment, Disharmony and Conflict, Health and Vitality, the Richness of Love, Enemies and Friends. Alone and bored to tears, I would wait for Mum to emerge from the honourable doctor's office, hand in my assignment, and then troop out of the clinic. There were a couple of occasions when the doctor himself actually saw me.

One morning, instead of Mum doing her disappearing act, a distinguished-looking middle-aged man in a three-piece suit introduces himself to me.

"I'm Dr. Winterbottom. How about we sit down together and we do a little test today?"

Without waiting for a response or telling me what the little test was all about, he shows me a bunch of cartoon pictures. "What's wrong with that picture?" asks Dr. W.

"The cowboy is shooting at the Indian farthest away from him instead of the one about to chop off his head." Best to let go of my Sheffield accent for this occasion.

"Very good. Now, how about this picture?"

"The man is trying to milk the cow, but he's squeezing the cow's nose instead of its...erm, tits?"

"Teats, actually. Very good. This is going quite well. Now, next picture. What is missing from it?"

"The man has no...erm." I'm searching for the right word. Cock? Prick? Knob? No, I'll have to use that daft word that only kids use.

"That man has no...Tommy," I finally say.

"Well done, Roger."

After about twenty minutes of this nonsense, we revert to

the familiar protocol—Mum and Dr. W. in his office, while I sit in a room at the other end of the hallway drawing a picture of a dog on a long leash peeing on a lamp post while his owner stuffs himself with fish and chips wrapped in newspaper. Happiness is the theme.

The next time Mum had a tête a tête with the honourable Doctor, he told her that on the basis of the test that he had conducted on me, the cartoon test, his determination was that I had an average I.Q. and it would be unlikely that I would qualify for entry to Grammar School through the eleven plus examination. Of course, Mum proceeded to tell me this discouraging assessment right away. Just what I wanted to hear.

The second and last time I saw Dr. W. perplexed me no end. After his usual confab with Mum, he asked to speak to me privately in his office. I got to sit where Mum usually sat. "Roger, after speaking with your Mum, I think it would be a good idea to explain to you how babies are made. Don't you think that's a good idea? Is this something that's been troubling you? Perhaps keeping you awake at night? Bit of a stumbling block for you?"

How am I supposed to respond to a bunch of strange questions like that, I think. So, I shrug my shoulders. "Well," continues himself, unperturbed by my indifferent response, "I have a book here that explains the whole thing."

He proceeds to open up a large medical book, about the size of a world atlas. Drawing after drawing of human innards. A picture of a naked man and woman standing like statues side by side. Making love? Not in a fifties' anatomy and physiology text. A sterile and grotesque depiction of a natural process in which tenderness and beauty are intrinsic elements—the words nurture and love absent from the story.

"What's that coiled tube inside her belly?" I ask.

"Oh, that's just her intestine. We don't need to worry about that."

"Look at these little chaps. What do they remind you of?"

"Tadpoles."

"Of course. And they have little tails like tadpoles to help them swim. But they are called sperm. They're what your Daddy gives to your Mummy to make a baby."

I keep following Dr. W's patter, more confused about why we are talking about the topic than about its details. When he gets to explain how the little tadpoles get into Mummy's body to say hello to the little eggs, he shifts uncomfortably in his seat, clearly more comfortable with the book of drawings in which this scene is missing.

"To show his love for your Mummy, Daddy puts his penis in Mummy's vagina. That's called intercourse. You might have heard it called by a slang name around the school yard?"

He's waiting for my response. Dare I say it?

"I think it's called a shag," I mutter.

"Oh. Is that so?" Has Dr. W learned something new?

When we get outside, I tug at Mum's arm.

"He wanted to tell me about babies being born."

"Oh, that would have been interesting," says Mum.

"Will you tell him not to talk to me anymore about that? I'm not interested in it."

~~~~~

During my last year at elementary school, Mum and Dad started to argue. Behind the scenes, there may well have been shorter, minor skirmishes that preceded the era of the major battles—a nose out of joint, a finger pointed tenaciously, or a tongue let loose of its bridle. However, as kids, such occurrences escaped our notice, so it seemed to be an all or nothing situation—calmness or all out, raging warfare. The episodes were always at weekends, beginning on Saturday morning, and ending late into Sunday. We were never told what the arguments were about and since we were never there when they started, it would have been pointless for us to speculate. "Keep out er it," was our admonishment. Mum was the aggressive, demonstrative participant, Dad the compliant, reserved one. She ranted and raved, threw crockery around, slammed doors as she raced from room to room. Dad responded to her through mild mutterings of disagreement, stone silence, or pleas to call a truce.

"Tha't nowt but a sponger, a bleedin' layabout. Tha dun't know what it's like ter make a real livin'."

"Now, come on Nell, it's gone far enough." Dad reaches out to her to her, touches her arm. Mum swiftly recoils.

"Get away from me, yer bleedin' chuff."

Mum races out of the kitchen, up the stairs, into her bedroom, weeping, yelling and slamming doors as she does so. Dad quietly leaves the house, sits on the front steps, then after a while picks up a spade from the outhouse and starts to tidy the garden. Trevor and I are spectators to all of this.

But were we? For the entire time, our home was off limits to anyone. If we heard a knock at the door, a friend wanting to know if one of us wanted to come out to play, Trevor or I would rush to open the door a crack, embarrassed at the scene within. Once out, we'd head off as far as possible from our house and make sure that the friend didn't set foot on our property on the return journey.

"Got ter go now. Dinner'll be ready," say I, one hundred yards from home. I race off before he can say anything.

But dinner was never ready on those weekends. We all got by, piecing together scraps from the pantry, managing the best we could. Sometimes, Mum would make a simple meal such as bacon and eggs for Trevor and me, but Dad was not on the guest list.

The arguments always culminated in Mum leaving home, carrying no personal effects, on Sunday afternoon or evening.

"I'm gone. An' I'm not comin' back."

"Nell, be reasonable. Tha dun't need ter go. Think abart t'kids."

But being reasonable wasn't on the agenda.

"Where do yer think she's gone, Dad?"

"Don't know. Not far I expect. Don't worry. She'll be back."

Half an hour or so later, in she walks.

"I only came back for them kids sake," she blubbers.

"Come 'ere Nell." Dad walks toward her, they embrace, and it's all over. Now we can have a normal carry on.

My brother Trevor and I got on reasonably well together, but we weren't close. For whatever reason, my parents chose to divide us by over-emphasising or concocting perceived strengths and weaknesses and playing them one against the other.

"Thee brother Trevor's got a 'art er gold. 'E's got more feeling in 'is big toe than tha's got in thee entire body." Mum or Dad to me.

"Tha'll never amount ter much. Tha't too busy carryin' on an getting' inter trouble ter be any good at thee schoolwork. Our Roger can knock socks off thee." Mum or Dad to Trevor.

I was characterized as the brainy, unfeeling elder brother, while Trevor was the scholastically inferior, caring sibling. Even if there were a grain of truth in their discernment, why use it so destructively?

It was during my last year at the West, early 1954, that Mum decided to work in a downtown machine shop, Pneumatic Components Limited, to save money toward a new car so that Dad would be better able to do his job as a sales representative with Hallamshire Electric. He was commuting from customer to customer by bus. Hopefully, a car would enable him to be more efficient and he would rise in the ranks. She took a job working a lathe—a dirty, smelly, strenuous job. She worked alongside bulging, muscled men, all performing the same job, and, in those days, it was considered perfectly reasonable to pay women at half the rate as men. Whose idea was it that she should take the job of a machinist when, with a Grammar School education and eight GCE "O" Levels to boot, she was qualified for a more intellectually-challenging and less arduous occupation?

The home was left abandoned during the weekdays. We all went our separate ways—Trevor and I to our separate schools, as he had transferred to the new Stradbroke Elementary; Dad to his white-collar job; Mum to her "roll up the sleeves," blue-collar one. For Trevor and me, school fare—usually, sloppy messes—replaced midday dinners at home. We would arrive home, one by one, to the remnants of breakfast, dirty dishes, unmade beds, and carelessly scattered items of clothing reminding us that it was a house that had not been inhabited. Mum would come home in her raggedy work clothes, hands still grimy with machine oil, and Dad, suit, neatly pressed shirt and tie, briefcase in hand. Mum cooked our tea, Dad did the dishes. In between, there was a stilted conversation around the old wooden kitchen table.

"'Ow did tha get on at school?" Mum to me.

"Oreight."

"An' 'ow did tha get on. Din't get in ter any trouble did tha?" Mum to Trevor.

"No."

"Owt interesting 'appen on thee travels?" Mum to Dad.

"Not much. Saw Sidney Grinstead before I went out on me calls this mornin'. Told me that Mr. Wiseman's 'appy wi' t'work I'm doin'."

"Should be an' all," says Mum, "They're payin' thee next to nowt an' expectin' thee to do thee job travellin' on t'buses."

"Turn t'radio on Pat. Let's listen ter t' *Archers*."

My last year at Woodhouse West was a turbulent one in several respects.

# Part II: Adolescent Years
## (1954–1961)

# HIGH STORRS

Ninety percent of our schoolwork was aimed toward the infamous eleven plus examination, a series of standardized tests carried out by the School Board to determine whether children were clever enough to proceed to Grammar School or, by inference, dumb enough to continue on in the secondary modern school system. It was administered to children in the final grade of elementary school when they were between eleven and twelve years old. Proceeding to Grammar School carried with it the possibility of moving on to university and entering a profession; secondary modern school children were excluded from a university education. They could look forward to a career in one of the trades[16] or in the unskilled workforce. The exams were challenging— English grammar, comprehension, arithmetic, and an aptitude test that was supposed to test your intelligence. The pass rate in a working-class school like Woodhouse West was around ten percent. Further weeding out was done within the Grammar School System through "O" and "A" level examinations, so that only about three percent of the nation's eighteen year olds attended university. The system was unfair and elitist because irrevocable decisions were made at an early age, and since academic performance and socioeconomic status were linked, students from middle- and upper-class backgrounds predominated within universities, to a lesser degree within the Grammar Schools. The education system was a powerful tool in perpetuating the British class system.

Nonetheless, it meant everything to me to pass that eleven plus exam. My academic capability was a source of pride. I envisioned myself as a physician or schoolteacher, someone respected by the community. I was afraid of what the future may hold if I were to fail the exam because I wasn't much good at anything involving the use of body parts other than my brain. There was a gap of several weeks between taking the test and learning the results. I remember panicking, convincing myself that I had blown it.

"Why dun't tha go an' see Mr. Vaughan?" asks Mum. "'E might know summat. Put thee mind at rest."

So, I did. In his office, Mr. Vaughan kindly told me, "I thought you would pass the test, Roger." About all he could say.

Depending on where one placed the emphasis in that sentence, "thought" or "pass," it could be taken either of two ways. Since a nuance in communication such as this was beyond me at that age, I just had to wait. The school board mailed decisions out—positive ones in large brown envelopes, negative ones in letter-sized white ones. Just before school recessed for the summer break, on a dull Saturday morning in June, a brown envelope was delivered to our house. I had been selected to go to High Storrs Grammar School for Boys, the second highest, arguably the co-equal of King Ted's,[17] in the city. I was relieved and proud; Mum and Dad were pleased also.

Yet, negative ones that emanated from turbulence within the home offset these positive feelings. Sometime over the summer of 1954, Mum and Dad, in what had become a typical behaviour pattern, spent the whole weekend arguing. It was an especially nasty flare-up—epithets and crockery being thrown around by Mum, Dad his usual passive self, Mum leaving on a sunny Sunday afternoon (ostensibly for good, in reality for a walk around the neighbourhood), Trevor and I caught up in the whole mess, distressed to the core.

After Sunday tea, Mum tried to break the awkwardness of a conversation replete with single phrases and sentences punctuated by long periods of silence. "I know what we can all do ter make us feel better. Let's go up an' take a look at our Roger's new school." Perhaps not the shot in the arm that our Trevor might have preferred, given the unfair intellectual comparisons that he had endured, but at least it would bring the four of us together for a few hours. So, we travelled together on two double-decker buses to the opposite side of the city from where we lived to an upscale part of Sheffield called Ringinglow. We stepped off the bus and turned the corner on to High Storrs Road, to look the building squarely in the face.

"Just look at it," I said excitedly.

It was a mesmerizing sight all right—a two-storey brick structure that extended about a hundred feet or so back from the pavement and parallel to it like two tentacles of a dead octopus. Light rebounding from the abundant spacious windows that festooned the walls of the building from a still powerful sun. Concrete decorative columns around the three entrances—boys, staff, and girls—provided an elegant accent to what at first appeared to be a purely functional design. Then, in what might be thought of as the middle of the octopus, directly above the staff entrance, was the building's distinctive clock tower, sprouting like a miniature version of Big Ben from the roof.

"It were built just before t'war," said Mum. "Used ter be in an old building in t'city centre."

"Wow. It looks smashin'. I can 'ardly wait," I exclaim.

As we moved back around the corner past the bus stop on Ringinglow Road and continued to walk around the perimeter of the school, it became apparent that the building and its endless expanse of manicured playing fields took up what in North America would be termed a city block. It was secure from intruders, surrounded by brick walls, wrought iron fencing, and gates. I was later to discover that it was of the art deco architectural style—lots of frills, very elegant, but very practical. A very impressive structure. I was excited, filled with anticipation and awe, but also anxious. At what, I was unsure.

～～～

September 1954. It's a bright sunny morning, a change from the depressing summer we've just had. The rain washed out the cricket Test[18] series between the heavily favored England side and underdogs, Pakistan. In the end, the teams drew, shaking hands and conceding defeat to the weather. Mum was right about the meat prices going up after the end of rationing. Sheffield was not hit as hard as London, however, where the butchers at the Smithfield market caused what the media referred to as "price chaos."

The start of another school year. High Storrs is at the opposite end of town from where I live. This means a one-hour journey on two separate buses—public buses; no such thing as "school buses." I'm sitting on the upper deck of the Number 93 bus headed toward town, Dad alongside me, a miasma of cigarette smoke swirling around us, Dad contributing his share of noxious fumes to the smoggy atmosphere as he puffs away on a Woodbine. As the smoke condenses on the window next to me, I periodically wipe away a porthole in the slimy, opaque film that continues to form. I peer at the uninspiring scene outside. Housing estate after monotonous housing estate, row after row of identical red brick semis, plumes of sooty smoke emanating from their chimneys. Bed shirts, bloomers, and bras hung out on washing lines. The clusters of people queuing at bus stops stare disinterestedly into space—women with cotton scarves tied over their heads, men with stubble covered chins and grubby hands, adolescents in their school uniforms. It's as if everyone in this city is programmed to follow a lifestyle of drudgery, their minds on automatic pilot, the working poor conceding the better part of their lives to the better-offs that run the steel mills, the cutlery and machine shops.

The bus stops with a jolt at Manor Park Shopping Centre. I look around the bus and through the smog I can make out the occasional school cap and bonnet, hallmarks of the various grammar schools. Bedecked in the green and navy blue colours of High Storrs Grammar School for Boys, I am feeling proud, yet a little nervous. Will I know anyone there? How will it be different from the West? Will I do well? Will I fit in?

The bus arrives at the Pond Street bus terminus in the city centre and everyone disembarks. Dad walks with me to the opposite side of the busy transit hub to the queue for the bus to Bents Green. It's easily discernible by virtue of all the navy blue and green headgear—green berets for the girls, comically designed navy blue and green caps for the boys. Split down the middle like two halves of an apple pie, one side navy blue, and the other green. Had the blazer been similarly designed, the effect would have been that of a clown's costume. Thankfully, the blazer was navy blue, with a badge of the Sheffield crest on the breast pocket. Short, above the knee grey trousers, grey socks, black shoes, grey shirt, and navy blue and green striped tie and everything must be just so.

The atmosphere on the Number 28 Bent's Green bus is healthier. Most of the passengers are pupils, so there's no cigarette smoking, except for one gentleman wearing a grey raincoat, his silver hair sleeked back with an abundance of Brylcreem. He hangs on to the post on the platform at the back of the bus and on to his cigarette for the entire journey. I later discover that he is Mr. Littlewood ("Woody"), the gym teacher. He takes it upon himself to watch over the flock as they journey back and forth. Woe betide anyone falling out of step. The bus is noisy, abuzz with chatter about summer holidays, Sheffield Wednesday, Sheffield United, the latest flick, and speculation about who the new form master may be. As the bus stops by the school, there is an almighty clamour to leave it. Boys jostle with one another, schoolbags catching sitting passengers in the face. Woody bawls, with minimal effect, to try to stem the surging throng. When most of them have vacated the bus, Dad says to me, "You'll be oreight now. Good luck." Several other first-year kids played out the same scene with their chaperones.

Off the bus, I follow the crowd into the schoolyard. Kids ranging in age from eleven to sixteen congregate in clusters, each one representing a different year of progression, second to fifth formers. Sixth formers are in their classrooms. They don't have to wait for the bell to ring. The first years, like myself, look lost, ambling around between the groups, hoping to recognize someone, be recognized, or be welcomed by a stranger. The catchment area for the school is the entire city of Sheffield, so friends are at a premium for the newcomers. Then, I recognize Jimmy Earnshaw from way back at Manor Lane Elementary, a lifetime ago. Here comes Peter Hinchcliffe, the other boy from the West selected to go to High Storrs. We chat among ourselves—the awkwardness is diminished.

Clang, clang, clang. The bells at the two entrances into the school ring. Boys at either end of the yard stampede through the doors, pushing and shoving one another, streaming along corridors and up flights of stairs as if another Diaspora is in progress. They, like I, are en route to their form rooms. I have a piece of paper that tells me the room number of Form 1B. Without much difficulty, I join my other thirty or so future classmates milling around the rows of desks, making schoolboy small talk. "Which school did you go to?" "Where do you live?" "What's your Dad doing for a living?" Then, a short thirty-something-year-old man wearing a black gown enters the room and silence descends. He approaches the blackboard and chalks "Mr. Presgrave." He then turns around to the class.

"Good morning boys. Every boy here should have been told he is in Form 1B. If you have been told anything different, come to the front now and I'll tell you how to find your correct form room." Two or three boys troop up to talk to him, and then leave the room with their marching orders.

"When the bell rings, you will follow me to the assembly hall for the daily morning service. Then, after the Headmaster has spoken to you, you must come back to this classroom. You will be assigned desks in alphabetical order, starting at the doorway with the beginning of the alphabet."

Off we go to a huge assembly hall and stand facing the raised platform in the second row behind the kids in 1A. Standing in the two rows behind us are the 1C and 1D kids, then the second year A to D, and so on. An older boy is playing the piano over to one side of the hall. Then, a distinguished looking barrel chested, grey-haired man, hair style a bit like an older version of Tony Curtis, clad as are all the teachers in a black gown, struts confidently into the hall, up the stairs and onto the platform. An older boy, the anointed head boy for the school year, follows closely behind him. What follows is a religious service, à la Church of England, replete with hymns, prayers, and a recitation from the Bible read by the new head boy. Then, a few words of general welcome by the Headmaster, followed by his admonition to all the first-year boys to sit down on the hardwood floor and stay behind to listen to his words of wisdom.

"You boys have been chosen to be educated at High Storrs Grammar School for Boys, the finest grammar school in the city. Represent it with pride wherever you go. You will wear your full school uniform going to and from school. That includes your school cap." I groan inwardly.

The Headmaster, Mr. George Mack, pontificates for what seems like an interminably long time, in reality fifteen minutes or so. We learn that not only is the school cap split down the middle, but so is the school itself. Closed glass doors separate the boys' side of the school from the girls' side. Boys are not to be seen talking to the girls, even during the small portion of the midday lunch period when there is an overlap of timing.

Not only are we prohibited from the girls' section of the school, but there are certain sections of the neighbourhood that are off limits, "out of bounds," at lunch times. The "roughs," an area of wooded, uncultivated terrain at the back of the school is singled out for special mention.

We learn that corporal punishment, the gym slipper on the backside or the cane on the hands, is routinely practiced, as it is good for us. Detention after school, or writing five hundred to a thousand repetitive lines about the errors of our ways are alternative forms of correction.

The stern figure at the rostrum goes on to explain about school prefects, selected sixth formers who are the Headmaster's soldiers on the ground, and about "houses" to which each student is assigned. These are aggregations of students from all levels of the school that compete in sporting activities. The houses are named after ancient tribes. I become a Jute. Sports include football and cricket, but also ones that I have not encountered before—"rugger" and "harriers." These, I later learn, are fancy names for rugby and long-distance running.

The teachers are all male and wear black gowns. We are always to address them as "Sir." The Headmaster is to be given a special form of recognition that involves everyone standing to attention when he enters a room. To give us practice, he makes us all stand in unison.

Before he dismisses us, he tops off his cheery monologue with a warning about a curious practice known as "fagging." On the first day of the school year, second-year students pick on first years ("fags"[19]) and subject them to some form of ridicule. The man with the clipped and polished accent asks us to grin and bear it, show a stiff upper lip.

After all this, I'm left wondering whether I've enrolled at a grammar school in a mostly working-class city or at an upper-crust boarding school such as Eton or Harrow.

I survived the fagging at morning recess on that first day. Shoes tied together, jacket put on backwards. Nothing much to it. Some fags had been forced to put their heads down into the toilet bowls while the perpetrators threatened to pull the flush. But that's all it amounted to, a threat.

My first term at school was troublesome. I did not adapt well at all. The special-occasion fagging was a nuisance, but like my classmates, I took it with a grain of salt. But, when it was superseded by all-occasion bullying within the class, I was not so sanguine. The more demonstrative element of the class decided to pick on boys who were on the shy side. Between classes, they grabbed hold of the boy of the day and tried to force him into a small cupboard underneath the teacher's bench at the front of the class. The boy would kick and scream, even cry. I knew that one day my turn would come and I had already decided what I would do.

Joe Collier, our German teacher, had given all the boys in the class German names. There being no direct translation for Gordon, I was named Schotte—Scot. On that fateful rainy morning, the class confined indoors at break time, someone started to shout, "Schotte in the cupboard." Then, more joined in the chorus, until the chant became overwhelming. A couple of boys started to grab hold of me. "No need for that. I'll go in t'cupboard," said I chirpily.

The bullies stood back amazed as I climbed into the cupboard and closed the door behind me. "Just leave me a gap er air. I'm fine in 'ere," I said, lying through my teeth of course.

In walked Mr. Presgrave, "Sep" as we nicknamed him, and the class scuttled back into their seats. I emerged from the cupboard just as Sep was about to start writing on the blackboard.

"Well, Gordon, you're full of surprises. Still like to play hide and seek, do you? Were you playing tiddlywinks in there?" Sep was in good humour and I took the ribbing.

The class was in stitches. Raucous laughter everywhere. "Sorry, sir," was all I could muster.

After that event, I never had any trouble fitting in, socially. The bullies in the class respected me. I'd gone along with their stupid fiasco, taken it on the chin, and not ratted on them.

Even years later, when passing one of them in the corridor, I'd hear a whisper "Schotte in the cupboard." We'd both laugh. I formed a fine group of friends during my seven years at High Storrs.

---

16    In the 1950s, the perception of trades was different than what it is today. Usually "blue collar" jobs, they were viewed as a "second best" career option to that of the professions.

17    King Edward VII Grammar School for Boys.

18    In cricket, a Test series is a sequence of games between two international teams, each game lasting up to 5 days.

19    In those days, the term "fag" did not carry the offensive connotation or meaning as it does today. It Britain, it was either a slang term for a cigarette, or as in this case, a somewhat demeaning term for a first year student at a Boarding or Grammar school.

# STORMY WEEKENDS

High Storrs Grammar School gave me breathing space from a tempestuous home life that had become entrained since that last year I spent at Woodhouse West—the year that Mum had made the decision to hit the factory floor. My teenage years were spent growing up in a house in which long periods of tranquility and stability were punctuated by weekends when my mother went berserk. She flew into tantrums, threw crockery around, and raced from room to room shouting, swearing, and crying uncontrollably, while Dad simply stood around, occasionally taking cover in another room or in the garden. Mercifully, the flinging and smashing of crockery occurred while my brother and I were in bed–a rude awakening–we were witnesses to everything else. Dad's demeanour was stoic, though his face carried a worried expression. He said very little, allowing Mum to rant and rave, only occasionally offering a mild correction to her diatribe, which for the most part was unfocused. A typical exchange might include references to Dad's war service, his manhood, white-collar job, and his encounter with polio.

"Tha't not a real man. Tha took a ground job in t' RAF.

Lookin after t'planes. But not flyin' o'er Germany–fightin' like a real man would."

"I at least served me country. All tha relatives stayed out er t' war altogether. Excused national service."

"Don't thee talk abart my family. An' 'ere's another thing. 'Ere I am workin' me fingers ter t'bone. Comin' 'ome night after night covered in machine grease. For what? Ter make enough money so that some fine day tha'll be able ter drive around in a car all day. Wearin' thee collar an' tie. I must be bleedin' mad or summat."

"Now, Nell, it weren't my idea for thee ter work."

"No, but din't tek thee long ter go along wi' it, did it? I spend all week workin' wi' real men, men who roll up their sleeves, aren't afraid er a bit a muck. They don't wear a collar an' tie an' walk around wi' a brief case like a chuffin' puff."

"Well, tha knows I can't do that kind er job on account er 'avin 'ad polio."

"Polio? Polio? 'Ow much longer are tha goin' ter keep on abart that? A small slump in thee shoulder. Anyone would think thar were spendin' t'rest er thee life in an iron lung."

Mum would often deflect her frustrations at other Grandma. "She cared so much abart thee she let thee be brought up by Auntie on Staniforth Road. Tha might 'ave got in t' way. 'Ow could she 'ave met Arnold wi' thee around?"

Keeping his silence, Dad just stood there, looking glumly at the floor.

"Bloody Irish tart. What do we need 'er sort for o'er 'ere anyway? She should er stayed back on the dear old Emerald Isle along wi' all them Irish navvies, layabouts that they are."

"She's me mother. I can't help that," said Dad in an unnecessarily apologetic tone. "I don't insult your parents."

"Neither tha should, Patrick Gordon. They brought me up t' proper way. Fed me on proper food, not parsnips an' pilchards. An' while she were feeding thee on food that were not fit for t'pigs, there she were givin' t'Father bottles er whiskey, like a good Catholic."

"Tha dun't know owt er t'kind," said Dad a little more assertively.

"Chuff off," yelled Mum.

Trevor and I just stood there at the other end of the kitchen, not daring to utter a word. It was certainly not the time to ask a question, like "Is it alright to go out to play?" or "Can we have our spending money?"—sixpence each a week to keep our rooms tidy, do the odd errand, and help out with the dishes. Gingerly, we left the kitchen and headed upstairs to the relative safety of our bedrooms. Dad left the house, ostensibly to do some gardening. Mum continued to seethe and rage within the confines of the home. The affray would either die of natural causes or escalate into another weekend-long war.

I was confused by Mum's anger. I suppose it must be a bad thing for someone to be Irish. But what does that have to do with Dad? He wasn't born there. Was my other Grandma?

(Actually, as if it mattered, she wasn't—but we were led to believe otherwise). But, what's a pilchard anyway?

Envy also came in to the picture. The vast majority of my mother's relatives were too poor to own property, so they lived in rented quarters. On the other hand, Teresa, through her marriage to Arnold, lived in a modest semi-detached home that Arnold owned. The neighbourhood was still working class, but home ownership was the norm in it.

"There she is in 'er la-de-da fancy 'ome, lookin down 'er nose at everyone else," she'd often say. "She dropped 'er 'andkerchief an' funny thing, who should pick it up but Arnold Lawson. That's t'only reason she's on Dovercourt Road. Otherwise, she'd be back where she belongs, slummin' it."

*Why was it wrong for her to have dropped her handkerchief?* I would wonder. I was unaware, as I am sure my mother was, that this expression had its origins in Shakespearean England. In upper-class circles, when a lady dropped her handkerchief and a nobleman picked it up, it signalled the beginning of a romantic relationship. My mother stretched the imagery to depict promiscuity.

⁓⁓

Trevor and I would be onlookers while all this was going on. Standing around. Not knowing whether to move to another room, leave the house, or stay rooted to the spot. We were never addressed by either one of them. They carried on, Mum mostly, as though we weren't there. We could go out, and often did so, but if we met any friends, we couldn't bring them anywhere near the house. We gave the house a wide berth, checking in at the end of the day. Usually, we discovered that the argument had continued to escalate.

We felt the tension every minute of those weekends. Even though time after time, there was a predictability about the whole scenario, we were always frightened that Mum would either leave with no plans in place for us, or that she would do something terrible to herself. To make matters worse, although Dad did nothing to provoke or heighten the rift between Mum and him, he would sometimes bring Trevor and myself into the affray as though we were adult sounding boards for his anxieties. On Sunday afternoon or evening, after Mum had done her usual slamming of the back door and barged into the neighbourhood with her "I'm gone. Don't expect me back" parting shot, Dad would often volunteer to the two of us that he didn't know where she was going and only hoped that she would come to her senses and return. Sometimes, though not often, he would give us the reassurance that we needed as kids that Mum was following a pattern and would be back.

During one especially violent argument, my mother locked herself in the upstairs bathroom. It was Saturday night, and Trevor and I had been out for an hour or so to try and wind down. We had taken temporary leave from the battle. When we got back, Dad was wrestling with Mum in the kitchen, holding her hands to stop her lashing out at him. His posture was defensive, hers decidedly offensive. She was crying uncontrollably, her body trembling with anger, her mouth spitting out one venomous insult after another. Then she broke away from him, raced upstairs, and slammed the bathroom door behind her. Dad marched after her up the stairs, one long stride after another, then started pounding on the bathroom door. "Nell. Please come out. We can talk abart this. It's gone far enough. Come out Nell."

This only provoked more hurling of profanities to complement her bottomless and continuous wellspring of bawling and blubbering.

After round after round of Dad's pleading, Mum's ripostes, Dad came downstairs, looked the two of us in the eye and said in a whispered voice, "I'm really worried. She's locked herself in there. There are all kinds of things in that bathroom. Scissors. Razor blades. She's in such a state she could 'urt 'erself."

Then, he pointed to the back door. Still whispering. "Look at them four 'oles about two feet from t'top er t'door. While you two were out, yer Mum threw a fork at me. T''fork stuck in t'door like a dart. If I an't ducked, it would er stuck inter me forehead. That's t'condition she's in. She tried ter kill me."

We looked at the holes mesmerized. Our adrenaline levels were on surcharge. We couldn't think of anything to say. The three of us sitting around the kitchen in silence watching the minutes go by on the wall clock, listening to Mum's sobbing, as it grew weaker and more spasmodic. Then, the sound of the doorknob from the bathroom upstairs, the squeaking of the door hinges as it opened, the padding of Mum's feet as she made her way to the main bedroom, and the clicking of the bedroom door as she closed it. We all breathed a sigh of relief.

That, and many other weekends, did have an ending. In fact, most of the time, life at home was relatively calm. It was the suddenness and the brutality of those weekend punctuation marks, four or five per year that kept my brother and I on edge, on our toes. Despite the extremeness of my mother's behaviour, my brother and I never considered her to be mad in a psychological sense. We always thought that though she never confided in us, there must have been a valid reason for her tantrums. Dad was calm, but too withdrawn within himself. He exuded no passion and attracted no compassion from us. He was just there, in but not of the world. It seemed like Trevor and I just happened to be living in the same house as him. And, there was the natural tendency of sons wanting to protect their mother, especially in the fifties when women were still looked upon by society as the fairer and weaker sex. So, while we never confronted Dad, we always took Mum's side no matter how she behaved.

Another way in which Mum's frenetic personality manifested itself was in Saturday house cleaning binges. Like the arguments, these, too, started during my last year of elementary school and continued right through the years of my adolescence. I would arrive home mid Saturday afternoon after a day of playing outdoors or in my later teenage years, flirting, chasing after, or spending quality time with the girls. The smell of bleach and floor cleaner would hit my nostrils when I was half-way down the pathway. Then, I'd arrive in the back yard to find Trevor kicking a football against the wall of the house, balancing it on his toes, flicking it in the air, bouncing it from his knees. Up in the air again, against the wall, onto his head, his feet, and so it would go on. Leather against brickwork, asphalt, and bone. Thump. Thump. Thump. I would know immediately what was going on.

"Don't even bother ter try goin' in. She just yelled at me. She's in one of 'er cleaning fits."

So, I'd just hang around the yard, pacing back and forth, while Trevor did his footballing routine. As the late afternoon dusk gave way to pitch black nighttime, I would begin the drill of cupping my hands together and blowing into them. Anything to get warm. Mum would usually choose the coldest days to flex her mop and broom. Clad until I was thirteen in short trousers, my bare legs had to take a full hit from the chilly night air.

"Soddin' cold innit," I'd say to Trevor.

"Ah. Stupid if tha asks me. Why can't we go upstairs outter t'road?"

"I'll see 'ow much longer it'll be," says I.

Knock. Knock. Knock. The back door flung open to reveal

Mum, mop in hand, scarf tied around her head. "What's tha want?" she asks menacingly.

"'Ow much long…?"

"I don't know. Tha'll just 'ave ter wait." She slams the door in my face.

So, on and on, the time would drag. Minutes into hours, literally. Sometimes, we would be outside up to three hours waiting for the all clear.

Then, like manna from heaven, the back door would open and Mum would shout, "Tha can both come in now. Both er yer, tek yer shoes off, go in ter t'front room and sit. Don't move."

If we were really lucky, there would be a fire burning and we would be able to thaw out.

After we had eaten our teas, a quick fry up, we would be dispatched one at a time to the bathroom. Our once-a-week bath could not wait. The scouring must include the occupants of the house as well as its walls and floors.

I didn't realize that Mum was starting to come unhinged and that it was revealing a most disturbing side of her character—one that would become dominant over time and be accompanied by deterioration in her state of mental health.

# GAS MEETS WATER

Aside from the bullying, which I was able to parry successfully, the second major issue that I had to confront during my first term at High Storrs was, surprisingly enough, my less-than-stellar academic performance. The West had prepared me well enough for the eleven plus examination, but it did not teach me how to study. I discovered at High Storrs that not everything is intuitive. Most new facts have to be learned, understood, and memorized. Intelligence alone is not good enough. So, I struggled. I came home just before Christmas with a school report that placed me twenty–fourth in a class of thirty-two students.

No solace at home.

"Tha'd better pull thee socks up. Tha weren't sent ter t'grammar school ter come back wi' a report like that," chastised Mum.

"Aye, it's time tha started ter frame," joined in Dad.

I did start to frame—I buckled down. So much so that at the end of the year I was promoted to 2A and stayed near the top of the class in the A stream from thereon.

I developed a keen interest in chemistry during that first

year at High Storrs. Acids poured down thistle funnels, sizzling powders in flasks, gases bubbling through water in pneumatic troughs, collecting in cylindrical jars, popping or extinguishing lighted tapers, or stinking of rotten eggs. Alchemy and magic. I wanted to replicate all of these intriguing experiments that our science teacher, Sep, had shown us, invent new ones, and make compounds and gases not yet created. Be a real scientist. A small group of us would gather together on Saturday afternoons in the garage of a house at Nether Edge, the home of Jack Martin, a close friend of mine over the High Storrs years. We would add a to b, c to d, x to y, a to b, c, a, x and y, standing back as frothing, spitting broths bubbled up the sides of test tubes, beakers and flasks, making sure we got a good whiff of whatever noxious fumes spewed into the air. It was exciting and fun, if a little on the dangerous side. I would save up my pocket money, some of which I had earned through an early morning paper round that I had taken on, then on Saturday mornings go downtown to Preston's, a chemical supply shop just around the corner from West Street, opposite the Glossop Road Baths. It was the main supplier for the various city schools. A man in a brown smock would peer out of a hatch, then go find the precious items of interest that schoolboys, amateur chemists, and schoolteachers requested.

"A 5cc pipette? Graduated or wi' t'bulb on it?"

"Sodium cyanide? No lad. Tha can't 'ave that. As ter 'ave special permission for poisons like that."

But few requests were denied.

"Bottle er sulphuric acid, son? Be careful wi' it. That'll be three shillings."

"Sodium hydroxide pellets? It'll burn thee if tha not careful. 'Ow much does tha want?"

I would then take my haul back home and store it in the outhouse where I had started to amass my personal collection of chemicals and glassware. The outhouse was fast becoming my own laboratory. My mind was buzzing with new ideas.

One day, I found myself staring at the gas outlet on the wall by the kitchen sink. What would happen if gas met water, I wondered. Two opposing forces. Would one win out over the other? Or would they cancel one another out? If I were to connect the cold water tap over the sink to the gas outlet and turn both on at the same time, that would give me the answer.

I ran the idea past a few friends at school. Everyone thought it was a great idea. Nobody tried to tell me how ridiculous it was. "A length of compression tubing is what you'll need," one of the group said. "I'll swipe a length from the physics lab."

May 1955. It's a rainy Spring evening. I've just arrived home from school to an empty house. Trevor was out playing. Mum and Dad had not arrived home from work. Just a kid's show on the telly, so I turn on the radio. It's the BBC news. An American scientist called Salk claims to have developed a vaccine against polio. That's what Dad had. It's a terrible disease. It has my attention. The Yorkshire coal miners are out on strike again. So what? There's nothing newsworthy about that. They're always on strike. The BBC announcer drones on, reciting a progressively less interesting sequence of news items. I turn off the set. Time for the scientist in me to make a breakthrough, I think. Now's the time for action. I bet nobody's ever thought of tackling this fundamental question before. No telling what applications it may have. What happens when gas meets water? What, indeed? I take the length of compression tubing out of my satchel, attach one end of it to the water tap, the other to the gas outlet, then count. One, two, three. I turn on the two taps. And wait. And wait. Two minutes go by. Nothing happens. Nothing I can see. What should happen? I suppose nothing. Failed experiment. I stuff the tubing back into my satchel, rummage around the kitchen cupboards and the pantry looking for scraps of food. Then, one by one, the other three quarters of the family arrive. Last to arrive is Mum. She hauls some meat out of her shopping bag and turns on the gas oven. Nothing happens. The pilot light doesn't kick in. She tries the burners on top of the oven. Same thing.

"Pat, would yer take a look at this oven? I can't get it ter work."

Dad repeats what Mum has just done, keeping his ear close to the burners.

"I can 'ear somethin' bubblin' in theere. That's strange. What can it be?"

Mum goes over to listen.

"What kind of liquid can it be? There's not supposed to be any liquid in a gas oven is there?"

Then it clicks. *Bloody 'ell. The gas oven is connected to the pipe leading from the gas outlet on the wall. I'd forgotten about that. When I hooked up the pipe, the tap water must have gone into the oven. I'm in for it now.*

Before I can speak, Mum turns toward Trevor and me and snaps, "You two don't know owt abart this do yer?"

Might as well get this over with.

"It's probably my fault. I wanted to find out what happens when gas meets water. An experiment. So I connected t'gas tap on t'wall ter t'cold water tap wi' some tubing an' turned both taps on. I din't know t'water would go inter t'oven."

"Tha what? Tha wanted to see what 'appened when t'gas met t'water? Bloody cooker is full er water now. I can't cook supper."

Dad joins in. "I'll 'ave ter tek it all apart. I don't even know whether I can clean out all them pipes. Oven might be ruined. Stupid bloody sod."

Mum lunges toward me. Starts hitting me, mostly on the back of my legs and my arse. "Get upstairs. Get thee clothes off. Right now. Get inter bed. I'll show thee what 'appens when gas meets t'water. Bloody 'ell." She's screaming now. Chasing me up the stairs into my bedroom. Starts to hit me again as I'm taking off my clothes and blubbering like a baby.

154 | ROGER GORDON

"I'm sorry. So sorry. Din't mean ter do it. 'Onest. I'd never 'ave done it if I'd known this would 'appen."

"An' it won't be 'appenin' no moore," she screams at me as I scramble into bed, dodging her blows. "I'll put paid ter thee chemistry set. I'll tek it down ter t'oller an' smash every bloody piece er it. That's all."

"Please don't, Mum. Please. Please. Not me chemistry set. I'll do owt ter make up for what I've done but don't smash me chemistry set." I'm crying and pleading at the same time.

She storms out of the bedroom and tramps downstairs. I'm thinking she's bluffing. She won't do anything so mean as to destroy my chemistry set that I've collected over weeks and weeks with my pocket money. Then, I hear her calling out.

"Trevor. Where does 'e keep 'is chemistry set? In t'outhouse? Tha can 'elp me."

Again, I convince myself that she really won't go through with this. She's just trying to upset me, make me feel even worse than I already feel. I settle down in bed continuing to whimper. Suddenly, I hear someone come charging up the stairs. Trevor appears at my bedroom doorway. "I've just been down ter t'oller an' smashed a long thin piece er glass wi' a swellin' in t' middle er it."

"That's my pipette," I wail.

"I'm 'elpin Mum. I'm on me way down ter break summat else," he declares, as he races back downstairs. Then it dawns on me. She really wasn't fooling. She's deliberately organizing the destruction of my chemistry set, drawing Trevor in to her spiteful scheme. A short while later, Trevor re-appears to announce the latest notch on his belt.

"That's my new thistle funnel. Please stop this." I'm just beside myself.

For about an hour, the process is repeated time and again. Re-visitation from Trevor. More pronouncements. I just can't believe this is happening. Then all is quiet. The reprisal has been completed. Nothing more to do or say. I'm left alone to ponder my sins. Were my motives those of a scoundrel? How about my mother's response to it? Did the punishment fit the crime? Her motives? Angry. Spiteful. Calculating. Disproportionate. Reckless. Can any of these adjectives be used to qualify her intents when she systematically destroyed my chemistry set? Yes—and a thousand times over.

It's dark now. Ten o'clock. Four hours since punishment was rendered. The tinkering of metal on metal stopped a while ago as Dad finished removing part after part from the drowned corpse of the oven. I can smell food.

"Tha can come down now an' get summat ter eat. Bloody fine time ter be 'avin us tea," Mum shouts from the bottom of the stairs.

As I enter the kitchen, head bowed, feet shuffling, she confronts me again.

"So what 'as tha got ter say for theeself then?"

"I'm sorry. I din't mean for it ter 'appen. But 'ave yer really destroyed me chemistry set?"

"Bloody 'ell. Listen ter it. Thee Dad's been on 'is 'ands and knees all night fixin' t'bleedin' oven an' all tha can think abart is thee soddin' chemistry set," she thunders.

"Should be ashamed er 'imself," offers Dad.

"Anyow, sit darn, get thee bacon an' eggs an' get back up ter bed yer self-centered bugger," growls Mum. "I'll tell thee what 'appens when gas meets water," she mocks, "Tha gets a bloody good 'idin'."

*And have my chemistry set demolished,* I think. *I couldn't care less about the good "iding," as she puts it.*

When I returned to school the next day, I was given five hundred lines by one teacher, *I must remember to do my homework as given to me by my Latin teacher.* No abbreviations allowed. Pencil and ball point pen forbidden. Fountain pen obligatory. Another teacher noted my name and advised me that should there be another occasion when I forget to do my homework, I'll be given detention. I couldn't tell either of them the real reason why I didn't do my homework.

Not long afterwards, one of my friends asked me if I'd carried out the gas meets water experiment. I told him about the oven filling up with water, then made light of it.

"Bet yer parents weren't too 'appy abart that," he chuckled.

"Not too pleased," I replied, forcing a smile.

August 1955. Three months have passed since gas met water. Since then, Anthony Eden's conservative government has been returned to power, much to Mum's delight, and a young woman, night club hostess Ruth Ellis, has been hanged for murder at Holloway Prison. But, at Buckingham Palace, Princess Margaret hasn't been able to decide on whether to go through with her controversial intention to marry divorced RAF Group Captain, Peter Townshend. My mind is closer to home. Sheffield Wednesday have now been relegated back to the second division, earning them the title of "yo-yo club" due to their bouncing back and forth between the first and second divisions in successive seasons. I am feeling relieved that I have been promoted to the "A" stream at High Storrs. After an unsteady start, my academic performance improved steadily throughout my first year. I'm looking forward to September and my new class of 2A.

After enduring a winter of perishing cold temperatures and lots of snow, we're having a dry and sunny summer. The four of us are on a week's holiday in Scarborough. To give Mum and Dad credit, through thick and thin, they've always managed to cobble together the money for us to go on a family holiday at the seaside. We have moved up in the world from the house-keeping chalet in Cayton Bay of earlier years to a real B & B.

We are standing alongside the wall that borders the

waterfront. It's high tide. A gentle breeze. We're looking down on the North Sea as it swishes gently back and forth, waves frothing against the other side of the wall. We take it in turns to put pennies in a telescope that is pointed out to sea. There are a couple of boats on the horizon. Closer to land, scattered groups of seagulls bob up and down on the surface of the water. Occasionally, a scattered one breaks from the group and takes to the air, squawking and flapping its wings. What has caught its attention? As I'm gazing at this seascape, I am startled from my reverie by a voice behind me. A deep voice, Sheffield accent undoubtedly, but with a rounded edge to it that conveys middle class.

"Pat. Nice ter see thee. 'Avin' a good 'oliday?"

I turn around. There's a middle-aged man wearing a tweed jacket, cravat around his neck, his hair moderately Brylcreemed, his hand stretched out as he approaches Dad. Alongside him is a forty-something lady in a pink woollen suit, matching high-heeled shoes, and hair immaculately set. Mr. and Mrs. Well-Heeled. This couple has cocktails before their evening meal, leather upholstery in their car, own a telephone, maybe even a fridge. For sure, they own their own home—a detached home, unlike any of the others around it. In the Dore or Totley districts of Sheffield, where the better off live. They've kept the skeleton of a Sheffield accent so that they can pretend to relate to the downtrodden working class folk who work for Mr. W-H.

"'Ow tha gerrin on," says Dad, shaking the man's hand. "Nell, this is Mr. Grimstead, a Director at General Electric. You've heard me speak of Mr. Grimstead."

One of Dad's bosses. Better not slip up here.

"Sidney Grimstead. Pleased ter met yer, Nell. This is me wife Betty. And who are these two young lads, then?" He's looking straight at Trevor and me.

Introductions all around. The usual small talk. The weather. Isn't Scarborough a nice place? Would you like a cigarette? Been to see the Castle?

"And 'ow are your boys at their schoolwork then?" asks the boss man.

This is Mum's territory. "Well, our Trevor, 'e's more inter sports than schoolwork. Our Roger's the brains. 'E's just finished 'is first year at High Storrs Grammar," she beams. "An' what does tha want ter be when tha grows up? A scientist," she continues, patting my head condescendingly. "Pat, tell Mr. Grimstead abart our Roger's interest in science and 'is gas meets water experiment." She's acting out a laugh now.

As Dad parleys the details of the scurrilous experiment, guffaws ringing out as punctuation marks, my face is growing redder. I'm pretending to see the funny side of it, but it's a charade. Inside, I am hurting and seething.

"So, the result of gas meeting water, I keep telling our Roger..." Mum pauses for the punch line. "It's a good smacked bottom."

Belly aching laughter all around. The facemask I'm wearing carries me through. Not too far below the surface, I'm thinking, *you forgot to tell him about the other result of the experiment, Mum. You know, the breaking of the glass—not just the beakers and the pipettes, but my aspirations and emotions. Glass is fragile.*

# HOUSE RULES

The household operated under a strict set of rules that were often concocted by my mother on the fly. As far as I can ascertain, the underlying principle for these rules was control. Mum insisted on being in control even when the prudent course would have been to stand aside and let me go through the awkward phases and symptoms of adolescence in my own way. It wasn't as though I had any criminal inclinations. All of the activities in which Mum interfered, ostensibly for my own good, were perfectly harmless and natural to the graceless period of transition known as puberty.

Such was the case when, as a young teenager, I started to take an interest in my appearance and naturally, wanted to be in vogue with the fashions of the day. There wasn't much I could do about my clothing, which was either school uniform or a toned down version of it. Long sleeved shirt, v-necked pullover, grey flannel trousers, and black leather shoes or sandals. Jeans, t-shirts, and sneakers, often called baseball shoes, were considered by Mum to be common—American rubbish. Nonetheless, I could at least do something with my hair, couldn't I? Imitating the film and rock stars of the fifties, I would cobble together enough money from my morning paper route to buy a bottle of Brylcreem. After daubing huge globs of this greasy white mush on my hair, I would then comb it back on either side, making sure that the two waves met at the back of my head to form a D.A., otherwise known as a Duck's Arse. Then, I would tousle the top and front in an amateur attempt to create a Tony Curtis look. In reality, it looked awful, but I thought at the time that it looked chic. Mum saw things differently. To her, it was an abomination. To Mum, there was only one hairstyle for boys and young men—short back and sides, with a parting on the left side, the hair stroked downwards on the left side and across the crown on the right side of the parting. Absolutely no hair creams, only water to hold everything in place. When I dared to deviate from Mum's approved layout, she would often make me wash the Brylcreem out of my hair, then sit me down in a kitchen chair and recreate her masterpiece. "Sithee. That's 'ow I want ter see thee 'air. Not like a bloody common Teddy boy."

In the 50s, young men considered it stylish to dress in the fashion of the Edwardian era, as men dressed at the turn of the twentieth century. With their odd costume-like clothing and greasy hairdos, they were known as Teddy boys. For the most part, though, Teddy boys belonged to the working class, which is why Mum looked down her nose at them and abhorred the very idea that I might in any small way be dressed even remotely like them.

Of course, once I had left the house, replete with Mum's equally ridiculous and childish hairstyle, the comb would come out of my pocket and I would do my best to undo what she had done. After we had moved to the Stradbroke estate, she insisted that I continue to have my hair cut by Mr. Clarke, the barber on Duke Street at the end of Talbot Place where we used to live. Two bus rides away. After I once came home from a visit to Mr. Clarke with a style that was something other than the authorized one, she sent Dad down to talk to him.

"Tell 'im not ter listen ter 'im. I want 'im to cut it just like 'e's allus done."

Unsurprisingly, Dad came back from his tête-a-tête to announce that good old Mr. Clarke could not agree to Mum's wishes.

"Mr. Clarke says 'e's a young man, a customer, and 'e 'as ter listen ter what 'e wants. I can see what 'e's getting' at."

But, while Dad may have seen the light, Mum's appetite to be in control of my hairdo was undiminished. It wasn't until I was in my mid teens that she threw in the towel and conceded defeat.

My relationships with girlfriends were also problematic for my mother. It all started during my very first romantic foray. It was the spring of 1956 and I was just thirteen. One Friday night, my friend Peter Hinchcliffe and I were walking home from the Rex cinema when we chanced upon a couple of young girls walking just ahead of us. We caught them up, chatted them up, split them up, and walked them home through Richmond Park. My prize was Jessie Snelgrove. I thought she was beautiful. Shoulder length fair hair, delicate thin lips, hazel eyes, dressed maturely as a young woman in mid-length coat, skirt just above the knees, and black, low-heeled court shoes. She was fifteen and worked as a sales clerk at Banner's department store. By contrast, in my navy blue gabardine raincoat and grey flannel trousers I looked every bit the schoolboy that I was. How could I have fluked into this, I wondered? Can't look a gift horse, especially a very attractive one, in the mouth. So, I arranged to meet her in Richmond Park on my way home from school one afternoon the following week.

It's five o'clock on an overcast afternoon. I am striding along the pathway through Richmond Park, a full head of stem on, when I see her standing near the bowling green about a hundred yards away. I am overjoyed. She really is there, I think. As I approach her, we look into each other's eyes and she starts to blush. Just then, a young girl appears from behind a bush and shouts in a taunting way, "Jessie's got a boyfriend. Jessie's got a boyfriend."

Jessie tells the little blighter to tek off, but she remains on or around the scene like an ornament you want to see the back of. After we have exchanged a few words, stilted sentence fragments, I ask her if she'd like to sit with me on the park bench. No sooner have we sat down, than little Miss Nosey Parker pops up out of the woodwork again. "Are you two goin' ter kiss each other? Jessie's goin' ter kiss a boy. Jessie's goin' ter kiss a boy."

Jessie gets up, says something to her that does the trick, and then sits down again. The imp is gone.

What happens next is clumsiness, embarrassment to the extreme, yet it remains one of the most memorable moments of my growing up.

Very slowly, excruciatingly slowly, I put my arm around the back of the seat, inching it closer against Jessie's shoulders until it wraps itself around her. Like robots we both continue to stare ahead. Silence. No conversation. Then, after what seems like an eternity I turn my face toward her, she leans back and we press our lips together. My very first kiss. Should I open my eyes or close them? I see that hers are closed which means that mine are open. The scene around me, some of which I can see, is a blur, the two of us vividly cast against it in high relief. We are the principal players, everything else the supporting cast. My heart is racing. I have never felt anything like this before. But, how long should I let it go on? And am I doing it properly? Should my tongue come into play? What about my teeth? Things feel awful dry at our meeting point. Eventually, we do come apart, reclaim our lips, and then revert back to the side-by-side, forward facing position. A pause would give the wrong impression. Can't leave it at one kiss, I think. Two seems about right. So, again we lock lips, and only lips, again

I re-experience that otherworldly sensation. I look at my watch. It's 6 o'clock.

"Blimey. Better get 'ome." I say, knowing that on the way home I'll have to think up an excuse for being late for tea.

So, Jessie and I arrange to see each other again, and then part our separate ways. Miss Pain-in-the-Arse, who was hanging around the park entrance, threw in her two pence worth. "Lovebirds. Lovebirds. What's 'is name then Jessie? Did yer like 'im kissin yer?"

After the climb up Richmond Hill, it was all downhill through the Stradbroke estate to number 23. I ran all the way, slowing down in time so that I wouldn't be panting as I went through the back door.

"Where's tha been till this time? Thee supper's gone cold. What's been goin' on?"

"Forgot ter tell yer, Mum. We had a 'ouse meeting at school tonight. Nowt I could do abart it."

"Sounds fishy ter me. Anyroads sit darn an' get thee tea. It'll just 'ave ter be cold."

In those days, a couple of generations before computers, email, and text messaging had been invented, courting couples sent one another letters. After all, within the same city, next day delivery was the norm. So, Peter Hinchcliffe and I got into the act. We each sent letters to our respective paramours via Jessie's address. Letters to Peter and myself were sent to me at my address. Later that same week of the first kiss,

I noticed an especially frosty atmosphere around the table at teatime. Scowls on Mum and Dad's face, few words passing across tight lips. Then, after the "please may I leave the table?" routine, my brother was told to go outside and play. My command was to stay seated. I knew something was up.

"I'll be back in a minute," says Dad. And so he is, clutching a couple of envelopes in his hand. He throws them down on the table. "What's the meanin' er this?" says Dad in an unusually aggressive tone of voice. "These came through our letter box yesterday."

As I stare at the opened envelopes, I see that one is addressed to me, the other to Peter Hinchcliffe. Both are covered in hearts and kisses. Without waiting for a reply, Dad starts to read mockingly from Jessie's letter. "My sweet lover boy. What a darling you are. I can't wait for our next kiss. You are my dream…"

Soppy, giddy, foolish crap, typical of adolescents. Harmless. More important though, crap that should not have been seen by either of my parents, as the letter in question was not addressed to them. They had no right to open the envelope.

"Who is this girl you've met? I want ter know," demands Mum, banging her fist on the table.

"'Er name's Jessie. She's fifteen an' she works at Banners," I reply, thinking this to be an innocuous explanation.

"She's fifteen? She works at Banners?" yells Mum, as if I had told her that I had consorted with a woman of the night.

"Tha't not old enough ter be 'avin girl friends. She's years older than thee. And besides, working at that Banners store darn Attercliffe—she must be common. Tha should be spendin' time on thee studies, not bothering abart girls. That's all."

Then Dad intones. "Anyroad, it might interest thee ter know that I've already been ter see Peter Hinchcliffe's father. I've shown 'im t'letter that t'other girl sent ter 'im. 'E were shocked and said 'e'll put a stop ter it too."

I am sitting there incredulous. Dad has opened and read a letter addressed to me, gone ahead and hand delivered my friend's letter to his Dad, then as I was about to find out, colluded and agreed with Mum on what the consequences should be.

"Tha'll not be seein' any moore er 'er," announces Mum. "'Er address is on t'letter so we know where she lives. If either me or thee Dad catch thee seeing 'er, thee Dad'll go round ter 'er 'ouse an' see what 'er mother an' father think abart their daughter goin' out wi' a schoolboy."

"What's wrong wi' me seein' 'er?" I ask. "And why did yer open a letter that were addressed to me?" I said, challengingly.

Mum rises, slaps me across the face. "Yer cheeky young bugger. Get upstairs, get inter thee pyjamas, get thee 'omework done, then climb reight into bed. That's all."

"That's alls" are flying around left, right and centre. Humiliated, inwardly fuming, I have to obey. But, I have no intention of obeying the restraining order. I'll write to Jessie, let her know what happened, suggest we don't try to see each other for a couple of weeks, then arrange a date.

I sent that letter, then another one, and then another one to Jessie. I arranged to meet her a couple of times but she never showed up. On each of the times that I tried to see her, I was cross-questioned when I got back home. Where had I been? To see a film? What kind of film was it? Then, the question that almost caught me out once, because I had forgotten to look it up in the newspaper beforehand—was it in technicolour or black and white? I guessed correctly. More than half the films back then were in black and white.

So, my parents clumsily crushed my first relationship with a girl. Perhaps I was a bit young, but I didn't see the harm. An enlightened way of handling it might have been for them to ask to see Jessie, show understanding and support, help to steer things constructively and sensitively in an age-appropriate direction. True, it was the 1950s—a time when parental and children's roles were more sharply defined than is now the case. Parents were authority figures within the family setting. Yet, Mum's propensity to micro-manage our lives went beyond the norm, even for that era.

As I got older into my mid-teens, the ban on girlfriends was lifted. Nevertheless, Mum always offered an opinion on them. Sally, my girlfriend for a couple of years "dressed like a tart," and "tried to look older than her age." In all fairness, Sal was a little risqué with her wardrobe. Long black hair resting on her frequently bare shoulders, low neckline, tight fitting mini skirt that hugged every inch of her curvaceous "bod," long, shapely legs covered in fashionable, see-through nylon stockings, ending with high-heeled shoes. She was a good dresser. Someone who would attract a second look. As she came to call for me one afternoon, Bill Withers and Dad in the Withers' yard below, the two of them stopped talking, whistled through their teeth and ogled her so lecherously that Sal stepped out of character and blushed.

"Dirty old buggers," she said to me afterwards.

Then, one night, when we were partying at Mum and Dad's friends, the Currans, Sal went into the living room where the adults were sitting around drinking. From what Sal told me, Percy Curran asked her to sit on his knee, then started feeling her up. She came back into the kitchen where we were gathered—quite distraught. When I barged into the living room and confronted Mr. C., he said it "were just a bit er fun," while Mum yelled at me to "tek me bloody 'ook."[20] So, I never took much notice of Mum's characterization of Sal. She looked fine to me and, so it seemed, to Dad and his friends too. Hypocritical? Jealous? Opinionated? The saying that if the shoe fits, wear it is apt. Mum wore her shoes well.

Mum thought I could do better than Dianne, who was almost literally the girl next door. She liked Liz and even gave me a piece of her mind when I finished with her. "What are tha doin' finishin' wi' a lovely lass like that? She's t'best one tha's brought round ter t'ouse." Kathy, a short-lived flame, won over Mum from the word go by bringing her a bunch of flowers. "What a lovely lass she is. Eyup, I do like 'er." What she didn't know was that Kathy, bless her, was one of the randiest girls around, which is why I thought her to be a lovely lass. Then, there was Sandra, my steady girlfriend for about three years. At first, Mum liked her, because she was polite, deferential, and wore a smile that would win over anybody. But years later, after Sandra ditched me and I subsequently had a nervous breakdown, Mum made no bones about the fact that she could not stand her and hoped I would never think of rekindling our relationship.

Mum's rigid application of a code of conduct that she herself had invented affected my relationships with my pals as well. On one occasion, she banned my best friend Jeff Morgan from visiting our home. What cardinal sin had Jeff committed? He had forgotten to say "thank you" after Mum and Dad had taken Jeff and me on an afternoon trip to Lincoln and treated him to an afternoon tea in a restaurant. Not the greatest of manners, granted, but issuing a ban didn't seem to be necessary. One day, when I ignored the edict and brought him back to the house, not inside it, I got a tongue lashing from Mum afterwards. "Din't I tell thee not ter bring 'im 'ere no moore? No moore means no moore? Don't let it 'appen again."

I thought it would be hard to continue my friendship with Jeff if he couldn't call upon me, so I decided to be straight with him. One Saturday afternoon, I told him. "I'm sorry Jeff. I don't agree wi' 'er. She's makin' a mountain out er a molehill."

I was so embarrassed. Jeff could not believe that something so minor and unintentional was being held against him in such an extreme fashion. "I'll go around right now an' square things up," says he.

I stand in the back yard while Jeff knocks at the door, asks if he can come in and have a word, then enters the kitchen. I can hear the conversation.

"Mrs. Gordon, I'm sorry if I forgot ter thank yer for that dinner t'other week. I appreciated it."

"Oh, that's oreight, love. I were glad yer came wi' us. Any time."

With that, the brouhaha was over. The sinner had repented and all was forgiven. Mum had made her point. The only thing she had succeeded in doing was embarrassing me. But, he could be my friend again.

---

20   A Sheffield variation of the expression to "take (or sling) your hook," meaning to go away.

# CAR RIDES

A new dimension was added to the ambience in our home sweet home occurred in 1957, six years after we had moved to the Stradbroke estate. I was nearing fourteen, in my third year at High Storrs. It's a foggy evening in March. The three of us, Mum, Trevor, and I are pacing back and forth between the kitchen and the living room, stopping en route by the living room window, peering intently up the street. Nobody around. The fog has driven them indoors.

"'E'll be 'ere soon," says Mum.

"'Ow come 'e's tekin so long, Mum?"

"'Cus 'e 'as ter sign t'papers. That's why."

"But it's 7 o'clock now," says Trevor.

"'E must er got 'eld up. 'Ope 'e an't got in any accidents," Mum says, fingers touching her temple.

Excitement? We are beside ourselves—on an adrenaline rush. Trevor and I have rushed home from school, Mum from work. No appetite for much tea—canned beans on toast, nothing more elaborate than that. Then, the vigil began and our collective fervour escalated.

"'Ere 'e comes," I shout.

"Ooh ar, just look at it," gushes Mum.

Dad pulls into the concrete driveway, the one that all four of us had helped to build, with a brand new car. Our first car. A shiny powder blue Ford Anglia, straight out of Brooke Shaw's showroom. A two-door saloon model, PVC covered seats, separate in the front, bench in the rear, dark blue interior upholstery to complement the exterior colour, three gear floor mounted gear shift, 36 bph side valve engine, top speed 70.2 mph.

We all race out of the front door and invade our new possession.

"In't it smashin'?" burbles Mum from the front seat.

"Does tha like look er it?" asks Dad from behind the steering wheel.

"'Ow's it drive, Dad?"

"Can we go for a drive in it?" Choruses from the back seats.

"It's reight foggy. Don't know whether it's safe," says Mum, staring Dad down.

"Be oreight. I'll just be careful," says Dad.

With that, he lights up a Woodbine and starts to reverse out of the driveway.

"Should tha be smokin' in t'car?" asks Mum, "Where will tha put t'ashes?"

Dad flicks out the ashtray tucked underneath the dashboard. We crawl around the neighbourhood streets in the thick fog (outside and inside the car) at twenty miles an hour.

"Be careful, Pat. "Can tha see oreight?"

"Slow darn a bit."

"Eyup, it's reight comfy, innit?"

"What's it like in t'back, you two?"

"They're sayin' that petrol's goin' off ration in a couple er months," says Dad. "We bought it just at t'reight time."

After a half hour or so, we pull into the driveway and into the toxic garage that Dad had erected from a kit consisting of asbestos panels.

"Cheaper than t'metal ones and besides which, it won't catch fire," he reasoned.

Trevor and I get out of the car to go inside the house. Mum remains in her seat.

"I just want to sit here a while," says she in a wistful tone of voice. Dad stays with her. A full twenty minutes before they come back into the house.

The government had placed strict regulations on credit. Too easy access to it would be bad for the economy, so the government said, so people could only buy cars by hire purchase if they coughed up a down payment that met the government's requirements. Mum had worked for two years, putting aside her wages week after week, to save for the deposit on that car—two hundred and fifty pounds, half of what the car cost. Her hands covered in machine oil and grime, day after day, she would come home on the bus from the downtown machine shop where she worked, then throw together a cooked meal for the four of us. She was entitled to her moments of quiet reflection and self-satisfaction.

⌒⌒⌒

The little four-seater regularly came into service at weekends for day trips to the seaside. Amazingly, we managed to cram six people into it—the four of us plus Grandma and Granddad Bonsall, the latter at over 300 lbs being equivalent to two people. Somehow or other, I would squeeze between Grandma and Granddad in the back seat, while Trevor would perch himself on Mum's knee in the front. When Granddad got into the car, the undercarriage sagged visibly. The suspension in that car gamely stood up to the assault on it. Though it was only a two or three hour drive to Skegness or Scarborough, our preferred destinations, after an hour or so on the road, Dad would pull over and we would heave ourselves out of the two doors. Then, the folding table and chairs, Primus stove, and picnic basket would be hauled out of the boot. Once assembled, we would sit at the side of the road around the table, which would always be covered with a tablecloth, munching on sandwiches and biscuits, slurping tea, while other cars drove by, occasionally tooting.

During that summer, the car was used to take the four of us on a weekend trip to London, then with my Mum's cousin Lorna also on board, on a week's holiday in Torquay. The trip to London was memorable because Mum and Dad could only afford hotel accommodation for one night, so we tried to sleep in the car on the second night. Dad pulled into what he took to be a country lane and fastened newspapers to the inside of the front windshield to block out the moonlight. A short time later, we were startled with a metallic clanging sound followed by the roaring of a train passing by. We were next to a set of railway lines. This went on all through the night. "No point movin'. We might be just as worse off some where else," Mum said. Once daylight had arrived, and we sleepily moved away from the sleepover spot, it was time for the table by the road-side breakfast routine, this time complete with Dad, his shirt off, shaving as cars passed by.

This same weekend, Dad managed to go the wrong direction down a one-way street in the centre of London and get completely lost driving around the outskirts of the city, going around in circles through the village of Bray. But we all, Mum included, saw the funny side of these contretemps. The Torquay trip was likewise enjoyable, carefree, with no hint of a marriage in trouble. We even managed to befriend another family from Sheffield, the Schofields, and spend time with them on trips to the beach and other places of interest. My interest was in the Schofield's teenage daughter Claire. This time, my parents did not interfere as Claire and I indulged in a brief holiday romance.

The next summer, 1958, that little blue car was used to take the four of us on a week's holiday in Cornwall. This time, our destination was Perran Sands Holiday Camp in the small coastal community of Perranporth. The effects of the journey on Dad's health became a defining moment for both him and our family. Setting off in the pitch black, early hours of the morning, we were all the worse for wear when we began the long, arduous journey from Sheffield to the southwest coast. In those days, automobile travel was not the piece of cake that, by comparison, it is today. No motorways; poorly maintained, often narrow, roads. Innumerable cars that by today's standards would be deemed unroadworthy. Drivers who were inexperienced, many driving their first cars. Then, there were the traffic bottlenecks that had to be negotiated. On our trip, the infamous Exeter bypass was the gateway to Devon and Cornwall. We knew we had arrived there when in mid-afternoon, we were confronted by what looked like a long line of parked cars stretching as far as the eyes could see down the length of the roadway. We joined the line up. We waited. And waited. And waited. Under a scorching hot August sun. Every fifteen minutes or so, we would all get out of the car to stretch our legs, joining the hordes of others who had done the same, chatting and complaining in groups. Cigarette after cigarette. Occasionally, Dad crawled the car forward twenty feet or so. Some old clunkers had pulled over to the side, out of the line-up, their bonnets letting off steam. That gruelling experience at the Exeter bypass lasted well over two hours.

Early evening, we arrived at the holiday camp, too tired to

take in the surroundings. Dad collapsed into a chair in our chalet, complaining of dizziness, gasping for breath. I was dispatched over to the camp office to have a doctor called. When he arrived, Trevor and I were told to wait outside. After the doctor had left, Mum summoned the two of us inside. Dad was drinking a glass of whisky. I have no idea how he came upon it. Mum told us that the doctor had diagnosed Dad as suffering from severe exhaustion and he would be all right if he took it easy for a day or so. But, I later learned that exhaustion was just a symptom, not the disease. Some time after the collapse of his marriage, his psychiatrist told him that it marked the beginning of a mental breakdown, which he managed to keep in check, hidden from the rest of us for the remaining two years of his marriage. In reality, both of my parents were undergoing psychiatric stresses. Forever the introvert, Dad kept his emotions to himself, so I took him at face value. Mum did the very opposite, but I still failed to impart a medical connotation to her behaviour.

Perran Sands Holiday Camp was set in a beautiful location on a bluff overlooking a long stretch of sandy beach. But, it was a holiday camp in name only, consisting of a few dozen chalets grouped around a central office complex. The small hall attached to that office complex was the multipurpose entertainment centre—the venue for board games, nightly pubbing, a Friday night dance, the music for which was provided by a portable record player. The compère for all activities was a middle-aged man called Alf. One day, when Trevor and I decided to explore the premises, we found Alf sleeping on a mattress under the small stage in the multipurpose room.

The week went by without much in the way of organized camp activities. This was no Billy Butlin's[21] or Prestatyn, for that matter. One day, Alf organized a game of cricket on the beach, but since cricket is not a game designed for a beach, this feeble effort turned out to be a flop. In fact, the set up was such an amateurish attempt at emulating a holiday camp, that the campers considered it a joke.

One afternoon, my brother and I decided to go wading in the sea and lost track of time and what was happening around us. We hadn't noticed that the intertidal zone was festooned with raised sand bars. When the tide came in, this created a maze of shallow and deep zones. Paddling around on one of these sandbars, we experienced a false sense of security, which was dispelled as soon as we tried to head back to the beach. We were marooned, seemingly separated from the beach by swathes of seawater that was over our heads. Spurred on by Mum and Dad frantically waving at us, we gingerly, one foot at a time, felt our way back to terra firma through the shallower sections. The outcome could have been disastrous.

The main purpose of buying the little blue car was, of course, to enhance Dad's working conditions and prospects for promotion as a sales representative. In hindsight, the very idea of a sales representative with a sizeable suburban catchments area commuting by bus seems absurd. Dad thought that his employer, Hallamshire Electric Company, would be delighted at the opportunity for improving working efficiency. So, in March 1957, a few days after the car joined our family, Dad made an appointment to see Mr. Horace Wiseman, the managing director of the company. I remember the night he came home, his face bowed, long and worn, his raincoat creased and bedraggled. As he opened the kitchen door, his demeanour showed that the meeting had not gone well. "Yer won't believe this, Nell," says he.

"What's up? What did 'e 'ave ter say?"

"'E told me that I din't need a car ter do t' job an 'e's no intention er payin' for runnin' it. 'E won't even cover cost er t'petrol. If I want ter use t'car, I 'ave ter keep a log er where I've been an' 'e'll work out what I'd 'ave 'ad ter pay in bus fares."

"Chuffin' 'ell. Cheeky rotten sod. Ungrateful bugger. 'Ope tha tolled 'im what ter do wi' 'is bus fares."

"I told 'im it weren't good enough. I'd 'ave a lotter thinking ter do. But, that's it. I've 'ad enough wi' that firm. I'll look for another job."

"Quicker tha gets outer that place, better I'll like it. Ter think I've worked me fingers ter t'bone, grease up ter me elbows ter get thee that car so that tha can get ahead an' this is all t'thanks I get. Mr soddin Wiseman."

While Dad was dejected, Mum was irate. Well, she did have a stake in the whole business.

A couple of months later, a showery evening in May, I was sitting in the kitchen talking to Mum who was cooking our tea. Just then, Dad walked through the kitchen door, looking decidedly upbeat. He had got another job as a sales representative for Pyrene, the leading fire extinguisher company in the country. The job was not without risks. His salary was entirely sales commission, no base amount. But, they agreed to pay for all of his petrol costs and he would be part of a national team of sales representatives. Dad would be responsible for a large chunk of South Yorkshire. Dad proved his mettle and soon became one of the firm's top representatives in the country. Monthly sales figures issued by the company showed him to be consistently second or third among twenty or so representatives, trailing only those responsible for the more densely populated areas of London. His salary climbed to a respectable level, sometimes approaching twenty pounds per week. Dad was good at his job.

As the family income improved, Mum continuing to work as a lathe operator at PCL, the desire to climb upmarket from the little blue Anglia increased. Mum badgered Dad to look into getting a bigger car so that Grandma and Granddad could sit in it more comfortably on our Sunday jaunts to the seaside.

It's a fine evening in May 1958. I've arrived home from school and am sitting in the kitchen reading the newspaper while Mum is cooking our tea.

Just then, Dad bursts through the kitchen door, sporting

a big grin. He asks us to take a look at the new car he is thinking of buying in exchange for the Anglia. There it is sitting
in front of the house. A classy cranberry colour with a beige
flash down each side, two-tone no less, sleek, sporty and stylish, its tires hugging the tarmac. It looked like it had lost its
way home to one of the posher areas of the city, Fulwood or
Dore perhaps, and seemed ill at ease parked in the middle of
a corporation estate.

"We can't affoord that. What is it?" Mum lets out.

"It's a Singer Gazelle. Two years old. 1956. T'man at t'car
dealer's can gimme a good price on an exchange."

*Gazelle*, I think. The very name exudes sleekness and speed.

"Ooo ey," Mum exclaims, her eyes sparkling, "let's 'ave a
gander. It's even got four doors. Mum and Dad'll find it much
easier ter gerrin an' outter that."

"An' look at t'dashboard," Mum went on, "It's walnut. An'
ey, these back seats are smashin'," as she wriggles around in
them like her arse is on fire. The vinyl beige bench seats, tastefully matching the colour of the exterior trim, were decidedly
better padded, more comfortable than the little Anglia.

After the four of us took a royal spin around the neighbourhood, it was a case of the horse having already left the
barn. The Singer had left the showroom for good. Mr. Sargent,
a mechanic and car enthusiast from across the street came
strolling over, peered under the bonnet, gave it the once over
and pronounced it to be in fine shape. That luxurious gem of

Rootes wizardry took all six of us, grandparents included, on numerous Sunday trips to the seaside. But, it proved costly to maintain and after about a year, Dad exchanged it for a new Hillman Minx, a car made by the same company that was almost identical in its specifications, but lacked the classiness of the Gazelle. Needless to say, the trips to the seaside continued and proved a deciding factor in the choice of car.

"I would 'ave been 'appy wi' a Morris Minor or even another Anglia," Dad would often tell me while Mum was safely out of earshot. "But, your Mum said we needed a bigger car ter seat yer Grandma and Granddad." It was clear that this was a sore point to Dad. It was also evident that he felt powerless to go against Mum's wishes. In any event, when Dad finally did leave home for good, it was the Hillman Minx that ferried him away.

---

21    Sir Billy Butlin built an empire of military-style "holiday camps" in Britain. The first ones were built prior to WW 2, but the heyday of these camps was after the war, up to and including the 1960s. Some of the camps were used as military bases during the war.

# School Rules

Headmaster George Mack ran High Storrs according to the British public school, North American private school model.[22] Eton College was alive and well in industrial Sheffield. Rules were prescribed and they had to be followed. Or else. Classes were not discussion groups. The teacher, always male, ruled his domain and students were there to listen. Careless muttering among the backbenchers could bring about a public thrashing, six over the bum with a gym shoe. The teacher would haul the miscreants one by one to the front of the class, tell each one to bend down over a chair, then with a flourish take a swipe at the boy's backside. One teacher, Colin Smith, who taught Latin and Greek, was famous for taking a run at the bum from the other side of the classroom—much like a bowler in cricket trying to get more zap into the missile in his hand. Returning to one's seat after such an embarrassment had to be done with grace. No revealing to the rest of the class that it might have hurt, stiff upper lip. Then again, this portrayal had better not be overdone. Play acting such as shrugging of the shoulders, grinning, or hand gestures would result in a quick recall to the front for more of the same. Corporal punishment was the norm in those days and though I took my share of it, I never bore any ill feelings toward the perpetrators of it because with one or two exceptions, it was administered dispassionately and proportionately.

One exception to this was Mr. Littlewood, "Woody," the chain-smoking gym teacher. He harboured a sadistic streak. Playing noughts and crosses with his fingernails on little boys' bare chests, blowing cigarette smoke in their faces—these frivolities in front of the class. Twirling his bunch of keys, also at bare chests of unsuspecting boys, as he strolled around the gym. It soon became obvious why the gym uniform was shorts, gym shoes and socks, no clothing over the upper torso. It was Woody's target zone. One morning, he crossed the line with me. I was in Form 4A, a fifteen year old, waiting at the Pond Street bus terminus for the bus to High Storrs. I had decided not to get on the next bus because I wanted to wait for my girlfriend, Sally, to arrive and sit with her. Sally was a pupil in the girls' school at High Storrs. When I arrived at school, the door was locked. I was late. Woody was the late-for-school master. As always, he opened the door after assembly was over and told the group of us to line up facing him.

"Why are you late, Cruickshank?" he barked.

"Alarm clock din't go off, sir."

"You're in detention," he says, writing down the boy's name, "Next Monday night."

"Slater, no excuses from you. It's your third time late this term. Your name will be read out at morning assembly and you'll report to Mr. Griffen."

Mr. Griffen was the Deputy Headmaster who instilled fear into all who crossed his path. An ex-military man, he was the only teacher other than the Headmaster who used a cane. The hands were his favourite targets. The boy was made to hold out his arm, palm uppermost, while Griff swung at it with gusto. Better to look the other way, because if the hand moved to lessen the impact, the poor soul had to undergo a repeat performance. He and Woody were cut from the same cloth. Corporal punishment was something that they enjoyed doing. I just never got on the wrong side of Griff, because he was the French teacher and I was assigned to study German under one of the best teachers in the school, the highly capable and affable Joe Collier.

"Yes, sir," says Slater, head bowed. He was having visions of what was to come.

"Gordon, step forward," growled Woody.

He's picking me out of the line up, I'm thinking. What on earth for?

"And why were you late?"

"Missed the bus, sir" I said, believing what I said to be technically true.

"Gordon, you're a liar," snarled Woody, as he flung his fist into my face. I reeled back, temporarily blinded in one eye.

"You waited and let a bus go through. I was on that bus. You chose to be late."

After we were dismissed and told to go to our classes, the other boys gathered around me. "Are tha oreight, Gordon? 'E's gone too far."

Needless to say, my eye reddened, blackened, puffed up as the day progressed. Sitting around the tea table that night, my mother noticed it.

"What's 'appened ter thee eye? "

After I told her, she hit the roof.

"Bloody 'ell. 'E's given 'im a black eye. Pat, will tha go up ter see t'Headmaster an' tell 'im we're not standing for that? Bloody teacher's no right ter be givin' kids black eyes."

So, Dad went up to speak to George Mack. A day or so later, Woody asked to speak to me in his little alcove of a room beside the gym. He asked me how my eye was, told me that he didn't think it would swell up like that, almost but not quite apologizing.

The word "compulsory" was written into most of the rules at High Storrs. It was compulsory to attend after-school evening house socials, the annual school Shakespeare play, and speech night—a tedious evening at which members of the Board of Governors gave stilted, scripted speeches and prizes were given to top performing boys. It was compulsory to purchase the school magazine, *The Sheaf*, a compilation of selected articles and poems submitted by pupils of the school. In reality, such submissions were rarely spontaneous, but emanated from homework exercises. And, it was compulsory to wear the entire school uniform, including the silly looking schoolboy caps, and this applied to all boys, sixth formers included. One day, my friend Jeff Morgan and I came up with what we thought would be a great idea to ridicule what seemed to us to be a ridiculous rule. At the time, we were in Lower Sixth Science, sixteen year olds.

"The rule says we should wear our caps. It dun't say owt about whether t'caps are in good condition," says Morgan, as he takes a sharp pen knife and slices the crown of his cap from front to back, creating two flaps that hung over his ears.

"Gimmee that knife," says I.

I then proceed to slice away at the neb of my cap, so it hangs down in front of my face, swinging in the breeze.

Then, off we walk up to the bus stop at Bents Green, chortling away at our caper. Self satisfied. We'd taken on a foolish rule and weren't we having fun? Out of the corner of our eyes, we spotted a prefect looking at us.

"Nowt 'e can do," we both agreed.

The next morning, we were both sitting in Alf Ridler's chemistry class when the Headmaster's secretary appeared, note in hand. Alf took it, then proclaimed,

"Gordon and Morgan. Go immediately to the headmaster's office."

We knew immediately what had happened. As we walked

into his office, George Mack rose from his chair, to face us nose to nose. His teeth clenched, his command succinct.

"Bring me your school caps immediately."

We trooped back to our lockers to retrieve the offending headwear. No point substituting unblemished beanies from other kids. We knew that would make it worse. So, tail between our legs we trudged back into George's office to present him with our handiwork, two re-styled school caps. We waited while he handled, examined, rotated them, lifting up the newly created flaps as he did so. The silence seemed like an eternity. Then, he exploded.

"You boys have brought shame to this school. To all the boys who have worn the uniform of this school with pride. To boys of this school who have become pillars of society. To boys of this school who courageously fought for freedom in the war and who gave their lives in doing so. Boys who brought honour to this school. What do you have to say for yourselves? Gordon?"

"Very sorry sir. Didn't mean to be disrespectful."

"Morgan?"

"No sir. Like Gordon says, we didn't mean any harm."

"Do you realize what you've *done*? Do you *realize* what you've done?" (Just in case we didn't get it the first time around.) "You are both bright boys with a solid future ahead of you. But frankly, I don't know whether I can save you. Once the Board get a hold of these caps, they'll want to expel you."

*Bloody 'ell*, I think. Surely what we did wasn't serious enough to warrant expulsion, being consigned to a blue-collar trade, or unskilled labouring job for the rest of our lives. For, in those days, kids who were expelled from grammar school had nowhere else to go except into the workforce. No second chances. No university. It was final and terminal.

"Sir, we are so sorry for what we have done." By now, I was pleading.

"I don't know whether I can save you," he reiterated. Then, as he picks up his cane, "Bend over the chair. Lift up your jackets. Gordon, you first."

The six of the best[23] didn't bother us all that much, but the threat of being expelled did. Thankfully, it was never carried out. We each survived the sixth form, passed our A levels, and moved on to university. But, fellow students would often approach us to say that they had been talking to the Headmaster, who had shown them the two caps and given them the spiel. "Look what Gordon and Morgan have done." Then, the whole business about honour, pride, and serving in the Second World War.

At the time, we saw remodelling the caps as a bit of a lark. But to George, we had defaced, even desecrated that which was sacred. To George, it wasn't a silly looking uniform. It symbolized tradition, history, and a set of values that he and others had identified with the school. He might have been a bit over the top in bringing the Second World War into it, and yes, those caps did look foolish even before we had hacked away at them. But fundamentally, he was right.

Another incident that resulted in a trip to George's office was not as easy to understand. School dinners even in those days were not noted for being appetizing. Sickly stew, leathery liver, or grisly minced beef with lumpy potatoes and rock hard peas—bullets as we called them. Sometimes, smelly cabbage would be substituted for the peas. Prunes and watery custard or sago pudding that looked like frogspawn with a blob of jam spooned into it. Enough to turn any schoolboy's palate on to fish and chips. And that's what happened to several of us, pals in 4A, fourteen and fifteen year olds.

One Monday morning, we decided not to hand in our school dinner money, half a crown or so at the time. Instead, we sneaked out at lunch time and walked all the way down to Hunter's Bar, a couple of miles or so, to a fish and chip shop. Munching our tasty offerings wrapped in newspaper we strolled back to school just in time for the start of afternoon classes. After a couple of days of this, we were summoned to the Headmaster's office. George told us that a resident had reported us. For what, we were not sure. He then went on to give us the standard speech about having brought dishonour to the school. Making a public spectacle of us. Six of the best for each of us. No big deal. He could have queried our honesty in using money given by our parents for a purpose other than that which was intended. But, that was never mentioned. It was all about the image we had left within the community.

The trip to beat all trips to George's office, the one in which there was a very real threat of my expulsion from the school, happened while I was a fourteen year old in Form 3A. It was the spring of 1957. One Thursday dinnertime, a group of us were roaming around in the Roughs. It was actually out of bounds, meaning that we were not supposed to go there during school hours, but few people took any notice of this regulation that was not well enforced. It was crawling with High Storrs kids during the lunch breaks. A great place to hang out, smoke, hide away from the prefects, and be mischievous. Wortley, Garroty and I thought we were pretty smart pretending to be rougher and tougher than we really were. In those days, flick knives were the weapons of choice for the street gangs. What we each carried in our pockets were toned down versions of the real things, the hardware store variety, much like a modern day x-acto knife with a retractable razor blade. We slashed at the grass, at the trees, at the sky. A bunch of adolescents, pimply kids, on a testosterone high. But, it was all make believe. Or, so I thought. Out of nowhere, a young lad came running toward us, bedecked in the navy blue and white uniform of Greystone's Secondary School, which was located several miles away.

"What's 'e doin' 'ere?" muses Wortley. "I know. We'll ask 'im."

"Eyup young un. 'As tha got lost?"

"No. I'm on me way back ter school," says the timid lad.

He slows down a little as he passes us, looking apprehensively at the implements we hold in our hands. Wortley reaches out to stroke the back of the boy's jacket with his knife. A gigantic rip like an open sore stares us in the face. A blazer that had been cared for ruined. Was this still funny?

"Bloody 'ell. Tha's ripped 'is jacket Wortley. What tha do that for?" I ask incredulously.

"I meant ter stroke t' jacket wi' t' back er t' knife," he says. "I din't mean for it to rip t'jacket."

Garroty and I spent the rest of the lunch hour telling Wortley what an idiot he was and that we'd better not get into trouble for it. Wortley tried to shrug it off but we were all worried.

And for good reason. The following day, an overcast Friday morning, several teachers, together with a cadre of prefects, patrolled the schoolyard at recess time. The doors to the school were closed. The entire lower school, fifth form down, was contained within the schoolyard. We knew something serious was going on when a teacher blew a whistle repeatedly and when the clamour had died down, told us to line up form by form across the width of the yard. George Mack, accompanied by the young student from Greystone, strolled slowly down each line. Wortley, Garroty, and I made sure we were well separated in our line. As the pair patrolled the line ahead of us, the boy stopped and pointed at a boy.

"Take a good look," I heard George say. "You think it might be him?"

"Don't know, sir."

"Go immediately to my office," said George.

Then, the pair moved on to our line. Right past Wortley, then Garroty. Phew, I think, maybe we're going to get out of this. My heart is racing as they move along toward me. But, the boy stops, faces me, and points. At me. God. What am I going to do?

"To my office. Right now," snaps George.

As I take the long and lonely walk from the schoolyard to George's office, my mind is in high gear. *I'll just keep denying it*, I tell myself.

When I get to the outer office, Nina the young and attractive school secretary is there. Nina, every schoolboy's dream, but only on the surface. She was a strict enforcer.

"Hold out your arm," she says, stopwatch in hand. Then, she proceeds to take my pulse. The pulse was used much like a lie detector test on all boys who were sent to George's office for serious reasons.

"It's up," she says, not expecting an answer.

In all, four of us collect in the outer office and, after what seems like an eternity, we are ushered into George's inner sanctum. George, Greystone, and his Mum are gathered around the desk.

"Stand in a line," George barks.

"Starting from that end," as he points to one end of the line, "One at a time, step forward and say,

*Eyup young un. 'As tha got lost?*"

"And use your normal accent."

I'm number three in line. At each recitation, George asks the boy to listen hard.

"Is this the boy, do you think?"

"Don't know, sir."

When it gets to my turn, I put on the best show of my life, trying to sound as unlike Wortley as I possibly can. No gruff, low-pitched slurring. Clearly enunciated, Sheffield accent, no phoniness, delivered tenor style.

As I stare straight ahead, not wishing to make eye contact with Greystone, I hear him say those magic three words— "Don't know, sir."

After four "don't knows," George turns to Greystone's Mum.

"Sorry, but I can't do anything with 'don't know' answers. I'm afraid that's all I can do."

Then, turning to us,

"You boys go back to your classes."

For the rest of that day, Wortley, Garroty, and I were in shock. We agreed to keep our distances from one another for a while, especially at dinner breaks, in case we ran into young Greystone again. At home, I spent the weekend deep in thought. What if he had recognized me? What would I have done with the rest of my life? Will the incident go away or will it re-surface on Monday? I had just gone through hell and I couldn't believe it was over. But it was.

I spent plenty of time on the Green Hill during the weekend following the Greystone's incident, puffing away on one cigarette after another to dull my senses. Understandably, I was not allowed to smoke at home. However, at school, the regulation, which prohibited smoking anywhere at anytime while in school uniform, was not rigidly enforced. In the fifties, the health risks of smoking were just beginning to unfold and smoking was looked upon as chic in some quarters. Film stars, television personalities, and even some British football players smoked to cultivate their images or to feed their addictions. Newcastle United legend Jackie Milburn told the story of going to the toilets before the 1951 Cup Final at Wembley to have a smoke, only to find that four of his teammates were already there doing the same thing. Smoking on buses, trains, cars, in cinemas, restaurants, homes…virtually anywhere except public libraries, was taken as a given. It wasn't until 1956 that the Ministry of Education in the UK directed schools to instruct children that there was a relationship between smoking and lung cancer.

George Mack, a smoker himself, delivered this message to us in a half-hearted, dismissive kind of way. Smoking was not considered as great a sin as desecrating a school cap or eating fish and chips in public. Too bad if anyone wished to have a "slash" during recess times. All of the doors to the stalls in the latrines would be closed, great clouds of tobacco smoke billowing out from behind them, groups of boys huddled together having a fag. The Roughs were a great place to smoke, as was the lower end of the school playing fields. Prefects would usually look the other way or just tell the culprit to put it out. The extra year that some of us spent in the sixth form, S or Scholarship Sixth, was not rigidly structured and we were left with scads of free time on our hands. Times when we could smoke if we were ingenious enough. But we had outgrown the smoking in the bogs scene. We discovered an opening at the back of the school stage in the main assembly hall through which we could crawl and gain access to the space beneath the stage where theatrical costumes and supplies were stored. We spent quality time under the stage, looking through the grilles at the girls from the girls' school. They used the assembly hall for dancing practice, what would nowadays be called aerobics. We were eventually discovered when one of the prefects, someone involved in one of the drama productions, had cause to visit the under stage space one day. He found a cigarette stub. But, he just let the word get around that he was on to us and we moved on.

Occasionally, buffoonery would get way out of hand. Like the time when a bunch of fifth formers stole a double-decker bus from the city bus depot, hot-wired it, then went for a trip across the country. Not exactly going under cover. About as conspicuous as—well, a double-decker bus. The strong arm of the law caught up with them in Liverpool, waiting to get on the ferry to the Isle of Man. Of course, they were expelled—in absentia, but in public. One morning assembly, the entire school was forced to sit on the assembly hall floor and listen to a full exposé by an irate George Mack. On this occasion, perhaps the punishment really did fit the crime.

The last day of the school year was a traditional time for high jinks. A cadre of students would not be returning so they didn't have to worry about punishment. Underpants, on at least one occasion a pair of girl's panties, could be seen blowing in the wind atop the school flagpole. One year, probably 1958, the last day was marked by hordes of students marching up Ringinglow Road, purportedly to do battle with pupils at Silverdale Secondary School. Word had got around that the Silverdale students had issued a challenge. A challenge for what we were not quite sure, but listening to some of the chatter going around, it wasn't to play tiddly-winks. I would estimate that ninety per cent of the scores of youths who were caught up in the hysteria were there to watch. I was one of them. But, the showdown at high noon, mid-afternoon really, never materialized. As the procession moved past the Bents Green shopping centre, a posse of school prefects turned it back. All of a sudden, we were in retreat on our way back to school, ushered by prefects and several teachers. Notable among the latter was Mr. "Polly"

Sanford, a chemistry teacher, who patrolled the line on his bicycle.

We were escorted en masse into one of the dining halls, where we were told to stand alongside the tables. The place was filled. Mr. "No Nonsense" Griffin marched up and down the centre aisle yelling and shouting. "No sitting. No talking. Think this is funny? Try me and see."

When George Mack entered the hall, you could have heard a pin drop.

"You are all a disgrace to the school. You have brought shame upon our good reputation. You deserve no mercy. I should expel the lot of you…"

And on it went until finally we were dismissed.

In my last year at High Storrs, I was among a bevy of students who spent part of the afternoon drinking in the yard of a local pub. Another boy from the school stopped by to warn us that prefects were on their way down and we had better move on. Most of us heeded that advice and made our way back to school. But, word went around that a few students who stayed were expelled. On the last day of school.

Lest there be any misunderstanding, I was not a problem student during my seven years at High Storrs. Except for the initial settling-in period, I was consistently at, or near, the top of the class, especially in biology. For my scholastic endeavours, I had the dubious honour of receiving book prizes on Speech Night several years in a row. Although I ran afoul of the rules and strayed across the line from time to time, I was generally well behaved and regarded by my teachers as someone on a university track. I just was not part of the small group of studious students, referred to as "swots" back then, the equivalent of present day "nerds."

For the longest time, I had aspirations to be a medical doctor, and during free periods would spend my time reading library books with titles such as *How to Live with your Gall Bladder, You and your Prostate Glands*, and *Maintaining a Healthy Bowel*. Needless to say, this aroused some curiosity and leg pulling from my classmates. Word must have got around the school that I was a doctor-in-waiting because one day, a fifth-form student approached me and asked me if I knew how to perform an abortion. His girlfriend had a bun in the oven and he wanted to stop it baking. I felt flattered, so I told him that while I didn't know how to do the operation, if all else failed, I'd read about it and would give it a try. Of course, this was just unrealistic bravado. I was thankful that he didn't approach me again so I didn't have to renege on the offer.

---

22    The term "public school" in the UK refers to a small group of independently operated, fee-charging schools, traditionally patronized by the upper class and aristocracy. In North America, this term carries the opposite meaning, as it is used to refer to state-run schools, which the vast majority of the general public attend.

23    A widely-used idiom during the era of corporal punishment in schools, it refers to six solid whacks on the pupil's backside with a cane.

# RECREATION

Sports and gymnastics were never my strong suits, failings that the chain-smoking gym teacher never overlooked. In the lower grades, my bare chest was his playground for key chain flicking and finger nail noughts and crosses games; my face a captive receptacle for the jets of cigarette smoke that he would blow at it. For organized sports, forms would compete against each other, three teams per class. Teams were selected based on sporting ability by the athletically gifted students. Hence, I was consistently in the third team for football. The jocks automatically assumed that I would be just as inept at cricket and I was put into the third team. They made a mistake. I was a decent bowler. On my first outing, I took eight wickets. Word soon got around and I was moved into the second eleven. I spent most of my first appearance in the field, chasing down balls. Then, with the team struggling, the captain threw me the ball and asked me to have a go. I took two wickets in two overs.

Had it not been for my smoking habit, I might have been a better-than-average long-distance runner, or "harrier," to use George Mack's terminology. Every year, the entire school went on long-distance runs around the neighbourhood—through the school playing fields, the usually off-limits Roughs, woodlands, country lanes, and residential streets. The courses were selected according to age levels, with the longer courses for the older students. Points were awarded to the various school houses based on the final placements of the students. One year, I decided to break ranks with the rest of my mates who were strolling around the course chatting and smoking. I gave it a go. When I entered the finishing area in the school playing field, Mr. Presgrave yelled out in amazement, "Hey, it's Gordon. Come on, boy. You'll earn the house a point." And I did. Not in the first dozen finishers, but a strong enough finish for a point. I still carried on smoking until my mid-thirties.

In my mid-teens, I became a keen traditional jazz fan. The great trumpeter Louis Armstrong, Satchmo, could walk on water as far as I was concerned. I was also an ardent admirer of Pat Halcox, the highly talented cornet player in the up and coming Chris Barber Jazz Band. As I sat in the City Hall with my second cousin Lorna watching the band, I could imagine myself riffing and improvising like a real pro. My grandiose aspirations took on a measure of possibility when I saw a Selmer Lincoln® trumpet in the window of Philip Cann's music store on Dixon Lane. The price was seventeen guineas. Using some of the money that I earned from my newspaper round, I could save up a down payment and pay off the rest in weekly instalments. When I ran this idea by my parents, I got a much better response than I anticipated. Dad went down to Cann's music store, found out the name of a trumpet instructor and agreed, with Mum's consent, to cover the cost of the bimonthly lessons if I paid for the trumpet. With the help of donations from my aunts, I managed to pay for the instrument on what was then called the never-never, credit as it is known today. Of course, I never did become a second Pat Halcox, the trumpet being harder to master than I thought, but I did learn to play and it stood me in good stead when I entered university and joined a jazz band. In the meantime, my trumpet could be heard blaring out all over the Stradbroke estate as I practiced in my bedroom. Unlike a piano, a trumpet calls out for other instruments around it to make it sound pleasing. The neighbours were very tolerant.

I also had a keen interest in the new genre of music that had crossed the Atlantic—rock and roll. On a cold February morning in 1959, we are all sitting in Sep's, Mr. Presgrave's, "calculus for beginners" class. He is writing on the board, his back to us, differentiating some inconsequential cosine expression. One of the students in the class puts his hands up, yells out:

"Sir."

Sep turns around.

"Yes?"

"What did yer think ter t'news this mornin' that Buddy Holly, Ritchie Valens, an' the Big Bopper died in a plane crash?"

"And who might they be or were?"

"Rock an' roll stars, sir. The best."

"Oh. Well, I'm sorry. What else can I say?"

"But, sir. Could we have a minute of silence for them?"

"Oh, I suppose so," says Sep, in a bemused kind of way.

Eventually, Sep breaks the silence.

"Now getting back to differentiating that…"

None of us could care less about that stupid calculus stuff on the day the music died.

⁓ ⌣ ⌐

I may not have been athletically inclined during my years at High Storrs, but I did develop an outdoor recreational activity that may be loosely described as a sport—caving, otherwise known as potholing or spelunking. It was in March of 1959 that twenty-year-old Oxford university student and potholer, Neil Moss, lost his life in Peak Cavern, a limestone cave in the picturesque Peak District that borders Sheffield. Trapped upright for forty-one and a half hours in a narrow shaft of the cave known as the Devil's Arse, he suffocated on a mixture of foul air and his own carbon dioxide. The on-the-spot press reports were graphic. Pitch black, damp and fetid, narrow passageways leading to a subterranean maze of dripping wet chambers, underground rivers where the water often touched the ceiling, vertical shafts that disappeared downwards into the unknown. Who would want to enter such a place? Well, at the age of sixteen, I did. Whether it was to cater to an untapped sense of adventure, or to escape from a home life that had uncertainty and strife written all over it, I don't know.

It wasn't easy to garner much interest in my new sport among my school friends who found life above ground more appealing. So, against my parents' wishes, I would often go alone, exploring the caves around the village of Castleton. Eventually, one of my friends at school, Jack Martin, decided to give it a go and the two of us joined the British Speleological Society.

While I was in the sixth form at High Storrs Grammar, Jack and I had planned to spend the 1960 Whitsuntide long weekend camping in the Yorkshire Dales. The Bradford Pothole Club, as was its custom, was set to operate a winch to allow cavers access to Gaping Gill, a monstrous pothole that surfaces on the limestone slopes of Ingleborough through a 344-foot vertical shaft. We were chomping at the bit to go down one of the most famous caves in the country. We even planned to overnight in the cave. But, a trip like that was more than I could afford out of my pocket money. Since my early years at High Storrs, I had stopped receiving pocket money from my parents and had relied on my own resourcefulness. Delivering newspapers, Christmas mail, bottling milk at a dairy, general dogs body at a furniture store—I acquired a variety of skills. At the time of the Gaping Gill trip, I was a cloakroom attendant two nights per week at the Embassy Ballroom on

Mansfield Road. But, the seven shillings and sixpence that I received for this job was barely enough to cover my week-to-week expenses, chief among which were cigarettes and credit payments for the trumpet that I purchased. Additional money would be needed to cover the rail fare, camping, and sundry other costs of the trip. Along came Ron Storey, manager of the Embassy Ballroom. During the first week of our Whitsuntide break, he set Jack and me to work with picks, shovels, and rakes clearing a piece of land at the back of the ballroom, then spreading red shale over it to create a car park. For that, we were each paid the princely sum of four pounds—enough, but just enough, for our trip.

Mum and Dad knew weeks in advance that I was planning the trip and that the backbreaking car park assignment was to pay for it. Nothing was said until I came home with my wages, just a day or so before I was due to depart for the Yorkshire Dales. One of the four-pound notes that I received in my wage packet was a Scottish pound note, which I had never seen before. Innocently, I showed it to Mum and Dad, who were sitting around the fireplace.

"Oooh aye," says Dad, a sardonic smirk on his face, "A Scottish pound note? In't that just marvellous? Be nice ter 'ave one er them."

"Aye, specially since tha an't given us owt for thee room an' board," chips in Mum. "Bloody cheek er it. Does tha think it costs nowt for thee ter live in this 'ouse?"

When I explained to them that this was the first I had heard of them wanting room and board, that they knew what I had been working for, and that I would have to forgo the trip if I gave them money that I had not considered to be needed, Dad passed the pound note back to me and Mum began her tirade. "Ungrateful sod. Tek thee bloody Scottish pound note an' stick it up thee arsehole. Ter think I work me fingers ter t'bone ter keep yer at bloody grammar school an' that's the thanks I get. Chuff..."

Then, along came Dad with the sucker punch: the comparison between my brother and me. The wedge that my parents wielded so effectively. "I'll tell thee what. Tha might be good at thee schoolwork, but that not a patch on our Trevor when it comes ter bein' kind 'arted. Our Trevor's got more feelings in 'is little toe than tha's got in thee whole body. 'E's got a 'art er gold. Tha's not even got one."

I left the room. No point talking. But I felt like shit. Why the hell didn't they forewarn me about this? I might have even been able to put in an extra shift or two in the cloakroom. They didn't look like they needed the money. They were doing all right with Dad selling fire extinguishers. And if I hadn't been going to the Yorkshire Dales, I wouldn't have sweated and toiled building the car park. There would have been no wages. I would have willingly given over a portion of my wages if a need had been brought to my attention. This was just a mean attempt to scuttle the trip. It didn't work. I went on that caving trip. Thankfully, little more was said about it on the home front.

Jack and I would explore caves and potholes around Castleton and on one occasion, in the Yorkshire Dales. Sloshing along underground water courses, upright or on our hands and knees, crawling along narrow passageways known as cat runs, descending deep shafts using nylon or rope ladders, clambering or chimneying up ascending slopes, we relished in it. The problem for me was that I was not very adept at it. Blame it on my smoking, but I tired too easily and on one occasion, had to be hauled up rope ladders by the other cavers. Another caver gave me a shot of brandy once I made it above ground. On another occasion, as I was trying to dive under and through a sump, a place where the ceiling of a passageway dips underneath the water for a few feet, my helmet jammed in the architecture of the place and my head became stuck under water. I had to be pulled out backwards. Then, there was the time when Jack and I went in a cave, against all expert advice, during a day when it was raining heavily. We were far underground when we noticed the water in the stream that coursed through the cave rising. We only just made it out in time, our heads tipped sideways to access the few inches of air between the water level and the ceiling of the main passageway. The air pocket was rapidly diminishing to zero. Potholing was fun while it lasted but I very wisely decided to pack it in when I went to university—lest it get the better of me.

# Didn't Frame

During the 50s and early 60s when I was a student there, High Storrs provided a first-rate education, the likes of which one would have to pay for today. Alongside its strict code of behaviour, it evinced a no nonsense approach to its curriculum. Rigour, thoroughness, knowledgeable teachers and above all, good study habits were the hallmarks of what High Storrs had in abundance. Homework, which from the fourth form up amounted to as much as three hours per night, weekends included, was compulsory. Note taking in class was simply expected. A student staring into space would be brought to task. Science laboratories were carried out with meticulous attention to detail and we were taught how to write essays. Not only did we learn mathematical concepts, but also how to calculate. The nearest things we had to a calculator back then were a slide rule and a book of log tables and algebraic functions. I breezed through my G.C.E. "O" levels, passing in eight subjects, doing so in the accelerated 4A class, which took their exams a year ahead of the rest of their peers.

When it came time for me to slim down my subjects to

three in the sixth form, I chose biology, chemistry, and physics, with the intention of applying to medical school. I excelled in biology, was very good in chemistry, but alas, struggled with physics. We were made to take G.C.E. "A" level exams set by the Oxford and Cambridge Examining Board. One stipulation of the Board was that in order to pass a subject, a student must pass every single theory and practical exam in that subject, regardless of the aggregate grade achieved in it. The first time I took these exams, in July 1960, I sailed through the biology and chemistry exams, thought I had done enough to pass the physics theory papers, but had a rough ride in the practical exam. A few weeks afterwards, I knew I was in trouble when I started to get plain postcards from the universities to which I had applied stating that I had been rejected. Then, came that awful postcard in the mail telling me that I had achieved "A" grades in biology and chemistry and only an "O" level in physics. I needed to pass all three of my subjects at an "A" level standard or better to secure a place at a university.

Subsequently, I had to endure humiliating verbal abuse by my parents.

"What the bloody 'ell 'as tha been doin'? Bloody disgraceful."

"Tha's been spending too much time wi' thee bloody girlfriend, not enough at thee studies."

"What are tha wastin' our time for? 'Ere we are working ter keep a layabout like thee in t'school. Tha should be ashamed er thee'sen." Mum certainly laid it on.

"Abart time tha started ter frame." Dad's contribution.

"Aye an' while that framin,' remember who's payin' for thee room an' board while tha't at t'school. That's all," Back to Mum again.

What a load of shit. I had tried my damned best to pass those exams, studied hard. But no understanding or empathy was shown.

After talking to a few of my friends, I discovered that I was not the only one who had failed physics, so we all agreed to stay on another year and give it another try. When I reported to school, George Mack told me that I had passed both physics theory exams comfortably, failed the practical by two percent, and had an aggregate score over the pass mark. For two lousy percent on one exam, I was held back another year and entered the "S" or "Scholarship" stream of the sixth form.

When I discovered how close I was to passing, I realized how close I was to garnering my parents' admiration as opposed to their scorn. But, like many other facets of home life, there was a hard and fast line drawn in the sand and I had fallen on the wrong side of it. Once I discovered that I had only technically failed to meet the grade in physics because of a quirk in the examination regulations, I made sure that Mum and Dad understood this. To give them credit, they did not lean on me to quit school. As long as I started to frame, I might as well stay on.

That year proved to be an uninspiring one as we attended

classes that embellished what we had already learned, a curriculum that was designed for students wishing to apply for entrance to Oxford or Cambridge University. I had no such intention. A group of a dozen or so of us had plenty of free time on our hands—time to smoke under the school stage and look at the legs of the girls as they pranced around the assembly hall, time to visit the betting shop at Hunter's Bar, time to spend an afternoon in nearby Ecclesall woods, purportedly studying ecology, in reality playing like little kids, rerouting the little streams that wound between the trees, just for the heck of it. On a sunny Friday afternoon, May 5 1961, we lazed around in the woods listening on a portable radio to the broadcast of Alan Shepard's successful fifteen-minute flight into space aboard his space capsule, Freedom 7. History was being made. The first American in space. We were just biding our time.

# BREAKING POINT

Christmas 1960. On the world scene, the soviet Foreign Minister Andrei Gromyko issued a call for a second summit conference with the western leaders and offered an optimistic prognosis for improving relations with the U.S., once newly elected President Kennedy had taken his oath of office. In Sheffield, Christmas shoppers were in a buoyant mood, as they descended in droves on city stores to ring up record sales. The upbeat holiday spirit was evident in the offerings at the cinemas and theatres. *Puss in Boots* was the pantomime playing at the Lyceum, while films around town included *White Christmas* at the Park cinema, *Sword of Sherwood Forest* at the Hippodrome, and a Norman Wisdom film at the Gaumont. Inexplicably, *Jack the Ripper* and the *Curse of Frankenstein* were billed at the Cinema House. Those whose minds were not focused on the shopping or theatre-going were thinking of young Doug McMillan, the nineteen-year-old Sheffield Wednesday player who had his right leg amputated while in the wreckage of a team bus that had overturned on the A1.

Friday, December 23. A cold, crisp, still day. It was the

calm before the metaphorical storm that attacked and eventually wrecked my parents' marriage. Once triggered, the storm snowballed in the space of less than an hour into an out of control hurricane that sent them both over the precipice. There was no turning back. Nineteen years of marriage, a marriage beset with problems, though not (I believe) irreconcilable ones, tossed aside. Neither of them had anything left to put into the union, no will to keep going. Both wanted out. December 23 was also Dad's birthday. I arrived home in the early evening after putting in extra hours at my Christmas break job bottling milk at Express Dairy. Mum was sitting at the kitchen table crying like I have never seen her do before, heaving and sighing, her head bouncing up and down in her hands, her upper torso shaking like a blob of jelly. Trevor was standing beside her, grim faced.

"What's up, Mum?" I say, rushing over to her.

She takes her head out of her hands, looks up at me, and through the blubbering and spluttering coming from her tear-stained face, she begins to answer my question. "Thee bloody father, that's what's up," father pronounced like lather. "'E's just come 'ome drunk as a bloody Irish navvy and told me that 'e wished 'ed never married me. Said 'e should er married t'other one, whoever she might er been. 'E's upstairs now on t'bed sleepin' it off. Just wait while 'e wakes up. 'E'll get what's comin' ter 'im."

That's how the story was related to me at the time. I wasn't there when the incident happened. I wasn't able to fill in the blanks. But, it all sounded so out of character for my Dad, mild mannered man of few words, to have, without provocation, turned on my mother in such a belligerent fashion. Many years later, a more benign version of my father's behaviour on that night was related to me. He had been drinking and driving. Back then, such a toxic combination was commonplace. But, he entered the kitchen with a broad, inane smile on his face, the kind of smile that just stays there as a statement of insulation, indifference, and inebriation through whatever may be thrown its way. To almost anyone other than himself, he would have looked like a jackass, but a harmless one. But, not to Mum. She railed into him. He had no right to come home in that condition. Who did he think he was? As he protested, at first mildly, that it was his birthday and he was just having a drink after work, her ranting became more abusive. Finally, Dad stood his ground and with the grin now wiped from his face, gave as good as he got, culminating in that fateful statement of regret that he had married my mother instead of someone else. My mother would never forgive him for saying that. It was the end.

"So, what caused 'im ter say that ter yer, Mum?" I say.

"I don't know. I've tried me best. I don't know what I've done ter deserve this. I've worked me fingers ter t'bone comin 'ome night after night covered in muck an' grease ter get 'im that car an' this is all t'thanks I get for it. Nice Christmas present."

"Don't worry, Mum, we'll stand by yer. We know what yer've done for 'im an' for us." I'm hugging her closely and letting her tears stain my jacket.

Through all of the turbulent times, my brother and I had inwardly sided with my mother. She was such a dominant force, my Dad so deferential, that her perspectives, her sense of rightness and wrongness prevailed. I never knew who my Dad really was. He kept his feelings so well hidden that he conveyed the impression of indifference toward us. By contrast, my mother was many things–tempestuous, emotional, irrational, and often verbally abusive—but she was not indifferent. She had her moments when caring and warmth floated to the surface. The sight of my mother coming home night after night, her hands gnarled and smeared with machine grease, the knowledge that this was done to enhance Dad's status in his white-collar job, were telling points. Why did she make this sacrifice in the first place? Why didn't she stop doing it rather than let resentment build up? Why didn't she use her eight "O" levels and change to a white-collar job? Why hadn't she sorted all of this out with Dad instead of periodically letting it all hang out and making it a family issue? None of these questions occurred to us.

With Dad as an unwitting accomplice, we were subjected to a brainwashing regime. Like Mum, we saw everything in black and white. For many years, I even adopted many of her views that were out of synch with the working-class population that she was part of. The Conservative Party was the only one that knew how to govern. The Labour Party was inept and full of socialist bleeding hearts. Unions were stopping the country getting ahead and were led by communists. The Royal Family and the British Empire was what made Britain the greatest country in the world. Thankfully, I later rejected some of Mum's most bizarre and distasteful views. Contrary to Mum, I never believed that Americans were a mongrel race or that the Irish were an inferior race to the pure blooded British. Nor did I believe that Catholics should be avoided because they are a different breed of people than us Protestants. I was wary of communists, as were many people in the fifties, but I did think that Mum had taken things to an extreme when one day, I brought a loaf of bread home and she sent me back to the store with it. "We want no Fletcher's bread in 'ere. That firm's run by a communist." Well, the company was founded back in the 1920s by George Fletcher, who was a communist, but mixing politics with bread sounded to me even sillier than mixing politics with religion.

So, here I am two days before Christmas standing shoulder to shoulder with Mum, fully convinced that she had been severely wronged by Dad. I had bought into that black and white world in which Mum lived. Mum, ever the righteous one, had been hurt by Dad. Therefore, he must be despised.

"'Ow are we goin' ter get through Christmas now?" asks Mum. "'E's not goin' ter be part er it. I'm goin' ter 'ave ter tell yer Grandma an' Granddad ter stop 'em comin' up ter t'ouse for their Christmas dinner."

"We'll sort that out tomorra," say I.

The following morning, Christmas Eve, everyone woke up with a hangover, even those of us who had not been drinking. Dad, head bowed, slouched into the kitchen where the three of us were gathered around the table. Mum just looked up and sneered. "Look what t'cat's spewed up. So what's tha got ter say for thee'sen now? "

Dad started to speak when, fists clenched, Mum rose from the table. "I don't want ter 'ear owt abart it. Not interested. Get thee'sen outer t'ouse. Tha spends Christmas by thee'sen."

"Not much point in sayin' owt then is there?" mumbles Dad as he closes the kitchen door behind him and shuffles down the path toward the car, which, somehow or other, had made it as far as the driveway after Dad's happy hour. That was the last we saw of him and the car until Christmas was over.

"I think we should pack our things and go down ter yer Grandma's. We'll spend Christmas down there," says Mum. And that's what we did. After Mum had told Grandma and Granddad what had happened, including her pronouncement that the marriage was dead, there were long faces all around the table. Grandma's wailing interrupted this.

"Oo dear. What are we goin' ter do? 'Ow will we get o'er this?"

Granddad, wise as ever, brought her back down to earth.

220 | Roger Gordon

"Shut thee'sen up. Tha'll be doin' nowt. It's for our Nell ter do what needs ter be done. If owt needs needs ter be done."

Everything else that happened that Christmas is a blur. My Aunts Ray and Buddy, along with Uncle Carl, came around on Christmas night as usual—more people added to the sombre scene. On Boxing Day, the three of us went home to an uninviting empty house. Dad rolled in later in the evening.

No words are exchanged as he walks upstairs.

After a while, Mum follows him.

"I'll let 'im know where 'e stands," she announces to Trevor and me. "'E does not sleep in that bed."

Trevor and I wait at the bottom of the stairs, ready for action if anything should go wrong. We only hear Mum yelling, no sounds from Dad. Sobbing and shaking, Mum comes back down the stairs to rejoin us, shortly followed by Dad. For the first time, Dad speaks to my brother and me. "I know what yer thinking, but I can assure yer it's not like yer think it is. There's two sides ter every story an' one day yer'll see it."

"Don't you dare talk to them kids like that. They know what tha art. They've seen it wi' their own eyes. Tryin' to influence 'em." growls Mum.

"They deserve ter know that I'm not all bad. There's a lot gone on they don't understand." A dispassionate rejoinder from Dad, his body language that of reason.

"Get outter me sight."

"I will. Before I go, I'll say one more thing." Dad turns to face my brother and me. "One day, I firmly predict, each of yer will come to me an' tell me 'ow sorry yer are that yer could only see yer mother's side. I understand yer want ter protect yer mother. But, yer'll realize that I'm not the person yer might think I am an' yer'll want ter shake me 'and. I'll be there for yer."

All the time, Mum keeps up a teeth-clenched chant that gets louder and louder, insuring Dad's words of prophecy are set against a background of "Get out," "Get out."

So Dad did leave and took off in the car that was the result of Mum's hard labour. To where, we never knew. He probably spent Christmas and New Years at his mother's. The rest of the time, his frequent car journeys were to destinations unknown. Surprisingly, the car that had become a lightning rod for much of my mother's resentment and anger did not become a point of contention at this stage. Mum never balked at him using the car over the months in which the marriage was in irreversible decay. He even took the car with him when he finally did leave for good.

New Year's Eve 1960 was spent as per usual at Aunt Bud's flat. The jolly partygoers were Mum, Grandma and Granddad, Aunt Bud, Uncle Carl, and Trevor and me. The conversation was subdued to say the least. When it got to midnight, we all stood up with our glass of sherry to welcome the New Year.

"Well, it's a funny New Year, this one. I don't know what

222 | ROGER GORDON

ter expect. But, 'appy New Year everyone," says Mum with a measure of grace.

"Whatever 'appens, tha'll allus 'ave us ter fall back on. Tha'll allus be t'apple er me eye," says Grandma, her eyes filling up as she hugs Mum. Aunt Bud doesn't seem pleased at the apple of my eye part. Our Nell's always been her favourite, I can hear her thinking.

"'Appy New Year, everyone," I finally say.

# Taking Sides

In Sheffield, 1961 came in like the old one went out—
amid a potpourri of good and bad news. Shoppers carried forward their spending spree into the New Year sales,
taking advantage of bargains at the city stores. At Robert
Brothers, a boy's blazer could be bought for 12 shillings and
6 pence, a girl's blouse for the meagre sum of 7 shillings and
6 pence.[24] Two new roundabouts were constructed in the city
centre. Sheffield's Deputy Minister of Health issued a statement
to the effect that polio had been almost wiped out among the
city's population, but he warned people that they should get
vaccinated and not to become complacent. Against this generally positive backdrop, the miners at Grimesthorpe colliery had
gone on a one-day strike in protest against the mine operators
who had suspended a bunch of workers for taking time off during New Year's Eve. It was not a good start to the New Year for
Sheffield University's Pro-Chancellor, whose house was broken
into and burgled for jewellery and it couldn't have been a worse
beginning for the family and friends of that young mother of
four, whose murdered body was found among the bushes in the
graveyard of St George's Church next to the Jessop Hospital.

My New Year's Day chore was to carry the message to friends of my parents that we would not be joining them for the usual New Year's get-together.

"What shall I say to Mrs. Curran," I ask Mum.

"Make summat up. No. Tell er t'truth. I've nowt ter be ashamed o'er."

So, I find myself in the kitchen of Mr. and Mrs. Curran's home, embarrassed as a peeled beetroot, facing Mr. Curran, a burly man, whose strong points were his talents as a builder, not as a marriage counsellor.

"Joyce in't in," he says, in a matter of fact way.

"Me Mum sent me ter tell yer that we won't be comin' o'er tonight. Me Mum and Dad are breakin' up."

Awkward silence, then stroking his chin while looking down at the floor, he offers words of empathy.

"What? Oh. Oh. I'm sorry. Joyce'll be sorry an all."

Job done, I realize that what lies ahead will involve me in ways not of my choosing and in ways that align me fair and square alongside my mother. It's a three to one gang up against Dad, who is absolutely, one hundred percent the guilty party here. How dare he hurt our innocent mother so deeply? How dare he show his ingratitude for all that our mother has done? And how dare he bring all this on at Christmas time?

My brother and I had no choice but to position ourselves squarely with one side or the other. And the other was not even in play. My mother was omnipotent and faultless,

my father emotionless and blameworthy. Besides, he offered
nothing tangible to us—companionship, a roof over our
heads, for example. Mum had pledged to stand by us. Over
the next three months, while both parents were still aboard
the ship, my brother and I had to make our allegiance clear.
There was no middle ground, no sitting on the fence. At the
time that all this happened, I was seventeen, my brother
almost fifteen. I was repeating my last year in the sixth form,
my brother in his last year of secondary school and about
to enter the work force. So, we were not kids. But, neither
were we free wheeling, self-reliant adults. We needed some
measure of parental support to move ahead in our own lives
and only Mum was offering any. Too bad her support came
with strings attached, hateful and callous ones.

For three months, Dad was sent to the proverbial Coventry.[25]
None of the three of us spoke to him unless absolutely necessary and then only in terse sentences or sentence fragments.

"Goin' out tonight?" I would ask.

"Later on," his reply.

"Seen today's paper?"

"Mum's readin' it."

"She in t'kitchen?"

"Yep."

So, off I'd go to borrow the *Sheffield Star* and read the latest news about the South Yorkshire coal miners' strikes, the
Sheffield flu outbreak, or the sentencing of that man who had

killed the young woman in St. George's churchyard over the New Year.

Dad did not eat with the rest of us. After the three of us had finished eating in the kitchen, he would rustle himself up something like beans on toast or eggs and bacon, and then eat it by himself in the living room. For three months, he slept on the sofa downstairs while Mum occupied the marital bed.

Pretty soon, a pattern started to emerge. Night after night, they would take their separate exits from the house and go their divergent ways. Dad took the car, Mum strolled up the street. We never did ask them where they had been. Didn't seem to matter. The marriage was in free fall, the bond that once held the four of us together severed irreparably. Dad even vacated the house entirely at weekends, probably but not necessarily to his mother's. Then, one night in early March, as the three of us were sitting at the kitchen table, about to eat our tea, Dad incongruously hovering around in the background instead of biding time in the living room, Mum came out with a bombshell.

"I think I should tell the pair er yer. Yer Dad already knows abart it. I'm seein' a new man. 'Is name is Brian an 'e's a Canadian."

"So that's where tha's been all these nights on thee own?" Trevor asks in a confrontational tone of voice. "Goin' out wi' a fancy man."

I am less affronted by the revelation. "Is it true that you know abart this?" I ask Dad.

"Yes. I've know abart it for some time."

*And what does "some time" mean,* I think. *Since Dad came home that night at Christmas?* It never occurred to me that it could have been going on before then and my mother might have been the instigator of this sorry mess.

"'E works at PCL, where I work," says Mum. "'E's a mechanic."

"So is that who yer see when yer walk ter top er t'street every night?" I ask.

"Aye, 'e picks me up in 'is car, a little Volkswagen Beetle."

"That's great. All me friends'll see yer getting' in ter t'car," says Trevor.

"They might. What does that matter? Yer might as well get used to it. Me an' yer Dad are finished. I 'ave ter think abart t'future."

That's pretty much how that conversation ended, with Trevor registering his disapproval, me taking a laissez-faire approach.

A few nights later, Trevor and I arrived home late in the evening to find Mum and Dad sitting at the table. We joined them. Why not?

"Yer Dad's been ter see Brian. Brian invited 'im for a chat an' yer Dad went up t'road an' sat in 'is car."

"Is that really true, Dad?"

"Yeah. 'E seems oreight. 'E's from Nova Scotia. We used ter call em Bluenoses when I were in t'forces."

"So, what did yer talk abart?"

"Oh, this and that. Nowt yer need ter know."

"Just ter let yer know that everything, whatever it is, is being done in a civilized manner," says Mum. "I'm goin' ter meet Brian's wife. Everythin' above board and proper."

*Oh, right,* I think. *Everything about this whole fiasco is all so civilized and proper? At no time have my brother's and my feelings and needs been given the time of day, except for vague platitudes now and again from Mum that she'll stand by us.* But, it didn't enter my head that the whole atmosphere to which Dad had been subjected was not only uncivilized, improper, but also unnecessarily judgemental and cruel. Trevor and I did not hesitate to join in the spirit of the times. We ostracized Dad.

It wasn't long after Mum's affair had been aired that Brian spared us all the courtesy of picking Mum up at the top of the street and parked his late 50s orange beetle right outside our house. Dad was still at home. The indignities and humiliation that Dad endured and my acquiescence in most of it have stayed with me. But, I stayed silent. Somehow or other, while all this was going on, I made time to study for my repeat A levels and to carry out a relationship of sorts with my girlfriend Sal (the leggy girl with tight fitting skirts, low necklines, and a flirtatious look about her).

One night in late March, Sal and I were sitting on my bed in my bedroom upstairs talking. All of a sudden, we could hear voices downstairs, Mum and Dad. Where they had come from, heaven knows. We thought we were in an empty house. We could hear much of what Mum was saying because she was on higher volume. Dad's words were almost impossible to discern.

"I told 'em at work, I'm not a *fuckin'* machine."

Sal and I looked at each other open mouthed. We crouched down, ears to the floor.

"So when are tha goin' then?"

"Oh. And when did tha decide this?"

Sal wanted to carry on listening. To someone uninvolved, maybe it was fun. Not for me. I just wanted to leave. So, we descended the stairs and entered the kitchen. Mum and Dad at the kitchen table. "Where did you two come from?" she asks in an uncharacteristically mild manner, not really caring about the answer.

"Just went upstairs ter get somethin'," I said, knowing she wouldn't want to query even an answer as bad as this.

"Don't be long gerrin 'ome. Me an' yer Dad 'ave summat ter tell yer."

Hand in hand, Sal and I walk back to her home in the New Stradbroke Estate, a half hour's walk away. I know exactly what news awaits me when I get home. I'm in a sombre mood, in contrast to Sal who seems to think it's exciting, a bit out of the ordinary. I drop her off at her home and decline to go inside. The walk seems to drag on though I pick up the pace on the way home.

Mum and Dad are both sitting at the kitchen table, Trevor not home yet. Nonetheless, Mum loses no time in seizing the moment. "Yer Dad's decided ter leave," she snaps out.

"When?" I ask.

"Next Wednesday. A week's time." says Dad in a monotone, looking down at the table.

I pace around the room and finally sit myself down between the two of them.

My first reactions are both hostile and pragmatic. "Well, that's good. We'll be better off t'way things 'ave been. So 'ow much 'ave yer decided to give Mum in support payments?"

"Don't know. What do yer think?" It isn't clear to whom Dad is addressing the question.

"Four pounds a week?" offers Mum.

"I'd say five pounds." I'm making sure her interests are well attended to.

"Oreight," says Dad.

"Then let's see yer put it in writing," I say.

"Aye, that's a good idea," says Mum. "We'll have it in writing."

Was she just going to take him on his word?

Dad takes a piece of paper and scribbles down his commitment to send Mum five pounds a week. Just a few lines. No fancy stuff. Five pounds a week to eternity written on a scrap of paper, which Mum promptly seizes and stuffs in her purse.

The deed done, we all retire to our respective corners—

Mum to bed, Trevor, who has by now appeared, to his room, Dad to the living room couch, and I to my bed. We knew it was going to happen. Let's get on with it. Supporting Mum and despising Dad. But, oh, the shame of it.

～～～

The days ticked by slowly over the next week. The same daily routine unfolded—Dad was ignored, banished from the kitchen table and the bedroom, Mum and Dad separately savoured the night air. We were all oblivious to the events of the day that occupied the thoughts of ordinary Brits. Such free thinkers would have been worried about the government's threat to send troops into a far away country called Laos to fight communism. They would have been mystified by the intricacies of the unfolding court drama involving a couple known as the Krogers, who were supposed to have been spies for the commies. Then, on Saturday afternoon, they would surely have tuned in to the telly to watch outsider Nicolaus Silver win the Grand National, one of only two grey horses to have ever done so. The four of us carried on in our own little world like automatons, or maybe like one of the horses with blinkers on that lost the Grand National.

When the day of Dad's departure finally came, the week before Easter, it was treated with an air of indifference. Mum left to go to work. My brother and I got our breakfast as Dad stalked from room to room. As I stood by the desk in my bedroom, packing into my school bag the last of my home-work, I looked out of the back window, deep in thought. Overcast, cloudy weather. I turned to see Dad standing in the doorway.

"Yer know I'll be gone when yer get 'ome, don't yer?" he says.

"Yes, I know."

And that's how he flew the coop. Not so much as a good old Sheffield turrah, let alone a conversation, a shaking of the hand, or perish the thought, a hug and a kiss. Perhaps he was expecting me to say something more to him than my banal and hopelessly inadequate three-word response. "Yes, I know." Of course I know. Of course he knows. For different reasons, the two of us are resorting to sterile, unemotional utterances of the obvious. For my part, exposure of feelings, betrayal of even a tinge of sentimentality, would weaken my position in a conflict that recognized no shades of grey— only black and white, righteous and reprobates, villains and victims. Besides, bitterness had set in.

For his part, Dad was just unable to express his emotions. Yet, it never occurred to me that he was ill, locked away in a depression that like a leach sucked all the creative juices from his body. Unable to take on board any more emotional baggage than had been forced upon him over the years. The person not present at this parting scene, my mother, had the greatest influence upon it. But, she did not transform from a nurturing mother and supportive wife to a self-pitying, self-righteous nag without cause. An incident. An illness. A wayward gene—carried along the branch of Mum's family tree that goes back to Ireland and her great grandmother, my great great grandmother, the mother of Racheal Clancy. Yes, there was enough blame to go all around. We all could have done better. Then again, maybe we couldn't have.

I am sitting in George Mack's ethics class that morning pretending to listen to his paternalistic, patronizing prattle, my mind strays from time to time on the house that is no longer a home. I'm not interested in his admonishment about smoking. He smokes like a chimney himself. So do I. Nor am I the slightest interested in developing my personality by taking up a hobby such as rugger, listening to the opera, or reading about hovercrafts—whatever they are. As for his call to arms to all of us, if and when the socialists ever come to power, to stand shoulder to shoulder and barricade the entrances of the school against the creeping threat of it losing its status as a grammar school—well, why should I care?

As I look out on to the playing fields, the cloud cover, the overall greyness of the sky, the occasional spattering of rain drops driven by the wind onto the window panes capture my mood. Apprehensive, sombre, but not hopeless.

That evening, as the three of us arrive home in the steady drizzle one by one, the reality and finality of it all sets in. Conversation is muted. Brave fronts, grim faced but silent. Every room in the house feels cold and empty. Empty of what? Of Dad, the one whom we had ignored for so long, a man who innocuously kept his distance from us, only now and again sharing the same air space? No, not that Dad. For me, it was the Dad who went looking for firewood on the first night we moved into number 23, the Dad who sat around the fire playing hand shadows on the wall with us. The Dad who once stayed up all night with a cat to catch mice in the humble, little room that used to be our home. The Dad who didn't play cricket, but on a family outing rolled up his sleeves and bowled out our next door neighbour Billy Withers, a seasoned batsman for his firm's cricket team. The Dad who struggled through polio, who despite the hardships of the times, used to take us on family holidays even when he was the sole breadwinner. The Dad who wanted to get a better job because he genuinely wanted his family to benefit. The Dad who was committed to his family, even when he was not appreciated and bore the brunt of my mother's tirades. The Dad who was difficult to get to know, but was an integral part of what used to be a close-knit family unit. Where had he gone? Not literally, but figuratively. While he was around the house as an ornament, I was not forced to think in these terms. Now, I know he's no longer here.

None of us felt like eating. Eventually, Mum broke the silence. "Oo. It does feel strange. I think we should gather up our clothes lads an' spend a day er so down at yer Grandma's so we can get used ter things."

When we arrive at Grandma's house, Aunt Ray is there, sitting on the old sofa while Grandma and Granddad slurp tea at the table. The three of us take our places between Grandma and Granddad.

"Saw Poor Bill down t'market today. Lookin' like 'e'd just won t'lottery," intones Granddad.

"Allus remember Poor Bill an' 'is favourite saying, a belly full's a belly full," he continues.

"Did tha see in t'paper? Castles store down t'Moor are advertisin' two wardrobes, a dressing table, bed an' mattress for 69 guineas," chimes Aunt Ray. Heads shake.

"Forecast says it'll be rotten weather o'er Easter. Rain an' cold." Grandma's contribution.

After about half an hour of this nonsense, Granddad looks Mum straight in the face.

"Well, 'as 'e left thee then?"

"Aye, 'e's gone."

Then Grandma starts.

"Oh dear. What are we goin' ter do? 'Ow are we goin' ter live this down? 'Ow will we ever face..."

"Shut thee'sen up," barks out Granddad," It's not thee that's been left. Tha's got nowt ter worry abart. It's our Nell an' them lads. Never 'eard owt so bloody daft in me life." Granddad, a man whose few words always seemed to hit the right spot, had got things back on track again.

"So what are tha goin' ter do now?" asks Granddad.

Mum takes out a handkerchief and starts to wipe her eyes. "I thought me an t'kids might stay 'ere a day or so," she says.

Aunt Ray then chips in.

"An' then what? Tha's got ter think abart t'long term. An' t'long term means them two lads. I'll say this an' then shut up. I don't like what Pat's done, but two wrongs never did make a right." Aunt Ray's pulling no punches.

"I will be lookin' after them lads. That's why we're all darn 'ere together. As for two rights an' wrongs, I'm doin' things carefully, not galavantin' abart. Brian's a decent bloke. But I'm not rushin' things."

Aunt Ray looks disgusted, Granddad shakes his head, while Grandma resumes her through the teeth whistling. We've only just put the fifties behind us. In merry old England, marriages are not supposed to break up and if they do, spouses, especially women, are expected to wait a respectable time before getting into another relationship.

After school the following day, I stopped by the house we had all vacated. When I arrived there in the early evening drizzle, everything was as we had left it. A few clothes here and there, some dirty dishes in the sink, a newspaper and an electric bill pushed through the letterbox and lying on the floor in the front hall. But it was too quiet. What noise was missing from the background? I walked back into the kitchen and then it hit me. No chirping. I looked over at the cage that housed our pet budgie. I couldn't see him. When I went over to the cage, I saw a little green and yellow-feathered mass lying on the bottom of the cage. Billy was dead. As I reached in to lift him on to the palms of my hands, the poignancy of the moment hit me like a ton of bricks. Billy died on the very night that Dad went. There was a message to be found in this, at best a message of gloom and despair, at worst a message of life not worth living. But, somehow, I saw a message of empathy. Incredible as it may seem, that little bird that had been sick for months had finally had enough, just as his two legged owners had. I started to cry. I took Billy out to the back garden and buried him there in what used to be our vegetable patch, tears streaming unashamedly down my face and splashing on to the earth, mixing with the wet soil from the overhead rain. When I got back to Talbot Place and told everyone that Billy had died, there was little reaction. Perhaps I had taken symbolism too much to heart, or maybe others were too preoccupied with other thoughts.

We stayed at Talbot Place one more night, and then, on Good Friday, we trooped back up to the Stradbroke estate and reoccupied number 23. The forecasters were right. It was gloomy weather—rain showers and overhead cloud. Cold, wet, and damp, in tune with the way we all felt. Easter had become passé to my brother and me and Easter 1961 was just as unmemorable as the one or two Easters that preceded it—focused entirely on chocolate eggs, with no religious con-notations, Dad's five-pound note arrived in the mail as due. His next contribution was slashed to three pounds, then two pounds, then none at all. The ones that did come were post-marked from different locations—all part of the cloak and dagger game in which his residence was kept secret from us. It seems astonishing that during all the weeks he was on bor-rowed time living at home, we never once asked him where he would be living. Perhaps this was to convey a message to him that we didn't care, but now we didn't know where to find him. My first reaction to the cutback in weekly payments was to announce to Mum that I was going to quit school and get a job to help support her. I just couldn't see myself being sup-ported entirely by Mum's paltry salary as a female lathe oper-ator in a machine shop while I lived off her meagre earnings continuing my schooling.

"An' tha'll be doin' nowt er t'kind," she asserts, finger wag-ging in the air, after I told her of my plans. "Tha'll make sum-mat er thee'sen. Tha's got what it takes ter get out er this mess. Tha dun't 'ave ter live like this."

But she saw that she hadn't convinced me and she was tak-ing no chances.

A day or so later, I was twiddling the stopcock on my burette in Alf Ridler's chemistry laboratory, fully engaged in the volumetric analysis problem of the day. There was a tap on my shoulder.

"The Headmaster wants to see you," says Alf, the usual impish look in his eye.

What have I done now?

Nina, the secretary, ushers me into George's office. He's sitting with his elbows on the desk in front of him, cradling his chin with his hands. He looks pensive but not threatening.

"Sit down, Gordon," as he points to the chair directly in front of him. Then, he leans back, crosses his legs to take up a more informal posture.

"Your mother came in to see me yesterday. Told me about the family situation. She's very concerned about you. Says you had told her you were thinking of leaving school. Asked me to have a word with you." Then, without waiting for me to respond, he continues.

"Look, you are close to the time when you'll be taking your A levels again. Don't throw in the towel now. You owe it to your mother to knuckle down, stay the course, and go on to university. Once there, you'll get a grant to support your needs. But, your mother sees that you can climb out of the mess your family is in now and I am strongly suggesting you do it."

When George Mack strongly suggests something, you do it.

"Yes, sir. I shall take your advice. And thank you for speaking to me, sir."

"That'll be all then, Gordon. And good luck."

As I'm leaving the room, he adds.

"And if there's anything further I can do, feel free to contact my office and arrange an appointment to speak to me."

"Thank you, sir."

The issue of to leave or not to leave school had been settled. Thanks to Mum's clever intervention using an authority figure whom nobody dare question.

Eventually, the A level exams rolled around, and yet again, I found myself looking in despair at a bunch of wires, batteries, electric switches, and related gadgetry in the examination room where the physics lab exam was being held. Not again, I thought. What am I supposed to do with this? What do I connect to what? In the end, I asked one of the invigilators for help, knowing that it would cost me a heap of marks. I spent the next few weeks resigned to a repeat performance of the previous year's results. Then, to my astonishment, I began to receive offers from several universities. I could have studied medicine or zoology. Then, the magic postcard came. I had scored distinctions in biology and chemistry and a passing grade in physics. I must have squeaked through that physics exam by the slimmest of margins. But, I was now free to go on to university.

---

24    About $1 U.S. at the exchange rate that prevailed.

25    A British idiom meaning to ostracize someone by not speaking to him or her.

# FALLOUT

After somehow or other completing my A levels among
all the goings on at home, I chose to study zoology at
Sheffield University, where I could keep an eye on the home
scene at a time of uncertainty. Against the odds, I received
the sixth form school prize for excellence in biology during
my last few weeks at High Storrs.

With the school leaving option no longer in play, if it ever
was, I considered taking another approach to Dad's reneging
on his weekly payments. One early evening in May, the three
of us are standing around in the kitchen.

"No money again this week, lads. That's yer father for yer.
Yer wonderful father," rails Mum.

"Me an Trevor'll track 'im darn an' confront 'im, won't
we Trevor?"

"Aye. We'll get t'money out er 'im," says Trevor.

"I don't think yer should go causin' any trouble," says Mum.
"But I don't see why two sons shouldn't go ter see their father.
Nowt wrong wi' that."

Words of encouragement indeed.

"Where would 'e be though, Mum?"

"'E might be wi' that woman an' her son darn Pitsmoor. That one that used ter invite 'im in for a cup er tea while 'e were on 'is travels wi' Hallamshire Electric."

So, without any cogent plan in mind, Trevor and I take the buses down to Pitsmoor and knock on the back door of an old stone terraced house. A busty old lady, sporting a hairnet and an apron, built like Ena Sharples of *Coronation Street*, stands in the doorway, arms folded.

"We 'ave reason ter think that our Dad, Patrick Gordon, might be 'ere," I say.

"No, 'e's not," says Mrs. Arms and Elbows.

"I don't think yer tellin t'truth," I say.

"Don't you dare call me a liar. Who the bloody 'ell do yer think yer are?" Mrs Chest and Abs has her dander up.

"Well, when yer do see 'im tell 'im we've been lookin' for 'im. We want ter know why 'e's stopped givin' our Mum support money. Tell him 'e's a louse."

"Yer Dad is a true gentleman. Which is more than I can say for you two." Mrs Hairnet slams the door in our faces.

We found out many years later that Dad was in the house and overheard the entire exchange.

To complete the evening, we journeyed up to other Grandma's house, had a similar doorstep exchange. I had not seen other Grandma for at least six years.

My last memory of her is of her standing with Arnold

in the front lobby of their home. Trevor and I, two angry teenagers, confronting them.

"How nice to see you both," said other Grandma.

"Where's our father? Is 'e stayin 'ere?" I growled.

"Isn't he at your house? Don't understand," they both said almost in unison.

"Yer must know 'e's left us," I snarled. "Can't believe yer don't know."

"No, we honestly didn't," they chimed.

And so went the exchange until I said, "Let's go on. We're getting' nowhere."

As we were about to leave, other Grandma approached us and pressed a pound note in each of our hands. Never forgetting our training, we resisted. But, I do believe we took the pound notes in the end.

Dad's whereabouts were a mystery and he wanted it kept that way.

Finally, the issue of maintenance payments was settled in court. It was a sunny weekday in July, around the time that I was sitting my A level examinations. I took a day off school to accompany Mum to court. Aunt Ray came along for support. Mum was into her second lawyer. The first one had tried to be fresh with her, so she fired him and chose someone without a penchant for playing the field. Mr. Fenoughty-Ashton, small in stature, grey haired, fifty to sixty-ish, highly respected legal counsel.

The three of us enter the lobby of the courthouse located in Castle Gate, downtown Sheffield. Small groups of people are huddled throughout the atrium. The three of us soon form another one and are quickly joined by Mr. F–A. Then, out of nowhere, Dad strides right by us accompanied by a tall, red-headed lawyer. No acknowledgement, no eye contact. We all stare at him. When we shake ourselves, we notice that Mum's lawyer has disappeared. Minutes later, he is back.

"Your husband's lawyer wants to settle out of court. He's offering three pounds per week as maintenance payments. I advise you to agree as there's no guarantee of what might happen in court."

With that, it is all over. Dad strides out of the courthouse again, saying nothing, except through his body language— a "Keep Away" message.

As Aunt Ray, Mum, and I stood outside the ABC Cinema on nearby Angel Street, unhappy with what had transpired, I suddenly had the urge to find Dad and confront him. Against Aunt Ray's protestations, I raced back down to the courthouse and scouted the area but he was long gone. I have no idea what I would have done or said if I had found him.

⁓

The financial uncertainties that the three of us faced in the weeks following Dad's departure reinforced our col-lective belief that Mum had right on her side. Dad was heartless to cut those payments, we all agreed. Hence, in this adversity, we were drawn together, to paraphrase the musings of the famous nineteenth-century philosopher Soren Kierkegaard. Nonetheless, discord and outright rebellion erupted due to differences between the rest of the family and myself in our perceptions of Mum's conduct—the new man in her life, the public spectacle of the car outside the house, all before Dad had left. One man waiting in line to take another one's place.

My brother was disgusted and made his views plain to Mum. At this point everybody in the family felt that Mum's behaviour was licentious and brought shame to the family. For my part, I was not happy with the pace at which events had unfolded, but I reasoned that Brian should be given a chance. If he did turn out to be a decent bloke, as Mum insisted, he might give her some happiness. Dad had turned his back on her, so what harm was there in someone else offering her companionship? I even went to meet Brian at his invitation—in his car, thankfully parked at the top of the street, not outside the house. An unstriking sort of a man. Unmistakably middle aged, average build but carrying a bit of a paunch, thinning hair, a mixture of silver and ginger, sleeked back with lots of Brylcreem. He spoke in a bit of a drawl, which I interpreted to be of Canadian origin. He had lived the better part of his life in Sheffield, having moved back with his parents as a teenager, but had kept the accent of his childhood. He drove me

246 | ROGER GORDON

around the estate, talked to me about his honourable intentions, and came across as a genuine person. He asked me to do whatever I could to bring Trevor onside, a task that was hopeless. When he stopped at the top of the street, he took a couple of minutes to give me a few tips on driving, something that came to be known in a derisory way within the family at large as my driving lesson from the fancy man.

A shouting match erupted one evening in Aunt Bud's flat.

"Roger, according ter our Trevor, tha dun't think there's owt wrong wi' thee mother carryin on wi' another bloke. Even befoore thee Dad left she were out carousing wi' 'im. I'm surprised at yer."

"Aunt Bud, I'm only…"

"And ter top it off tha's even been for a drivin' lesson wi' t' fancy man. I've never 'eard owt like it. An't tha got any backbone?"

"Let me explain, Aunt Bud. I just don't think…"

"Don't think what? That tha can stand up ter thee mother? Afraid she'll kick thee out er t'ome? Stop thee schoolin'? Tha't just thinkin' er thee'sen. At least our Trevor's got some principles. I never thought I'd see t' day…"

*I've had enough*, I'm thinking. Now, I'm good and mad.

"Me mother does what she wants to do. Me Dad's left 'er. What point is there in fightin' anymoore? If t'other feller can make 'er 'appy, why should I stop it? Anyow, yer can believe what yer like, who yer like. It's no use talkin'. I'm gone."

With that I rushed out of the flat, Aunt Bud yelling behind me.

"Go on then. Get out if tha wants. Everything me and yer Uncle Carl 'ave done for yer." The yelling turned into sobbing.

A few days later, I went back to see Aunt Bud. We embraced one another, cried together, and agreed that nothing that was happening at home would come between us. Both my aunts were very good to me and there was part of me that had to admit that some of what Aunt Bud was saying had a ring of truth about it. I could and should have taken a more thoughtful approach and been a little less welcoming to the new geezer. For what it's worth, by Christmas of that year, Brian had visited all of the family members, grandparents, aunts and uncles, and endeared himself to all of them. His easygoing manner, unpretentious attire, and straightforward yet gracious way of speaking reeled all of them in. At Christmas and New Year's festivities, he took the place that two years earlier Dad had occupied.

Reaction to Mum's philandering ways was not confined to blood relatives. In the socially conservative times that we lived in, morality was high on the agenda of the working classes. No matter that the tabloids were filled with racy stories about the upper classes. Lady Titillate found in bed with Jives the butler while Lord Cock o' the North goes grouse hunting, or so he says. *The Daily Tattletale* has it on good authority that Lord Cocky was with a different kind of bird, none other than new society debutante...Them upper gentry. And their ways.

But not our ways. We're proud folk. But, was it prudishness born out of an innate sense of moral rectitude or was it the lot in life of the working classes, thrust upon them over the years by their betters out of fear that a breakdown in the moral order might lead to, heaven forbid, a breakdown in the social one. A coal miner caught in bed with another worker's wife might not be the best working companion for the aggrieved husband as they both attacked the coal face with their pick axes and jackhammers.

So, I was unable as kids nowadays can, to share my domestic situation with my friends—except for one or two close pals at High Storrs. I was ashamed and felt stuck out like a sore thumb. My parents were the only ones in our entire neighbourhood whose problems had become public. Everyone else was either problem-free or problem-hidden. So, one Sunday afternoon, as Trevor and I walked up the street to catch the bus to take us to Grandma's, we had to thread our way on the pavement through a motley crew of teenagers, headed by Barry Hughes, a nondescript youth of no particular consequence to us.

"Yer mother's a tart," yells Barry.

We both stop in our tracks and turn around.

"Say that again," I say.

"Nowt, really," backpedals Barry.

"Just watch thee'sen," says Trevor, totally unruffled and that was that. Good for him.

But, not for me. I was caught flat-footed on a couple of occasions during the dying days of my time at High Storrs. One morning, I was outside the assembly hall when George Mack caught sight of me and waved me over.

"How are things at home, Gordon? How's your mother?"

"Fine, thank you, sir. In fact, she's found another man." I blurted out, immediately embarrassed. What have I said?

George seems taken aback. He pauses reflectively. Too long for my liking.

"Very well, Gordon. As long as you're both all right."

"Thank you, sir."

As we head off in opposite directions, I'm thinking that whatever Mum told him that day when she asked him to talk to me, it didn't include Brian.

Not long after he'd had flown the coop, Dad materialized in the flesh and not by design. Mum and Brian were still seeing one another every evening. Brian's VW pick-up service had moved from the top of the street to outside the front door, exacerbating the public ridicule that my brother and I felt. I was still working at the Embassy Ballroom selling tickets at the door. One night, I looked up from my glass booth to see that the man who had just said "One, please," was my father. He just said hello and went into the ballroom, on the prowl for a middle-aged maiden. Given what my mother was up to, I can't explain why this encounter troubled me but that was the case. Once I had finished my stint on the door, I tracked

Dad down in the ballroom and asked him to come outside for a word or two.

"What are yer up to? Yer actin like a teenager," I said.

"I don't know what yer mean," replied Dad. "I'm a single man now."

A nonsensical exchange followed out there on the street, in which the obvious was stated by each of us. Dad tried to be conciliatory but his demeanour was impassive and unpersuasive. I was hurt, angry, and hostile. As we went our separate ways, he back on to the dance floor, and me back to home sweet home, he gave me a parting shot.

"Roger, I know yer stickin' by yer mother now and that's understandable. But I predict the day will come when yer'll come ter me an' want ter shake me 'and. That's all I 'ave ter say."

"You're dead wrong," I growled.

But he wasn't.

# TRANSITIONS

B y September, four months after Dad's departure, Brian moved in. The Volkswagen became a permanent fixture outside the home. He and Mum's inner sense of decorum led them to sleep on the sofa in the living room. The master bedroom was vacant. Life went on much the same. Polite indifference bordering on acceptance on my part. Hostility by Trevor who had by now left school and begun an apprenticeship with a printing firm. Instead of Dad eating by himself in the living room, Trevor chose to do so. Nothing much had changed with respect to the overall ambience, just adjustments to the players and their parts. I had taken a summer job at Express Dairy at their plant on Broadfield Road, under the watchful eyes of Aunt Bud and Uncle Carl who also worked there. So, I was able to help out at home a bit financially and by working long hours and spending lots of time with Sal, I was able to relegate the home scene into the background. Every once in a while, a flare-up would occur involving Trevor with Mum and Brian to remind me that my home was anything but a normal one.

One day, we all awoke to find that the contents of the

dustbin[26] had been strewn all over the yard. Leftover bits of food, cans, cartons, paper, all manner of refuse. Covering the entire asphalted surface. None of us had heard anything during the night.

"That'll be one er t'neighbors," says Mum, matter of factly.

"Probably that woman up at number 17, next door ter t'Hughes family. Working class people, especially lower working class let yer know if they don't like what yer doin'. They have their morals and I suppose I've tramped on 'em. That's a message to us. It's an old custom. Trash the dustbin."

I never did find out whether the dustbin incident was the act of a self-righteous neighbour, a member of the morality squad, or whether it was my Dad who had done this. Dad was certainly sneaking around home base in the few weeks after he had left. Creepily. His comings and goings had a sinister ring to them. Acquaintances of my mother reported that he had been seen driving around the Ravenscroft area of the estate, a short mile from our home.

Then, one night in August, I returned home alone around ten at night. I had been to see my girlfriend Sal perform in an amateur production of the stage play "The Boy Friend." The house had been empty for at least three hours. The light in the kitchen was on, which was how we all had left it. But, something was not right. What was it? Then, I noticed that small puffs of steam were coming out of the spout of the kettle on the stove. When I felt the kettle it was hot, full of water that was near boiling. There was only one explanation. Dad had been back, entered the kitchen and either made himself a cup of tea and put away the cup or I had interrupted him before the kettle had chance to boil and he had switched it off. I roamed through the house gingerly room by room in case he was hiding somewhere. Then, I went into the darkness of the night and scoured the yard and gardens. As I was doing this, my heart was beating a mile a minute. What kind of mindset would a man have to enter the home that he had left to make himself a cup of tea? If I had arrived an hour earlier, what would he have been doing? Sitting at the kitchen table? Rummaging through drawers? What was he looking for? And how did he know that we would all be out that night?

The next night, Sal and I kept watch in my bedroom from dusk until around ten, all lights in the house out, hoping he would make another show. We kept hearing the odd creak, thump, whistling of the wind, but the mind games got the better of us and at Sal's insistence, we called a halt to the vigil.

Then, on a windy September night, just after Brian had moved in, we were awakened by a crashing and smashing sound. The sound of glass shattering. Trevor and I got quickly dressed, rushed downstairs into the back yard, where Brian joined us. The window in the garage had been smashed and it was no accident. We scouted the exterior of our home and those of neighbouring ones. Nothing to see. Nobody around. Silence. We all went back into the living room, where Mum waited, scared out of her wits. Was it a hooligan, fed up of throwing rocks at streetlights? Another message from one of our prim and proper neighbours? No, in this case it was definitely Dad. I discovered this many years later. He was hiding next to the wall, camouflaged, and in among the rose bushes in the small triangle of land directly behind the garage window. We looked there but never saw him.

⁓⁓⁓

Sal and I broke up just before I started my university studies. I met Sandra on September 16, 1961. I was walking through the Pond Street bus terminal with a group of High Storrs friends on my way to Bramall Lane football ground to watch my team Sheffield Wednesday, the Owls, play Sheffield United, the Blades, in a derby match. United had just been promoted to the First Division while the Owls had been laying in wait there for the past couple of years, having been promoted after the 1958–59 season. In fact, the previous season, 1960–61, was one of the most successful on record for the Owls as they finished runners up to the mighty Tottenham Hotspur, who won the league and FA Cup double that year. So, I fancied the Owls' chances that day, as did most of my friends who were also Owls supporters. Then, as we swaggered past the Woodhouse bus stop, one of my friends Terry Hutchen said hello to a girl who was standing waiting for the bus. I looked again. A girl. A pretty girl. A petite and pretty girl, no more than five feet tall, her long ash coloured hair tied up in a ponytail. Wearing high-heeled shoes, presumably to make her look older. She was daintiness personified. To top it off, her body was…well…curvaceous.

"Who's that girl?" I ask Terry.

"Sandra Archer, my next door neighbour," he says.

"Yer next door neighbour?" I ask incredulously. "Then I must have a date with yer next door neighbour."

"She's on the phone. Look her up. Give her a call," says he.

I was on my way back home from the match, passing again through Pond Street. The match didn't go well for us. Our optimism was not rewarded as centre forward Derek Pace snatched a last minute goal for the Blades to give them a 1-0 victory in front of over 38,000 spectators.

"Wonder 'ow that neighbour of yours would take to a phone call?" I ask.

"I know," says Archie Fosdyke, another of the High Storrs lads, "Wouldn't it be a lark if I phoned her and pretended to be you. Bet you half a crown I can get you a date."

"You're on," I say. Why look a gift horse in the mouth?

So, in his refined middle-class accent, Archie, a boy from a more affluent area of the city than me, did his stuff. "Oh yes. Lovely to talk to you. That's wonderful. I am so looking forward to meeting you tomorrow night. Thank you so much, Sandra."

Down went the receiver. "Seven o'clock tomorrow night

at the Woodhouse bus stop right here in Pond Street," says he, strutting around like a peacock, a big grin from cheek to cheek. All the lads were doubled up, beside themselves. I am down half a crown.

"And what will she say when she notices that Gordon's accent is nothing like Fosdykes?" one of them splutters.

"Oi could always troi to imitate him. Put on my jolly old airs and graces," says I, nose in the air, pretending to be Lord Archibald.

The next day, as I stride across Pond Street to the Woodhouse bus stop to meet Sandra, I notice her there. Wearing a short navy blue raincoat. What an appealing sight she looks. So cute. Wonder how old she is?

"Hello. I'm Roger. I hope you haven't been waiting there long."

"No, not at all. I'm Sandra."

A stereotypical first date then follows. We see *Ben-Hur* at the ABC—one of the downtown cinemas. Holding hands. The occasional sideways glance, sometimes in unison so that our eyes meet. Lots of cigarettes. Then, a ride home on the bus back to her house in the village of Woodhouse.

"I'm fifteen," she offers, "But soon to be sixteen."

"Oh. I'm eighteen." What else is there to say?

As the bus is going up City Road driving past the City Road Cemetery, I point downwards at it. "All my relatives are buried in there," I say.

To which she says the only words that can be said. "That's interesting."

When we get back to her house, she introduces me to her mother, Eileen ("Mrs. Archer" to me), a tallish grey-haired woman with a friendly demeanour. I knew she liked me and the feeling was mutual. Sandra and I spend some time in the front room together. The handholding moves on to snogging. I own up to the phone call, Archie the impostor. She thinks it's funny. "I thought your voice sounded different." Then, we arrange to see each other again.

"I could even come over to your home?" she asks.

I am embarrassed. "Oh yes. But when you do, don't be surprised if you see a man around the house. He's not my Dad."

"Oh," she responds.

After we have been going steady for a while, Sandra told me that the thing she remembers most about our first date is the comment about my relatives being buried in City Hall Cemetery. What was that all about? Also, the remark about the man hanging out at our home. Who is this man? Is he safe? How unusual, she would often remark as we did what lovers are prone to doing—looking back together on their first date.

For the next three years, Sandra was a major part of my social life. That's not to say I didn't have other interests. Playing trumpet in a traditional jazz band was my main extracurricular activity, but Sandra was always there, either in person or in my thoughts. My introduction to Sandra preceded the commencement of my university studies by a matter of a couple of weeks, and shortly after receiving my B.Sc. degree, Sandra and I parted company. Hence, my undergraduate life and my relationship with Sandra went hand in hand. Most evenings during the week, I would walk over to her home, a thirty-minute walk from where I lived on the Stradbroke estate, to be ushered into the front room by her mum.

~~~

I spent the summer of 1961 moving from job to job, trying to make enough money to pay my board at home and keep body and soul together until my university grant arrived just prior to the autumn term. I carried dustbins for the city council for about a week, and then threw the towel in on that job after I got fed up being a gopher for the regular crews who used the students as an opportunity to slack off. I worked at Fletcher's Bakery for a week or so, not worried in the slightest about Mum's prejudices against a bakery run by a communist. Then, after getting laid off, I managed to find a labouring job on a building site on the outskirts of the city—Lodge Moor. Tasks that should have been done more carefully included handling glass wool insulation with bare arms and no gloves, as I broke out in an awful rash, and using a jack hammer without ear protectors, a probable contributory factor to my hearing impairment in later years. There was nothing I could have done about that, anyway, because no ear protectors were provided in those days.

While I was making the rounds of the meagre job opportunities, Sheffield was undergoing some changes. A victim of the television age, one of the oldest cinemas in the city, the Cinema House, closed down. On the development front, a conglomeration of concrete blocks of flats known as the Park Hill Flats was officially opened. They were located near where I used to live on Talbot Place, replacing the quaint old stores that had so much character on Duke Street and it has to be admitted, slum housing at the back of Duke Street. But, those flats dominated the skyline and looked hideous. They still do.

---

26    Garbage bin.

# PART III: UNIVERSITY YEARS
## (1961–1969)

# FIRST TERM

I took my first term at Sheffield University very much in stride. As was customary, the opening to the university year started in October with the Rag Parade—a Mardi Gras-style procession of floats and marchers, carried out by students dressed up in bizarre costumes. The parade, along with the events and pranks that the students carried out around the city in the week preceding it, were done to raise money for charities. One highlight of Rag Week was a beer race, in which the course consisted of a circuit of pubs, each a pit stop where a pint of ale had to be consumed. Then, there was a balloon race, in which members of the public paid to have gas-filled balloons launched, the one that travelled the farthest winning a prize for the purchaser.

The Beatnik Ball, held at the City Hall, was for genuine beatniks as well as those who wanted to imitate the genre. Just before the 1961 parade, the students pushed the envelope a little far when they kidnapped two Sheffield United football players, Joe and Graham Shaw, and held them overnight at one of the students' residences. The police were briefly involved in enabling the players to be released without charges being pressed.

264 | Roger Gordon

The parade began on Western Bank at the university and wound its way downtown to the Town Hall, where the Lord Mayor stood proudly to greet it. People lined the streets and threw coins at the floats, all the monies going to charity. One float was fashioned as a Trojan Horse, another a Mississippi river steamer; one carried a mediaeval catapult, yet another offered a variety of goods, including a "do-it-yourself slave girl kit." People were dressed up as doctors, nurses, ballet dancers, hockey players, Arab sheiks, and naturally, as beatniks. In the days long before cross dressing became associated with gender issues and making a statement, Jack Martin and I dressed in ladies' dresses, hats, nylon stockings, high heeled shoes, and we even put on bright red lipstick. We received a few priceless comments from regular patrons when we went to use the men's underground urinal in Fitzalan Square. I stood outside Walsh's store, went around the pubs, selling copies of the *Twikker*, a racy magazine put out by the students.

The academic side of things seemed straightforward enough, though I found myself with a little too much spare time on my hands. In any event, there was no way for me to know how well I was doing because the lecturers provided no feedback until the end of year exams the following June, by which time it was too late to remedy any shortcomings. You either passed or failed. A pass meant you could proceed to the second year. A fail meant being "sent down," dismissal from the university.

Managing a budget was my greatest challenge during that

first term. The education authorities covered all of our tuition fees. In addition, each student received a small grant, a lump sum at the beginning of each term, to cover text books, stationary supplies, and other day-to-day expenses, from midday meals, the odd pint of beer, and cigarettes to dissection kits, lab coats, and deposits on breakable chemical glassware. Out-of-town students who had to pay lodging expenses were given a higher amount. The amount I received during the first week in October was around a hundred pounds. I did not spend extravagantly, confining my purchases largely to the intended ones. It had all gone by the end of November. I still had to get to Christmas and my job delivering Christmas mail before any relief would come.

So, I went to see Aunt Ray, who like the good aunt that she was loaned me a twenty. I paid this off as soon as my January grant came in. In those days, the banks did not loan students money or allow them an overdraft. There was no such thing as a student loan system. What was given as a grant was the entirety of it. And it was not enough. My award was certainly not enough for me to be able to pay Mum and Brian room and board, as they kept hinting at me. For that, I would have had to receive the additional emolument given to out-of-town students. Unless in-town students could prove extenuating financial circumstances, their parents were expected to bear the costs of their room and board. With both Mum and Brian in respectably paid machinist positions, owning a car, soon to be purchasing their own home, and Mum, at least to my knowledge, receiving some form of maintenance payments from Dad, they would not have qualified for the room and board coverage. Over time, this became a bone of contention within the home and I was made to feel like a sponger.

It was on the way home after one evening at Sandra's house that my Dad appeared out of nowhere—our second encounter, but the first time he had actually wanted to be seen since he left seven months previously. I was walking along the pavement that runs by the New Stradbroke Estate, a corporation estate lying midway between the original Stradbroke one and Woodhouse village. A damp, foggy November night, a chill that penetrated the bones of my body. Drops of vapour condensed and ran off the tip of my nose like a dribble of snot. The amber light from the sodium street lamps refracted off the droplets of mist, forming pumpkin like spheres around the bulbs. Outside the pumpkins, the darkness and dankness took over.

It was hard to see the details ahead. I looked about fifty yards ahead, and could just make out something underneath a streetlamp. An amorphous form. Then, it started to move, a person. My thoughts started to race. Better step up the speed. Whoever it is can't be up to any good standing under a street lamp this time of night and on such a night as this. As I neared the street lamp, the form started to move toward me. Then, I saw the crumpled beige raincoat, the upturned collar, the slumped shoulder, and the outline of a face that I instantly recognized. That pointed nose that Mum used to mock him about, something his mother had passed along to him. As far as noses go, it wasn't that bad at all, but it was distinctive.

"'Ello, Roger," says the voice from out of the fog.

"What are you doin' 'ere?" My defences are up.

"I thought we might have a chat, that's all."

"Abart what? I've got nothin' ter say ter yer."

"Just wanted to know 'ow you are doing."

Then, I launch into my tirade. "'Ow are we doing? Very well, no thanks ter you. Walking out. Cutting back t'payments. 'Avin ter take yer ter court. Thanks for nothin'."

"I notice that Brian King's moved in wi' yer now. What more can I say? So soon after I left. Speaks for itself. Anyow, I 'ope things are peaceful."

"Yeah, mostly. Once in a while, Mum goes off her 'ead." Why did I just say that?

"I know. I'm out of it now. I don't 'ave ter put up wi' it any longer," he says with a big grin on his face.

"Anyow, I just wondered. Yer know that sideboard in t'front room? I just wondered if it were needed now. I'd expect Brian King will be bringin' in 'is own furniture."

*So, that's why he's here,* I thought. Not to see me, but to try and use me as a messenger. He's after the furniture.

"I don't know. None er my business."

With that, I stalked off, picked up my speed, raced home.

Then, heaven knows why, but I spilled the beans about the entire encounter to Mum and Brian, who were sitting by the fireside in the front room.

"Furniture's what 'e's after," says Mum.

"And 'e's glad 'e dun't 'ave ter put up wi' me anymoore, is 'e?" Mum grits her teeth then takes another drag of her cigarette.

⁓⤳

The world has many reasons to remember 1961. A young American President with fresh ideas, John Fitzgerald Kennedy, was sworn in, inspiring his nation, giving hope that a new way of doing business was at hand. A Soviet, then an American, then another Soviet astronaut circled the globe in outer space, leaving people with the thought that it was better to compete out there for a noble cause than on earth for an ignoble one. But the new President got off to a rocky start, supporting half-heartedly an ill-fated invasion of Cuba by Cuban exiles at a place called the Bay of Pigs. Then, later in the year, the East Germans began to construct a concrete wall around West Berlin to isolate it from East Germany. The Cold War got a little colder when the U.S.S.R. set off the largest hydrogen bomb explosion ever in an obscure archipelago in the Arctic Sea. And feelings of horror and justice served surrounded the death sentence handed out by the Israeli courts to WW 2 Holocaust architect Adolf Eichmann.

In Britain, betting shops were legalized, The Beatles started to become known, and contraceptive pills were made available within the National Health System. Sheffield put on its first display of Christmas illuminations. Thousands of overhead lights and set display pieces ran the length of the downtown shopping area from the Castle Market to the bottom of the Moor, a main shopping street in town, putting Christmas shoppers in the holiday spirit. On the negative side, in Glasgow, a stand collapsed at a football game between Glasgow Celtic and the Rangers, killing three people and injuring more than ten times that number. Large numbers of protesters were arrested at Ban the Bomb rallies staged in London and at break-ins at US Air Force bases around the country. The steel industry in Sheffield was in a recessionary phase. The year's events were truly a mixed bag.

On a smaller scale, and at a more personal level, the year left me with the same diversity of feelings. A memorable year. No doubt about that. Despair, rejection, anger, and anxiety. The destructive manner in which my parents' marriage collapsed and the way in which my brother and I were drawn into the drama left me with all of these negative emotions. But, there were signs of hope. I had moved on to university, the start of what could become a promising career path. I had met someone whom I really cared about, most importantly who reciprocated my feelings for her. By the end of the year, with Brian now installed as the male head of the home, there seemed some semblance of steadiness there. Perhaps there would be blue skies ahead.

# FIERCE GALE

Thursday, February 16, 1962. It is late in the afternoon. I am perched on a stool in one of the zoology laboratories at Sheffield University. Midway through my first year of undergraduate zoology studies, I am not particularly enthused about this anatomy practical class. I am more captivated by what I am seeing through the windows than by the smelly rat that I have pinned out on my dissecting board. As dusk begins to fall, there is an ominous look about the sky. A red sky at night may be a shepherd's delight, but this is a lilac sky, almost but not quite purple. Never seen anything like this before. What does it mean? All month, the weather has been pretty mild. A rain shower here and there, a light dusting of overnight snow now and again, the odd blustery day, nothing out of the ordinary. Are things about to change? Or, is it all just an optical illusion, an atmospheric phenomenon, photons up in the stratosphere going through their paces, colliding with one another and with whatever else is out there—reflecting, refracting, diffracting, the laws of physics having an astronomical work-out.

Two hours later and darkness has set in. I am sitting on

the crammed-to-capacity upper deck of the bus taking me home from the university, soaking in the smoke and nicotine from cigarettes all around me, puffing merrily away on my Embassy filter tip. First- and second-hand smoke to feed the brain cells. The scenery within the bus, what can be seen of it through the miasma, is uninspiring. Pairs of heads and necks sit shoulder-to-shoulder, neatly arranged in rows, like a phalanx on either side of the centre aisle. The heads are uniformly covered. Men are wearing drab, well-worn flat caps; the women scruffy headscarves tied and knotted turban style. There is a sprinkling of schoolboy caps and schoolgirl berets to break up the silhouette. The chatter is incessant. I am able to catch fragments of a common topic.

"Did tha see t'sky abart an 'our ago?"

"No. Tha dun't get too much chance ter look at t'sky where I work darn t'pit." Chuckles, spluttering, and coughing.

"Nor me on t'factory floor. Tha wun't be able ter see t'sky for all t'grime on t'windows. What were wrong wi' t'sky?"

"It were a purplish colour. Like t'man upstairs were trampling on a bunch er grapes an' t'juices were runnin' all o'er t'place."

"Eyup, tha't sure tha an't been drinkin' some er that stuff tha says 'e's makin' up there?" Loud guffaws. More wheezing and hacking.

"T'owdlad's reight. I saw it. I were just outside for me break. 'Avin a fag. It were weird. Lavender is 'ow I'd describe it."

272 | ROGER GORDON

"Tha' must do some gardenin' does tha? I wun't know 'ow ter tell t' difference between lavender an' a bunch er 'orse radish." A spittoon would come in handy, given all the laughing and throat clearing that this last comment brings about. Soon enough everything settles into a low-pitched, indecipherable buzz.

Around five the next morning, I am awakened by the wind rattling the windows of the house. A bit on the rough side out there, I think, as I retreat into my semi-comatose stupor.

Seven a.m. The alarm has now gone off. I dress and make my way downstairs. Mum and Brian are about to head off in the VW for work. My brother has already done so.

"Never seen t' wind as high as this before. Buses might not even be runnin'," says Mum.

As I look out the window of the front room, my sense of detachment from the world outside dissipates. I suddenly realize that this is no regular windy day.

A woman, her head down, is walking at a sharp forty-five degree angle, fighting against the force of the wind, as she struggles to walk up the pavement of the street to catch the bus at the top of the road. The privet hedges around the front gardens are making a swishing sound, as they bend back and forth in unison with the wind gusts. Fortunately, there are no mature trees in our neighborhood. As I look more closely at the pavements on either side of the street, I see the occasional shattered clay-pressed roofing tile. Looking up at the roofs,

I notice that the TV antennae on some of the houses have been bent over. In one case, the antenna is hanging off the chimney top by a thin wire. I see Mum and Brian struggle to the VW parked on the street outside the house. As they each open the car doors, they have difficulty hanging on to them as the wind threatens to blow them off their hinges. After they pull away, I move into the kitchen to make myself some breakfast. I have a mid-morning lecture, so I can take my time leaving the house. Just as well. I don't like the look of it out there.

The wind gains even more momentum during the next half hour or so. I periodically look out of the front room window to check on the mayhem. School kids taking two steps forward one back, satchels wrapped around them, hanging on to their school caps and berets in what seems to be a ridiculous battle to maintain the school-imposed idea of decorum. A man with an artificial leg and walking stick, his body arched over parallel to the ground, making little headway at all. Sheets of newspaper, escapees from the newspaper boy's delivery bag, blowing around from garden to street and back again. Then, a crash. That TV antenna is no longer hanging by its wire thread. It's in the middle of the street. Not a stray dog, cat, or bird to be seen.

Funny how so many of my childhood memories are viewed through the fogged-up windows of the smoky upper deck of the bus. It's eight thirty in the morning. The rush hour to the steel factories is over, so there are a few empty seats. The buses kept running, and the wind has subsided quite a bit, so the walk up the street to the bus stop was more of a squabble than a fight. Swaying from side to side, the bus meanders along its route to the city core through a succession of corporation estates, starting with the most recent, Stradbroke, then continuing through the Woodthorpe, Manor Park, and Wybourn estates, all three built partially or wholly in the 1930s. Stradbroke appears to have escaped the brunt of whatever hit the city last night, but a more devastating scene unfolds in the older neighborhoods. The pavements and roads are littered with huge shards of slate roofing tiles. I wouldn't have wanted to be around when these missiles were airborne. There are huge holes in the roofs of home after home where the old fashioned tiles have been blown away. Then, as the bus stops at a busy intersection on the Woodthorpe estate, everyone lets out a collective gasp.

"Bloody 'ell. Look at that."

"'As tha ever seen owt like that befoore? 'Ope t 'family are oreight."

We are looking straight into the bedroom of a two-storey, semi-detached house, a house that is otherwise a carbon copy of all the other brick-constructed homes in this housing estate. An entire wall has been blown out of the front upper story. The three remaining walls of the bedroom are staring us in the face, three walls of heavily embossed floral wallpaper encasing an empty room. The metal frame of the bed is hanging down from the gaping hole, drooping over the front wall of the house. There is no sign of any other furniture within the room or among the masonry rubble and glass shards that are strewn across the front yard. As we complete our journey into town, I can't get the image of that home out of my mind. I wonder what it was like to have been in the house when that happened? Were people in the room or even in the house at all? For several weeks afterwards, the hole in the bedroom wall was covered with a piece of polystyrene sheeting, while, according to rumor, the occupants continued to dwell in the home.

Arriving at the downtown Pond Street bus terminus, I prepare to walk across the city centre to catch a second bus to the university. Along with other commuters, my eyes are drawn to a remarkable scene on the hillside across from the bus shelter— the building site for the new College of Trades and Technology. A massive tower crane, ten stories high, is grotesquely twisted and doubled over, its jib at forty-five degrees to the mast and touching the ground. An upside down letter V, it looks like a gigantic pair of nutcrackers with the hinge pointing to the sky. As I head across town, I notice that Church Street is barricaded off. Policemen are explaining to puzzled pedestrians that there is a danger of falling masonry from the upper stories and roofs of the buildings.

Within the lecture theatre at the university, the pre-class chatter is abuzz with stories of en route experiences. Someone has seen a metal pre-fabricated garage being carried down a main road as though it were part of the public transport system. Someone else saw a chimney pot blown on to the roof of a car parked outside the house. Another person said he had heard that one of the giant floodlight pylons at Sheffield United's football ground had been brought down, thankfully crashing into the ground and not the houses surrounding the stadium. From the leafier areas of the city, students saw huge trees lying on the ground uprooted, in one case blocking the roadway. Tales of blocks of flats swaying, dustbin lids taking to the air, houses with entire roofs missing, becoming airborne—mercifully at the height of the gale when nobody was outside. The lecture proceeds in the Ivory Tower as though nothing has happened. Professor Roper, dressed as always immaculately with his suit and dickie-bow tie, is in full stride.

"Now, let's leave Professor Mendel and his sweet peas back in his monastery garden and talk a little about humans. Genetics plays a dominant role in our appearance, personality, predisposition to certain diseases, even what appear to be superficial activities such as rolling one's tongue or even kissing." Pause. "No, the department is not carrying out research into that activity." Laughs and groans from the class mask the seriousness of what has gone on outside.

Almost six o'clock in the evening, darkness has set in and I am walking along Talbot Place to Grandma and Granddad's house for the usual Friday tea. The old-fashioned gas lamps, long since electrified, provide dim lighting, so I have to pick

my way carefully among all the rubble that is strewn around—
a hodgepodge of shattered glass, slate roofing tiles, and house
bricks. I enter the house and walk into the back room,
where my grandparents spend all of their time. Mum, Brian,
Grandma, and Granddad are gathered around the table, slurping cups of strong tea and preparing to dig into the usual pork
pie, boiled ham, salad veggies, and pickled onions.

"Blimey. Looks like a lot er slates 'ave come off yer roof,"
I say.

"Aye. That's not all. Did tha see t'big 'ole where they came
off?" asks Grandma

"No, it were too dark. Good job it's not rainin'."

"I don't know what we're goin' ter do. Landlord's not even
been round yet. Rainwater'll come reight through t'house."

"Stop thee worryin'. 'E'll be round soon enough. Accordin'
ter t'paper there's people lost their 'omes, got killed in t'storm.
There's people worse off then thee an' me. Someone put t'news
on." Granddad, as always, the voice of calm and reason.

*This is* Scene at 6:30 *and I'm Mike Scott. South Yorkshire was
hit by a sudden and gigantic wind storm in the early hours of this
morning...A state of emergency has been declared in the city of
Sheffield...winds gusted at 96 miles an hour...Four people were
killed in separate incidents as a result of masonry falling within
or outside of their homes...falling slates...chimney stacks...trees...
cars were upended...prefabricated homes were hardest hit...entire
roofs blown off or entire homes leveled. We now switch to our*

*reporter who is on the Arbourthorne estate where an entire row of prefab homes was razed to the ground...*[27]

Regrettably, my grandparents did not have long to wait for the rain. It began two days after the gale as drizzle. This was followed by two months of more drizzle, continuous rain, sleet, and snow flurries. There was even a snow blizzard and a thunderstorm thrown in for good measure. Despite our attempts to stem the flow, water entered through the hole in the roof, then traveled through three stories to cascade down the inside and outside panels of the kitchen cupboards. The odd cold and frosty days were the only respite from the indoor water feature at my grandparents' home. For my Granddad, it was two months of trudging up and down three flights of stairs to the attic, emptying buckets of water, day and night. We helped him when we could, but it wasn't enough. Finally, the landlord managed to get someone to fix the roof.

Granddad fell ill that summer and he died on September 7. A few of us went back to Grandma's house after the funeral. Slurping her tannin-heavy cuppa, Grandma announced to all the assembled, "They can say what they like abart 'im 'avin' t'cancer. I'll tell yer what killed our Johnnie. It were that bloody gale. All them buckets er water. Troopin' up an' darn t'stairs. 'E were never t'same after."

The Sheffield Gale of 1962 was a major historical event for that bustling steel city of half a million people. Listed among the eighteen worst European windstorms of the twentieth century, it carried no precipitation, only unforecasted, extraordinarily high winds. Nowadays, it would be categorized as a borderline level two hurricane. Work carried on as usual in the steel factories, cutlery and small tool manufacturing firms, and down the coalmines. Somehow or other, a new four-storey Woolworth's store managed to open in the Haymarket area of downtown, its glass and mosaic outer shell unscathed. Yet, two thirds of the homes in the city, over one hundred thousand, were damaged and around two hundred and fifty people rendered homeless. The government provided no emergency funding to cover repairs and restoration costs totaling approximately five million pounds—a huge amount for those times. Amazingly, there were only four fatalities, all the result of chimneys collapsing and trapping victims inside their homes. According to my Grandma, the gale killed my Granddad as well.

---

27    Reconstructed from various news sources.

# ADJUSTMENTS

During my first year of university studies, I managed to strike a workable balance between social life and academic commitment. Not long after classes resumed in the New Year, I was invited to dust off my trumpet and join a traditional jazz band. From the outset, I didn't think that I was good enough for this. I hadn't played the thing for a year or so, had never played in an ensemble, and had limited improvisation skills. To add to my feelings of inadequacy, two of the band members, the clarinetist and the pianist, were highly talented. But the group, which eventually became known as the Addy Street Five after the street on which two of the six band members lived, was desperate and the lads gave me their confidence. It was like a dream come true. Playing my favorite kind of music—the genre, if not the quality, of Chris Barber, Ken Colyer and the likes. The band enabled me to focus my social activities. Toward the end of the academic year, we started to get the occasional gig, playing at student residence balls, college dances, and pubs. A great bunch of guys, they became good friends and the core of my modestly sized social circle throughout my undergraduate studies and into my postgraduate program. With a modicum of effort, I passed my first year exams. No chance of being sent down.

At home, the scene was relatively quiet. We continued to live on the Stradbroke estate, putting up with the disquiet that we felt coming from the neighbors around us—people who had once been cordial toward us looking away. For my brother and me the embarrassment was mutual. We were the only family in the grouping of streets around our home in which a marital breakup, let alone promiscuity, had occurred. I felt like I was tarred with the brush, the sins of the father, or mother in this case, visited upon the son. We stuck out like a blight on the depressingly uniform landscape.

Then, one day Mum announced that Brian and she had been looking at houses and had decided to purchase one in the Gleadless Town End area. "We can make a fresh start," she said. This didn't impress Trevor very much, but he was not a happy camper anyway. My first inclination was to look at a street map to find out how far away the new home would be from Sandra's house. Once I had figured out that it wasn't too out of reach, I thought that the move would be a good idea. We could leave the old baggage behind at number 23. So, in August of that year, a month before Granddad died, we moved to a semi-detached two storey on a cul de sac known as Herdings View. Though I never felt that it was my family home, it was the first privately owned home that my mother, my brother, and I would live in. But it was Brian's home, his mortgage, and all 3000 pounds[28] or so of it. I referred to it as the King residence.

I spent that summer the same way I spent every vacation—working at whatever job I could get. In those days, except for one or two seasonal activities such as delivering the Christmas mail and driving the summertime ice cream vans, it was not a widespread practice for employers in an industrial city such as Sheffield to hire students. There weren't as many students as there are today. University students were looked upon by the working population as a privileged upper crust. Though I was an exception to this perception, it was an arduous undertaking for me to find work, one I never looked forward to. There was no manpower file for student jobs, so I would spend the first couple of weeks of my summer break traipsing around Sheffield on bus after bus, to factory after factory, building site after building site, talking to an endless succession of foremen. I would be met with looks of consternation and occasionally scowls, like I had no right to be meddling where I didn't belong.

"No lad. We don't 'ire any students 'ere."

Then, he quickly turns away from me, to yell to one of the workers, "Eyup Fred. Watch what tha t'doing wi' them planks. Pile em in t'…"

I'm an intruder.

"Do yer know anyone who is 'irin'?"

"No," he snaps, without turning to face me.

Nonetheless, with a combination of my own legwork, together with leads passed along to my by relatives and other students, I managed to apply myself to a variety of jobs. Unlike some of my student friends, I needed the money to meet day-to-day costs and pay board to my mother. Though my student grant was not sufficient to allow me to pay at-home living costs during term time, I made sure that I contributed while I was working between university terms. Not a single vacation, summer, or Christmas went by when my sleeves were not rolled up. I bottled milk at Express Dairy, carried and emptied dustbins for the council, made pork pies at Davy's factory, and baked bread at Fletcher's bakery. I delivered Christmas mail, at a time when people sent Christmas cards to everyone and their dog, delivered tires to garages around the city, and worked on building site after building site.

In the summer of 1962, I mixed concrete on a building site for a new fire station at Intake. Workers were only ever laid off on Fridays. So, the custom was for labourers to find places to hide around 3 p.m on Friday afternoon, to escape the two-hour notice that the foreman was required to give to laid-off employees. The place would look like a ghost town. The first Friday I was there, the bloke who was shoveling sand and gravel with me told me to follow him and we hid behind a stack of bricks. The second Friday, I was half-way up a ladder with a hod of bricks on my shoulder when I heard, "Eyup, thee up there wi' t'od. Tha't finished at five."

It was the foreman standing on another ladder a few yards from me. I had my head down on account of the hod and hadn't seen him.

I managed to get another labouring job on a building site near Catcliffe. It was a large-scale project but none of the workmen seemed to know what it was they were helping to build. A factory of some sort. My job was to lie out burlap sacking over the newly set concrete foundations and pour bucket after bucket of water over it to prevent the sun from cracking the concrete. This meant trudging to and from a standpipe at the other end of the site to fill and empty buckets of water, one in each hand. Monotony. The builder's equivalent of watching paint dry.

⁓

Soon after Granddad died, Mum asked me to sleep over one night a week at Grandma's house. "She gets reight lonely. It'd cheer 'er up."

So, I took on this responsibility, though I never looked forward to the nights in question. That old house had changed since we all used to live there as a family. Now devoid of human warmth, save for dear old Grandma, its labyrinth of unheated, damp rooms, steep, dimly lit staircases, high ceilings, and Victorian-era furniture left me with a clammy feeling. The downstairs room that we used to live in was barren of furniture, filled only with piles of old newspapers, and the attic, where people at one time used to sleep and where I used to play, was a no-go zone. Nobody could say what might be up there. Its entranceway was a flight of stairs behind a door off the upstairs landing, but when I once opened the door, all I could see were spiders hanging down from the roof of the stairwell in cobweb after cobweb. The entranceway to the cellar, a steep flight of concrete stairs behind a door in the downstairs back room, was similarly forbidding. The spiders were beginning to take over what had once been a place where people used to gather during the WW 2 air raids, a place where until Granddad became ill, meat was stored. Only Granddad was brave enough to navigate those stairs. On a hook attached to the back of the door of the backroom, hung Granddad's hat, waistcoat, and jacket, ready for him to put on. His clothes stayed there until the day that Grandma died. This was a house for Grandma and ghosts of the past. An eerie place at night, where a cacophony of strange sounds—creaks, squeaks, thumps, and pitter patters—made for a return to my fitful sleeping pattern of days gone by.

"Mum," I said, "That 'ouse sounds like it's 'aunted by ghosts at night."

"I wun't worry abart that. If it's thee Granddad tha't worried abart, 'e were a smashin' feller. Tha should feel reight comforted that 'e's watchin' o'er thee."

Hard to argue with that, but it didn't help.

A clear dark Monday night. October 22, 1962.

Grandma and I are in the backroom supping tea.

"I want ter put t'radio on, love. President er America. 'E's supposed to be sayin' summat abart Cuba. Dun't look very good."

She turns on one of the knobs on the walnut encased radio, the same one that used to give out the news to the family during the Second World War. It might even have dated back to the First World War.

*Good evening, my fellow citizens...of the soviet military build up on the island of Cuba...A series of offensive missile sites... nuclear strike capability against the western hemisphere...a strict quarantine on all offensive military equipment...any nuclear missile launched from Cuba...full retaliatory response upon the Soviet Union...Clandestine, reckless and provocative threat... world domination...*[29]

"Blimey. I don't like t'sound er it." All I could think to say.

"Been through two world wars," says Grandma, her voice rising, pointing her finger at the ceiling, "I've no stomach for another un."

Not to suggest any connection between the two events, but it was a few days after this that Mum announced she was pregnant. Life goes on. To hell with Khrushchev, Kennedy, and Cuba.

28   About $9,000 U.S. at prevailing exchange rates.
29   From BBC archives.

# TIN LIZZIE

Nationwide, the winter of 1962–63 was horrendous—the coldest on record since 1795. From a day or so after Boxing Day until early March, the snow and the thermometer readings fell. At one point, it was so cold that even the beer and the diesel oil froze, as did the Thames and a sizeable stretch of the North Sea. The gale force snowstorms, one after another, brought down power lines, caused villages to be cut off, and livestock to perish. Saturday after Saturday, football games had to be called off, to the point at which there was talk of cancelling the season. In Sheffield, the merchants trying to sell fresh fruit and veggies at the old open-air Sheaf market had a hard time convincing customers they were not employees of Bird's Eye® foods, flogging the frozen varieties. Cabbages as hard as cannonballs, apples that could have come in handy on the summertime cricket pitch, and bananas that could deliver a blow.

The double-decker buses struggled around hilly Sheffield, as the conductors divided their time between collecting the fares and shovelling ashes under spinning wheels. Traction was hard to come by. On more than one occasion, South Yorkshire was cut off from its Lancashire neighbors as the Snake and Woodhead passes across the Pennines were blocked by drifting snow. Gelignite was used to clear a way through. Impassable roads frequently isolated the small Derbyshire villages around the city. In the city suburbs, a milk deliveryman's body was found in a snow bank and just north of Sheffield, the bodies of two climbers were found encased in a tomb of ice. When the thaw finally did come, water pipes throughout the city burst and tankers had to be rushed around slushy streets to provide affected homes with water. The workers at the power stations chose this time of national crisis to work-to-rule, to add insult to injury.

I had no inkling that all this was in store when, at the start of my second year at university, I decided to buy a car. It was a black, two-door 1947 Ford Anglia, license plate KWB 972—an old banger. Shaped like two boxes of different height attached end-to-end to one another, with a long bonnet extending like Pinocchio's nose from the tiny front windshield and fronted by a no-nonsense upright radiator grille, it was a carry over from the pre-war cars commonly referred to as the "sit up and beg" variety. Mum dubbed them "boxy doo-dahs." I called it "Tin Lizzie" after the original model T, though it wasn't even in the same ballpark where class was concerned. Advertised for twenty-five pounds, I got it for twenty.

Tin Lizzie came with a crank handle that I sometimes used because the ignition starter rarely worked. Most times,

STARTING TO FRAME | 289

I jump-started it by letting it roll in neutral down the steep hill that led down the street from our house then slamming it into second gear when it had picked up speed. Sometimes it didn't start and I was stuck with a broken down car at the bottom of the street. The car had a vacuum-powered wind-shield wiper that tended to slow down or stop altogether when I drove over forty miles an hour. But I knew Lizzie's limits and hardly ever asked her to go that fast. Other fea-tures that were not state-of-the-art included a manually con-trolled turn signal, which flipped a small orange coloured arm out from the side of the car, and a gearbox that was non-synchromesh between first and second gear. I didn't know how to double-declutch so I sidestepped the issue by not using first gear at all and starting in second. It was a heap of junk and the more I drove it the junkier it became. But, damn I loved that car.

My old KWB 972 motored, mostly spluttered, its way through that dreadful winter, sometimes starting, often run-ning out of petrol as I tried to avoid the cost of bellying up to the pumps. As my friends would point out to me, I was in denial. It really needed that petrol. So, I broke down in the most inconvenient places—at traffic lights, roundabouts, bus stops, the city centre and thoroughfares leading to and from it, and on one memorable occasion on a one in three hill that services the small coastal community of Robin Hood's Bay in North Yorkshire. That fateful incident happened late in

May 1963, during the Whitsuntide university break. I was on a week-long field trip to the marine station that was nestled close to the shoreline in the old village at the bottom of the hill. One afternoon, on my way back to the lodgings from the station, the car spluttered to a halt after managing only a few yards up the precipitous slope.

"Don't know what's wrong wi' it," I said absentmindedly, to one of my classmates walking alongside the car.

"Hey, come on everyone, let's push Roger's car up the hill. There's a service station with a mechanic up there."

So, a gang of half a dozen got behind Lizzie, huffing and puffing until she was about halfway up Mount Everest.

"Got to stop to catch my breath," says one bloke, panting like Lassie in heat.

Just then, a thought hit me.

"Eyup, I don't suppose it's run out er petrol?" I ask, as though this were a new concept for the old jalopy.

This brought jeers and cries of disbelief from my classmates, who could and probably should have strapped me to the boot of the car and let it slide back downhill. I didn't easily live this one down and I have as a memento a photo of me pouring petrol from a can into the car, which responded by starting right away.

~~~

In mid-July, Mum went into Jessop Hospital for about a

week. Nearing forty-one, she was considered to be an at-risk expectant mother. In those days, childbearing beyond one's mid thirties was not common. My half sister, Lisa King, was born on July 21. A few days afterward, Mum and baby Lisa were on their way home. But, parental rights being nonexistent at that time, Brian was not given time off work to bring Mum and baby home from the hospital. So, Tin Lizzie and I stepped up to the plate. It was a ride home that Mum never forgot.

"Mind where yer puttin' yer feet," I say to Mum who is sitting beside me clutching the baby. "T' floor is rusted through in places under t' dashboard."

"Bloody 'ell. I can see t' road."

"Oh, and while we're movin' would yer 'ang on ter t' door 'andle. T' latch is broken an' t' door can fly open."

"Ey. Am I safe in 'ere?"

As we get going, "It's a bit stuffy in 'ere. 'Ow can I open t' winder if I 'ave ter 'ang on ter t' door 'andle?

"Window 'andles don't work anyhow. Sorry, Mum."

"What were them scrapin' noises when we went round t' corner?"

"That were just t' wheels scrapin' on t' underside er t' wheel arches. Suspension's gone."

"Chuffin' 'ell. Never 'ad a ride like this befoore. What a start for our Lisa. I'd er got a taxi if I'd er known."

But, she did see the funny side of it once we all got home

and it made for good conversation when visitors dropped by to see the new arrival. "Eyup, tha'll never believe 'ow our Roger got me an' our Lisa 'ome."

# PERSONA NON GRATA

Spring 1963. Second-year university. I was thankful for Tin Lizzie. She provided a welcome relief from the home scene. The novelty of the four of us being together in a home that Brian had purchased, not a rented home or a council house, was starting to wear off and my brother and I were seeing through the smoke and mirrors. We were guests in the home, not family members. During the term breaks, there was civility. I was contributing a portion of my wage packet from my various jobs toward household expenses. But, as soon as the study term began and I was unable to afford such an ongoing expense against my bare bones grant, the jibes and cold shoulder treatment kicked in.

"'Ow late will tha be up there in t'bedroom studyin' then?"

"Don't know. Why?"

"Lights. Electricity, that's why. Money dun't grow on trees tha knows. Course, 'ow would tha know? Tha dun't have ter pay t'bills. Tha's got it made."

"I explained to yer that me grant weren't given to pay room and board at 'ome. I get a smaller grant because it's assumed that those expenses are covered at 'ome."

"Oh aye," snorts Mum derisively.

"To get a bigger grant I'd 'ave ter leave 'ome and show reason why it were necessary for me ter do that. I give yer t'room an' board every time I get a job."

"Give me room an' board? Only 'cus I shamed yer inter it. Tha't nowt but a sponger."

"Look. You went to see George Mack ter ask 'im ter persuade me to stay in school. Now I'm doin' it. What's t'big problem?"

"Shut thee face, what's t'big problem. Tha't t'big problem. Nowt but an ungrateful sod. That's all."

And that's all for me, as I gather together my books and head out the door to catch the bus to the public library at Manor Top. Peace, quiet, and lights for an hour or two anyway. When it was one of my study nights, I would often opt to study at Grandma's house, where she welcomed me as a relief from her loneliness. In this quid pro quo arrangement, I got the front room to study in, the upstairs bedroom to sleep in, with a few bumps in the night thrown in for good measure.

Between the taunts, I received the silent treatment. Sent to Coventry, as the saying goes. Mum and Brian adopted the policy of not speaking to me unless spoken to and only then by sentence fragments or one-word answers. This reached its peak at the time when I went on that Whitsuntide field trip to Robin Hood's Bay, one that was compulsory and part of my curriculum, with the other biology students and some professors. I'm sure that Mum and Brian thought that I was taking a one-week holiday—having a good time rather than working to pay for my keep. I left in old Tin Lizzie to go on that trip amid an atmosphere of silence and tension. I returned one week later to find that nothing had changed.

I pull up to the house in Lizzie and wander inside, where Brian and Mum are watching the telly. Neither of them looks at me, continuing to stare at the screen—a motorcar race from Brands Hatch.

"'Ello, I'm back," I say.

Grunts, followed by silence. They aren't intending to speak to me.

"Well, it was a good week. Learned a lot. Good facilities there." Since they weren't going to ask.

"That's nice," Mum rasps, clearly unimpressed.

"Well, I can see things are the same as when I went away," I finally say in exasperation, walking out of the room to unpack in my bedroom.

"Why would they be any different?" I hear Mum say to the floor.

Somehow or other, I managed to ride out this difficult period and pass my end-of-year exams, which were not as critical as the first year ones. I found consolation and comfort in talking things over with Sandra and especially her mother.

"Sooner or later, you'll need to get out of that situation," Mrs. Archer would tell me. "Is there anyone at the university who can help?"

Having just returned from a field trip in which I got to know some of the professors in the biology department, it occurred to me that Prof. John Ebling, deputy Head of the Department and a very approachable individual, would lend a sympathetic ear. After I had recounted my home situation to him as we sat together one day in his office, he told me that he would help. Not long after that, I went back to speak to him to let him know that there had been some improvement at home, so he held off acting on my request.

After the Robin Hood's Bay trip, civility gradually returned. Mum asked me one day if I would loan Brian five pounds, as he needed the money to make the car payment. I met Brian in town during his lunch break and he seemed genuinely embarrassed to be taking it. I also made sure that as soon as the university term was over, I got a job delivering tires around Sheffield and Rotherham, so I was able to pay board.

I was away from home for much of that summer. I had been chosen to work at the Wellcome Field Station and Laboratories in Tonbridge Wells, Kent. It was during my second year of studies that I developed an interest in the area of parasitology and my summer job in a world-class research centre for parasitological diseases of livestock was a perfect step along the road to turning it into a career goal.

In October, it was time to put the animal antics of the

summer behind me and begin my third and final year of study for my undergraduate degree. No more messing around. If I really want to become a parasitologist, I'll need to stay on for a postgraduate degree, a Ph.D. no less. That means that I must place as one of the top two students in my graduating class to be sure of garnering a scholarship, the only way I'll be able to afford the extra three plus years of study. Life at home is starting to deteriorate again and this worries me. Baby Lisa seems no trouble at all—not by any stretch of the imagination a cranky newborn. She sleeps, breast-feeds, poops, cries now and again like babies do, but she doesn't keep Mum on the hop. She's hardly a straw to break any camel's back. I'm practicing my trumpet in the Music Room at the university, so as not to disrupt the tranquility at home. Recognizing that there is a new focus to be respected, I am trying to be as inconspicuous as I can.

But Mum still badgers and sneers at me for not paying my board. Maybe she wants me to leave home, and then she won't have to worry about whatever expenses are associated with my food and light usage; I've already told her that in order to leave home I'll have to make a special case to the authorities stating the reason why. She either doesn't believe this is the case, doesn't believe that I can't afford to make a payment anyway, or is pushing me to leave. What she doesn't know is that I've already started the wheels in motion in case I have to do this. She could be suffering from postpartum depression, but her symptoms are the same as were displayed earlier in the year before she delivered and go back to the times when she was married to Dad, laying the guilt trip on me for not paying my way. Is she being pressured by Brian to lean on me? He's quietly ignoring me right now, joining her crusade in a less obsequious but nevertheless obvious way. No, I am convinced that he is in the running for the award as best supporting actor, not the star role.

Is there a pressing financial need that I am missing? Am I being insensitive and uncaring? Going back to the days of Mum and Dad, at the time that this became an issue they were both earning respectable salaries and we were living in a government subsidized rental home on a corporation estate. By comparison with others around us, we were doing all right. Her live-in arrangement with Brian doesn't strike me as a fiscally desperate one either. Before Mum stopped working, their weekly incomes as machinists would have been more than adequate to make ends meet. Then, maternity and child allowance benefits would have kicked in. If it's really not about money, what is it about? In any event, this hostile and volatile atmosphere does not auger well for the academic year ahead.

One evening, as I'm looking forward to going over to Sandra's house, I hear a fuss downstairs. Trevor storming around, yelling and shouting. I walk into the dining room. Mum and Brian sit at the table, Trevor is standing, hands on hips.

"Don't look at either er us," says Mum in a very matter

of fact tone, "We din't take yer money. Yer must 'ave left it around somewhere."

Seeing me enter the room, Trevor turns toward me, his face beet red, as he points to the sideboard.

"I left a twenty pound note on that sideboard. Now it's gone. What does tha know abart it?"

"I don't know owt abart it. I never took thee money," I say, flabbergasted and angry at the accusation.

"Tha took it din't tha?" He moves toward me. I stand my ground.

"I never stole yer rotten money," I assert.

With that, he grabs me by the collar and starts to punch me, knocking me to the ground.

As I struggle to get up, Brian finally rises from his comfortable seat at the table and in a weak voice, drawls, "Hey, hey. That's enough the two of you. Let it go now."

"All I did was react to an insulting allegation that I'm a thief," I splutter. "You two just sat there an' watched all this 'appen. Did nowt." I am good and angry now. "That tells me everything."

"Get thee'sen out then if tha dun't like it in 'ere," shouts Mum as I storm out of the room to head out to the relative safety of Lizzie.

"Aye, and tha'd better stay outter my way," grimaces Trevor, gritting his teeth, "I worked bloody 'ard for that money."

Over at Sandra's, my eye is starting to puff up. He's given

me a shiner. Sandra's mum enters the room. "Roger, this is not acceptable. You really have to get out of there now. It's gone too far. This is an important year for you." I know she's right.

I can't even go back there tonight, I am thinking. So, I don't. With nowhere else coming to mind, I decide to go to Grandma's house. She'll be pleased to see me. She always is.

So, Grandma and I are sitting at in the backroom around the table having a cup of tea. She notices my eye. "What 'ave yer done ter yer eye, luv?"

"I din't do it. Trevor did it. 'E accused me er stealin' money from 'im, then started ter lay inter me. Mum and Brian just sat there and watched. Took it all in."

"Oo, our Trevor. 'E needs a good straightening out. Couple er years in t'army 'd do 'im good." she says.

"Ne'er mind our Trevor. What do yer think er me Mum and Brian just sittin' there doin' nowt ter stop it? Then tellin' me to get out er t'house?"

She starts to rise from her seat, wagging her finger at me.

"Now, I'll 'ave nowt said about thee mother. She's t'apple er my eye. When she were born I thought I'd got best that were *ever* born." Now she's on her feet. "She's 'ad ter put up wi' that bloody feller leavin' 'er. Left 'er no money. I could ring 'is neck. She can do no wrong for me. So don't say owt wrong abart er, 'cus I don't want ter listen ter it." Rant over, she sits down.

"Now does that want any more tea?"

*Is this family totally mad,* I think?

"No thanks," I reply.

# FLYING THE COOP

John Ebling was quick to react when I showed up in his office sporting my black eye. Within a day or so, he had obtained permission from the granting council for me to leave home on an award that included provision to pay lodging expenses. I looked at a couple of places and had no difficulty choosing a boarding house run by Marjorie and George Bailey, a middle-aged couple who, unable to have children of their own, had decided to take in a student for the company. They lived on Hollybank Crescent in the Intake area of the city in one of those asbestos-constructed prefabricated homes built just after the war as a stopgap measure to relieve the housing shortage. The location suited me fine because, like the other places where I had lived, it was not far from Woodhouse where Sandra lived.

It was also only a thirty-minute walk away from Herdings View, so it was a weird feeling for me to be moving into the home of a stranger located so close to where my own mother lived. I found myself struggling to explain to Marj why it had become necessary for me to move away from home at all to attend a university in Sheffield. In the early going, I passed it off as a mere desire on my part to flap my wings, an explanation which did not convince her. As time passed, I let her know that there was a domestic situation at home that was not conducive to my studying. She got the message.

George and Marj were a wonderful couple who treated me as part of their extended family. The three of us chatted freely, watched TV, and ate together, usually all three activities at the same time. Often, I was included in conversations when their relatives dropped by, though I was careful not to wear out my welcome and would excuse myself after a short time had lapsed. I took their dog Jane, a shaggy, friendly mutt, for walks around the neighbourhood and was on the scene when another dog uninvitedly tied himself on to her. I joined in with the fun when the resulting litter of puppies arrived. The hours I spent studying in my bedroom were never called into question, nor was my unmelodious trumpet playing which easily penetrated those paper thin walls and spread out over the neighborhood.

Marj was wonderful to me—George, a thoroughly decent bloke, a good friend. It was at the time the nearest approximation to a real family that I had.

Within a short while of my moving into my digs, the tone of the neighborhood took a turn for the better as I was forced to remove my dilapidated old Lizzie from its parking spot outside the Balls' residence and retire it for good. I had already been forced to pay a five-pound fine for being in possession of a vehicle in dangerous condition. A policeman stopped me one day and pointed out that the front wheel arch on the driver's side had a big rip in it and was about to part company with the rest of the body. I explained to him that a double decker bus had tried to overtake me and had caused the damage. Council had given me ten pounds as settlement. That explanation, which was perfectly true, only made matters worse.

"Think I'll ask yer ter tek me for a spin," says the man in blue, opening the passenger door and sitting in the passenger seat.

"What's this?" he asks, as he finds himself unable to close the door.

"Oh, yer'll 'ave ter grab that piece er string tied around t'door 'andle while I'm drivin'. That door lock dun't work," I explain.

"Hmmm. Interesting. Well, drive on then."

So we drive around the residential streets of Broomhill at around twenty miles an hour. I sense what he's going to ask me to do so I don't want to go any faster.

"Move 'er up to thirty," he says, not fooled by my tactics.

Then, "Stop," he yells. I bear down on the foot brake. The car eventually and painstakingly stops. Then, he asks me to cruise at 30 and stop on command using only the hand brake. Nothing happens. The car chugs merrily along.

"Sir, you'll follow me darn ter t'police station. I'm impounding this car for a complete safety inspection."

When I returned later that day, I was given a citation and permission to drive it to the nearest scrap yard. I drove it to one in a part of town called Heeley Bottom, where by mutual agreement, the owner did a cheap, half arsed job on the brakes, fixed the door lock and told me to buy a fiber glass repair kit to fix up the bodywork. This seemed to satisfy the cops down at West Bar police station and I drove around in the old girl for another couple of months. When it came time to put her through the ten-year road test though, even the bloke at the Heeley scrap yard drew the line in the sand. So, I let him keep what was remaining on the annual road tax sticker, and then we shook hands as I left old Lizzie behind for good.

Friday, November 22, 1963. It's just after seven o'clock George and Marj are sitting watching the telly. I am walking through the living room, about to head out the door to catch the bus to Woodhouse, when I am stopped in my tracks. On the black and white TV screen, there is a sombre, black haired man, whom I do not recognize.

*News has just come in that President Kennedy has been shot...open car through the streets of Dallas, Texas...blood on the President's head...rushed to hospital...no word of his condition.*[30]

After he has read his script, there is a pause, then normal programming resumes. Back to the *Tonight* show and Cliff

Michelmore. The three of us stare into space in disbelief, until Marj breaks the silence.

"I can't believe it. 'E's such a good man. Why would anyone do it? Oh, I do 'ope 'e dun't die."

He did die and like the rest of the world, everyone whom I knew was shocked and grief-stricken.

⌒‿‿⌒

As the Autumn term ticks along, I feel as if a load is being slowly lifted off my back. My studies are progressing well. Faculty and classmates are beginning to view me as a high achiever. My social life is just where I want it to be—a combination of weekend gigs playing in the jazz band and seeing Sandra. The state of affairs that I had left behind at Herdings View is no longer part of my life and there is much relief in that. Then, as the term draws to an end in preparation for the Christmas recess, the reality hits me. I am standing in the Student Union building with my pals from the jazz band.

"So, what are you going to do over the Christmas hols, Alg?" asks Adrian.

"Oh, I dunno. Read a few books. Just put my feet up and relax. Enjoy the warm comforts of home."

"Ah yes. Those comforts. Mum's cooking. Beats having to keep feeding the meter, doesn't it? How about you, Rog? Got any plans?"

I feel embarrassed, hurt, and jealous. I haven't told them

about my situation, so it's not their fault for assuming I have a normal home life with two caring parents, a dog curled up by the fire that blazes in the grate, brothers and sisters, nieces and nephews, aunts and uncles, sitting in a circle sipping glasses of egg nog. I haven't even thought about Christmas. But I'll have to go back home. It would be an intrusion to stay on with Marj and George—besides, my grant doesn't cover time between terms.

"No plans yet," I say finally. "'Ave ter give it some thought."

I returned home for the Christmas vacation with much trepidation. Surprisingly, I was not placed on the defensive and while affection and cordiality would have been too much to expect, the atmosphere was respectful. This was helped along by my taking leave of the home for the week before Christmas. I had obtained a job working nights at the Davy's bakery near the Midland Station in the city centre. To cut down on commuting times, I slept during the day at Grandma Bonsall's house, which was within walking distance. In those days, pork pies were a popular Christmas delicacy, so extra staff was hired for the additional demand. I learned how to toss balls of dough into pie molds and inject liquid gelatin into the space between the piecrust and the pork filling. Nights were long, but there was good camaraderie among the various students and regulars—and the pay was better than that of the Christmas mail delivery. On Christmas Eve morning I clocked off my last shift, slept for a couple of hours, then started my Christmas shopping.

After Christmas, life at home seemed to be going so well that I decided to give it another shot. I offered to pay Mum the amount of board that would otherwise have gone to Marj and George, a proposition which she gladly accepted. Of course, this meant that I would not disclose to the authorities that I had moved back home, or my room and board allowance would have been deducted. It was an illegal act that could have come back to haunt me, but Mum and Brian didn't seem to mind and I was wanting peace and quiet in the nearest approximation to a family setting. Too bad I misjudged what that setting would be. Within a week or so of the new term commencing, Mum began the nighttime "lights off" routine all over again.

I am trying to study in my bedroom. She appears. "It's ten o'clock. 'Ow much longer are yer goin' ter be?"

Five minutes later, she re-appears. "This electricity costs money tha knows. I'll put a stop ter it now."

She switches the light out. That's enough for me. Back to Marj and George's. I had some explaining to do, but they took me back. I left Herdings View on a Sunday and returned to pick up the remainder of my belongings the following morning. My mother was in a fit of rage that was frightening to witness. "What are tha 'ere for?"

"Come ter pick up thee belongings? Get thee belongings and get out yer ungrateful bugger. Get thee'sen o'er ter thee wonderful landlady. She an't 'ad ter put up wi' thee all these years."

"I din't come back ter get inter an argument, Mum."
I protested.

"No. Tha't like thee bloody father. A wolf in sheep's clothing. Dun't want an argument but wants everything thee own
way. All these years I've kept thee an' this is all t'thanks I get.
Marches out ter give someone else thee bloody board."

I raced upstairs and packed my remaining clothes and
books as quickly as I could. Amazingly, Lisa was sleeping
through all of this. As I appeared downstairs, Mum was throwing diapers in the washing machine, sobbing uncontrollably.
She turned to square up ter me.

"Out and never let me see thee face again."

Not wanting to come within even a foot of her, I stormed
out of the front door, suitcase in hand. I was shaken. She
hates me. Only wants my board. Doesn't make any effort to
understand why I have to study. The only people who show
me any semblance of worth are my girlfriend, her mother, and
my landlady and landlord. These are my thoughts that cold
January morning as I catch the bus to Manor Top to take
my paltry belongings the short distance to the little prefab.
Home, sweet home.

—✦—

I soon settled back into the routine at Hollybank Crescent.
And the winter term brought a pleasant surprise. The university jazz band that I played in, the Addy Street Five, performed

in the annual Inter University Jazz Federation competition at the Sheffield Students' Union and was selected to progress to the finals in Croydon, near London. In February, we took the coach trip down south with no great expectations of success, but surprised ourselves by claiming second place in the small band class. This was in spite of the fact that our regular banjo player failed to show up and we had to make a last minute substitution and as we discovered after the fact, our tuba player was suffering from appendicitis.

My course work progressed in an uneventful and generally optimistic manner. I was considered a strong contender for one of the two scholarships for postgraduate studies. Though I wasn't exactly breaking the back of the books, I was applying myself conscientiously. Then, in late March, the dreaded Easter break rolled around. I was not about to go back home again. Those days were over. So, to give the illusion that like the other students, the break was a time away from the normal routine, I moved into the one-room flat of one of the band members in a big old house in the Upperthorpe area not far from the university. I had a radio and a coin-fed small electric fire for company. When I ran out of money, I wrapped blankets around myself. There was nobody to talk to because the other students renting rooms in the house had gone home for the vacation. Then, of all things, we had a snowstorm. I was hemmed in and I felt miserable. After a few days of this and with my tail squarely between my legs, I trudged back to

Marj and George's house and spent the rest of the vacation there. Given all my comings and goings, that couple must have thought I was a wandering nomad.

April 17, 1964. A grey overcast Friday morning. I'm having my breakfast chatting with Marj, half listening to the BBC news on the radio. So, the Great Train Robbers, twelve in all, were about to spend a total of over three hundred years in jail. Some of them were going to the slammer for thirty years. Doesn't seem fair, I'm thinking. Murderers might get away with less than that. It's the money that got them the time, not injuring that poor railway guard. I glance at the morning newspaper. Two standout Sheffield Wednesday players, Peter Swan and David "Bronco" Layne, are in deep trouble for allegedly betting that their team would lose a game against Ipswich Town, which turned out to be the case. Tony Kay, now playing for Everton, but part of the Wednesday side that lost that game, is also under the gun for game fixing. Such talented players, I think. They'll probably be barred from playing for life.

The postman arrives at the door. He's early.

"There's a letter for yer, Roger," says Marj, handing me the envelope.

So, I open it, to find a birthday card from Aunt Ray. Ah yes, I'd almost forgot. It's my twenty-first birthday. In times past, there would be a big celebration. I would be given a key to the door of the house to show that I had reached adulthood.

*I'm twenty-one today!*

*Twenty-one today!*

*I've got the key to the door,*

*Never been twenty-one before.*

Or, so that old music hall song goes.

"I din't know it were yer birthday, Roger," says Marj. "Why din't yer say?"

*Because I knew it would be a let down*, I'm thinking. I show Marj the card from my aunt.

"Nowt from me mother, of course," I say bitterly.

"Maybe somethin's 'appened. Perhaps it got stuck in t'mail. Why don't yer call 'ome?"

Well, what could poor Marj say? She is only trying to temper my hurt feelings. But, she's right. I'll get on the phone.

An hour or so later, I am in a phone booth near the Town Hall in the city centre. Outside it's started to rain. Showers with sunny intervals was the forecast, but I haven't noticed the sun yet. I call Aunt Ray to thank her for the card. I mention to her that in spite of the fact that it is my twenty first, she is the only person other than my girlfriend and her mother who have bothered to acknowledge it. My own mother must have too many other things on her mind. I then explain to Aunt Ray why I left home in the first place and I bring up the turning off the light episodes.

"I wish I could 'elp, love. But I do know that electricity is expensive."

Good old Aunt Ray. Her heart is in the right place but she has to do a high wire act to avoid word getting back to my mother. She is the embodiment of a peacemaker.

My next five pence in the coin slot is a phone call to home. To my surprise it is Grandma who picks up the phone.

"Grandma, it's me. Roger. Where's Mum?"

"I think yer'd better come 'ome. Can't tell yer o'er phone."

"Why? What's wrong? What's 'appened?"

"Better come 'ome. That's all I'm goin' ter say."

"Did yer know it's me twenty-first birthday today, Grandma?" A long pause.

"Aye. 'Appy birthday." A begrudging recognition at best.

"Did Mum mention owt about it bein' me birthday? An' why can't yer tell me where she is?"

"Come on 'ome. A lot's been goin on."

So, I decided to wait until evening time to hear what had been going on from the horses' mouths. The grand mare wanted to play the suspense game and that's not where my head was.

Around seven that evening, I drop by the house. Brian, Mum, and Grandma are sitting by the telly, baby Lisa alongside them in her bassinette.

"Tha might 'ave noticed there's no car on t'driveway," says Mum. "They came ter repossess it on account er t'payments not bein' made. Man asked for t'keys an' drove off in it."

"Well, things'll get back to normal soon enough," drawls Brian, trying unsuccessfully to minimize his embarrassment.

"Soon enough?" bawls Mum. "Not soon enough ter stop me avin' ter go back ter work that lathe at PCL ter keep a roof o'er our 'eads." Then turning to me, pointing to Grandma, she continues. "Thee grandmother 'as ter sleep 'ere durin' t'week ter look after our Lisa while I go back ter work."

"'Ow come yer don't 'ave any money wi' Brian workin' an' child and family allowances comin' in?" I ask.

"Don't ask me. Ask 'im," she scowls, jerking her thumb in Brian's direction.

"It's just temporary," says Brian weakly.

"Temporary my arse." Then, as she confronts me," Course tha wouldn't know owt abart all this. Shut away in thee nice little bedsitter. Must be nice."

I stay around long enough to let them know that I'm sorry they're having money problems. I don't want to get into an argument, so I'll take my leave. Then, just as I'm leaving, I turn toward Mum. "Yer know it's me twenty-first birthday today, don't yer, Mum?"

A pause, as she takes a drag on her cigarette. "Aye."

Another pause, another drag.

"I ampt ad time ter think abart it."

That's my cue to exit. I head over to Sandra's home. It's raining again. I never did notice the sun today.

---

30    *The Independent.* April 9, 2014.

# Coming Unhinged

Back at George and Marj's, I hunkered down for the run-in to the final exams. I once stayed up all night studying my lecture notes, had breakfast with George when he got up for work, then crashed. As a study plan, that idea failed miserably. An endurance test—perhaps. Except for that ill-fated night, I made the most of whatever time I had available to study. I would often take Jane the dog for a walk around the prefab estate, leash in one hand, lecture notes in the other. My face was consumed with the notes, not the canine. June rolled around and with it, two weeks of final examinations. I decided to take the avant-garde approach and not study at all on the night before each examination. Was I out of my mind or overconfident? Nonetheless, the couch at Sandra's home, not the desk at the library or the table in my bedroom was where I spent my time.

On a fine Saturday morning, I strolled into the zoology department to find out how I had done. In those days, the results were posted on the department notice board for all to see—no such concept as privacy or student numbers. A couple of faculty members whom I encountered along the way gave me the "Well done" greeting. When I saw the result, my name was at the top of the leader board. Myself and another student had obtained a 2.1. Honours degree. There were no firsts that year. I was on my way to postgraduate studies.

I called Aunt Ray to tell her the news. She was overjoyed. I still have the congratulations card that she sent me. She even took me to Coles Brothers to pay for the sitting of my graduation photograph, something I would otherwise have dispensed with. When I told Mum, the response was mildly supportive. She accepted the invitation to attend my graduation ceremony. On Saturday, July 11, the sun was shining as I received my degree on the platform of the City Hall. Sitting together in the audience were an odd collection of my supporters—Aunt Ray, Sandra and her mother, Marj, and Mum. Mum did say to me afterwards that she found it a little strange sitting next to my landlady, but she didn't seem too troubled by it.

At the end of July, I was still waiting for the official news of my scholarship when Sandra told me that we were finished. She wanted to move on to other relationships. We had been inseparable over those three years at university, so I was shocked. Without her, I felt cast adrift. The profound sense of rejection that I felt was amplified by that which I had experienced already at the hands of my parents—a mother who spurned me when I became an inconvenience and a father who just walked away as though I didn't exist. I was unable to see at the time that I had unwittingly and unfairly transferred a lot of that emotional baggage on to Sandra during our years together. It was time now for her to flap her wings.

The marching order I received from Sandra was the straw that broke this camel's back. It triggered my first bout of clinical depression, a malady that would recur to haunt me from time to time. Without any religious inclination in mind, I went to see a priest for solace. I drank heavily, often alone. I saw everything happening around me as inconsequential, not part of whatever existence I was trapped in. Blackness, bleakness, and self-pity dominated my thoughts. *Why did this have to happen? What's wrong with me? Why is everyone else so happy?*

Soon, I began to entertain suicidal thoughts. I have no idea what might have happened had I not one afternoon decided to stroll into the emergency department at the Royal Hospital and announce to the nurse at the desk that I was thinking of killing myself. She looked at me strangely, asked me to sit down. Kept her eye on me until a man in a suit came to see me—the psychiatrist on call. I was admitted to Whitely Wood Psychiatric Clinic. My postgraduate studies were far removed from my mind.

Whitely Wood Clinic proved to be just the refuge that I needed, a shelter from the harsh realities and vicissitudes of the real world. Patients in need of love and attention and healing of the mind formed bonds in such a place, and located in a leafy suburb of Sheffield, with a view of the playing fields of my old grammar school High Storrs, it was ideally situated

318 | ROGER GORDON

for rest and recuperation. For two weeks, I was on a recovery path, content with where I was, not anxious to re-enter the real world. There was a soothing sensation about the uncomplicated routine of making my bed, looking at the roster to see whether I was posted to clean dishes or polish furniture, eating meals at prescribed times, and lining up for my meds. There was a friendly atmosphere within the place as patients participated in organized activities—bingo, animal, vegetable or mineral guessing games, charades. Once trust had been earned, patients in small groups were allowed walks in Whiteley Woods. I had started to see the sunshine even when it may have been raining. I started to see myself; my future.

Then, more drama. I developed a fever and a body rash. Confined to bed and segregated from the other patients, I was diagnosed as having measles. This seemed strange because as a child, I had already had measles—an illness that ordinarily does not recur. Despite heavy doses of antibiotics, my condition worsened, I was transferred to the isolation unit at Lodge Moor Hospital, where I became semi-comatose. Eventually, my mother, who had not allowed my illness to interfere with her caravan-touring holiday, came to see me and on seeing my condition, tracked down the doctors, who in her opinion didn't seem to know what they were doing. Dr. Sneddon, a specialist in dermatology and allergic diseases at the Royal Infirmary Hospital, was called in. He immediately ordered the antibiotic treatment to stop, insisted that I had never had measles in the first place, and arranged for my transfer to the Infirmary where I was treated for a severe drug reaction to one or other of the medications I had been prescribed.

I spent six more weeks at the Infirmary. My face puffed up so that at one stage, I could barely open my eyes. My entire body was covered in red spots and yellow pustules, my hair fell out, all of it in all places, I lost my finger and toe nails, and each day, I sloughed off another layer of skin. "Exfoliation," exuded Dr. Sneddon to the cadre of interns on their daily rounds. I once was wheeled over to a lecture theatre in the hospital as Exhibit A for the medical students to feast on. One of my High Storrs classmates was among the students. Eventually, I was re-transferred back again to Whitely Wood Clinic, where I was introduced to daily portions of a chalky, gag reflex-inducing beverage known as Complan®. I had lost weight and in those days, this was deemed to be a medical problem, not a virtue. Just before I was due to be discharged, I was called into a room where the Director of the Clinic, Dr. Stengel, and his staff were present. I was asked repeatedly if I had any intention of pursuing my mis-diagnosis and the drug reaction that I had contracted while in the care of the clinic. In the sixties, lawsuits against practitioners had not been invented so I was not sure what he was talking about. I just said that I wanted to forget about the whole business and get on with my life. I am left wondering whether I would have been discharged had I given a less mollifying answer.

# PLODDING ALONG

In the Autumn of 1964, militancy was the order of the day, moderation at a premium. The U.S. President, Lyndon B. Johnson, had ratcheted up the stakes in the Vietnam war by sending more troops into the region, while his more right-wing Republican opponent in the upcoming presidential election, Barry Goldwater, was running under the maxim that "extremism in the defence of liberty is no vice." The Civil Rights Act had become law, but that did not stop the white supremacist movement in Mississippi from murdering three civil rights workers, nor did it prevent race riots from breaking out in the streets of cities across the U.S.

The British justice system had exacted good Old Testament vengeance for one last time, taking two sets of teeth and eyes by hanging Gwynne Evans and Peter Allen for killing a van driver. The general election in Britain got underway in September. Aristocratic and aloof Sir Alec Douglas-Home had his hands full keeping at bay the opposition Labour party, led by the pragmatic, often witty, Harold Wilson. Sir Alec, the incumbent P.M., did his party no good at all when he remarked that he used matchsticks to understand economic problems.

Quintin Hogg, the Minister of Science and Education, added to the Tories' woes by suggesting that people who vote Labour are "stark, staring bonkers." Bonkers or not, the electorate gave Labour a slim majority of four seats and sent Sir Alec packing. Even my favourite football team, Sheffield Wednesday, had become restless over the summer and for the first time in its history, changed its team shirts from blue and white striped to all-blue ones with white sleeves. Had the world gone mad?

As I re-entered this volatile and inhospitable real world after my two months' "time out" in hospital, I was ready to embrace the second line from John Howard Payne's poem that declares "be it ever so humble there's no place like home." However, unlike the protagonist in that piece I was not seeking refuge from pleasures or palaces. My mother was not there for me when I was in a critical state, but she did resurface from her vacationing and provide support during my recovery. Once again, our on-again off-again relationship was on. Our relationship in my undergraduate years was like a pendulum swinging between closed door and luke warm "welcome back" positions. Perhaps she viewed me as the prodigal son and herself as the forgiving parent. She never would have considered herself to be part of the problem. In any event, with my postgraduate scholarship, I could afford to pay my board, so I didn't foresee any real problems. I was more or less right.

For the first and final years of what would prove to be a

four-year Ph.D. program, I stayed at home with few domestic incidents of real consequence. The middle two years I spent living away from the King residence with friends or in bedsitters. For much of those two middle years, I was sharing rooming houses near the university with Adders and Alg, two of my band pals from my undergraduate days. We even managed to get a new jazz ensemble together and played around the clubs and pubs. The camaraderie within the band and at the residences we occupied was just what I needed and I was generally content. However, toward the end of my third year of study, we all went our different ways and I succumbed to the loneliness and inhospitality of progressively squalid bedsitters. After another mental breakdown, I returned home for the final year of my program.

~~~

It was some time early on during my first year at home when I began to gain insight into my mother's volatile temperament. One night in particular, I was awoken in bed in the early hours of the morning by shouting coming from downstairs. I could hear struggling. Brian was yelling something undecipherable at Mum, who in turn was squealing, "Don't 'it me." I jumped out of bed, ran downstairs, to find an out of breath Brian towering over Mum, who was sitting on the sofa, hand over her eyes, looking down and sobbing.

"What's going on? 'Ave yer been 'ittin' Mum?" I ask.

"No. Nothing like that. Everything's under control," says Brian disingenuously.

"That's a lie. Yer 'ave so," mutters Mum.

"Better not do," I say as I stalk back to bed, not sure of how I would back up the implied threat.

Something definitely happened, a serious altercation with a physical confrontation at some level. But Mum's demeanour was quite different from the good old days when she would have hurled crockery around and thrown cutlery at Dad. Brian was no pushover. He stood his ground and then some, leaving Mum in an uncharacteristic state of submission. It must have been frustrating for her to have nowhere to channel her pent-up emotions.

Financial issues were somewhere in the mix, either as the source of the stress or as compounding factors. I never did understand why two wage earners with respectable working class incomes should have encountered financial distress. Then again, I was given no information. Lurking in the background was someone who was never discussed—Brian's legal wife. Inexplicably, she and he never divorced. At a time when common-law, live-in relationships hadn't been invented, Brian and my mother were in-the-closet groundbreakers. When Brian left his wife to move in with Mum, we were told that an amicable settlement had been made. It was a done deal, as far as I knew. Years later when Brian died, his wife re-surfaced to claim possession of the home that Mum and Lisa were living in. Of course Brian's wife had a continuing interest in his money. She was probably receiving alimony all along. Hence, the financial pressure, the hair trigger that set off Mum's adrenaline overload.

But, in the final analysis, it boiled down to an innate propensity to react to stress or even situations of disagreement in ways that went beyond the pale. The angry tirades against Dad, her offspring, now Brian. The hurtful way in which I was made to feel like an unwanted interloper in her life, blood not being thicker than water. The frightening manner in which she was able to suddenly and often permanently, transform into ice her feelings toward those she had loved. Money problems or indeed, any other combination of issues, cannot explain such behaviour. Other than knowing from later experience that my mother bore a proclivity to suffer from clinical depression, I shall never know the root causes of her behaviour.

My first year of Ph.D. studies set the pattern for the years that followed. It was an unsatisfying academic experience, one in which I scraped by in fits and starts and by the thinnest of margins. My supervisor, Dr. Eric Francis, was approaching retirement and not fully engaged in research. He retired midway through my studies. He taught parasitology, my area of specialty, and was one of the nicest individuals I have encountered. He always meant well, met my frustrations with even-tempered understanding, and offered advice to the best of his abilities. The main problem was that he was low on the departmental pecking order, so was unable to procure much in the way of resources from the Department Head, the guardian of the department's budget, to enable me to develop a worthwhile research project. I was forced to grovel for desk and lab bench space and for every chemical and bit of glassware that I needed to carry out my research. The nature of my research project was determined solely by financial constraints.

Prior to being admitted to hospital, I was given the impression that I could carry out research on parasites of trout that roamed freely in the Ladybower reservoir, the main water supply for the city. This had an appealing ring to it. When I returned to the department after my sojourn in hospital, Dr. Francis broke the news to me that he had been unable to procure the money from our tight-fisted Head for me to study trout. Insects were much cheaper. I should go out into the countryside and collect insects and find out if they had any parasites in them. I was not impressed. To make matters worse, I was not given a problem to consider. The approach was a shotgun one. Find a bunch of insects, tear them to pieces to see what is in them, and then figure out whether there are any questions to be answered. I rooted around in some of the city parks and woodlands, visited a mushroom farm in the Derbyshire countryside, and took a long bus ride to a field on the outskirts of the city. The grass in that field had on one occasion been used as food for our department's locust colony, which promptly became infected with deadly parasitic worms. Alas, everything I collected, whether insect, vegetation or plain old dirt was clean as a whisker.

I was floundering around without a goal in mind. Then, one of the other students told me that the animal housing facility in the basement of the building where I did my research was infested with cockroaches. Tough and disgusting domestic cockroaches. Shiny, black, almond-sized free-roamers that are repulsive in so many ways—thick exoskeletons that make a crunching sound when stepped upon, six long spiny legs that prickle the skin of the person they crawl upon, swivelling triangular-shaped heads with prominent black eyes that take everything in, and two tendril-like antennae that are constantly in motion sweeping the entire landscape. They are creatures of the night that scuttle away from light at high speed, seeking refuge in dark crevices in walls, behind kitchen cupboards and appliances, inside floor drains and sewer pipes... places where normal people would never go. Like mice, roaches emit an unpleasant, musty odour and their droppings follow them wherever they go. Yes, I had descended a long way from the trout in the local reservoir, moved several steps further down the ladder from the grubby but otherwise copacetic ambience of natural habitats—but I didn't exactly have too many other options.

So, the nightly safaris began. After several beers at one of the local pubs, my mates and I would trek across to the animal house, switch on the light, and then race around between the rows of animal cages scooping up as many roaches as we could from the floor into screw top jars. The little beggars scampered and darted in all directions as they headed for safety. Scooping up the roaches into the jars was not a foolproof exercise. The occasional one would escape custody and scurry up the arm of the handler, free to roam around at will inside his clothing. If the person, usually me, were quick enough, clamping the upper sleeve would prevent the beast from reaching the torso, but they moved like lightning and on numerous occasions I had to remove my shirt. When we remembered to do so, we removed our jackets and rolled up our sleeves before entering the arena—much like preparing for a gym work out. The beers that preceded the hunt added to all this frivolity. Unsurprisingly, given the unsavoury habitat of these hexapods, they were infected with parasites. Pinworms. Worms like infants sometimes get that live in the lower digestive tract. When people asked me what my project was and I told them that I studied parasites that lived in the arses of cockroaches, I got some very strange looks.

Eventually, the animal house supply diminished because they brought in the pest control people. Then, a technician in the department told me that a neighbour of his had reported seeing cockroaches in his home. So, since I could hardly carry out nightly, after-hours safaris on the man's home, I decided to use a cockroach trap.

Trap in hand, with Arthur the technician at my side, I knock on the door, afraid that the man might not appreciate hearing from us that his home was infested with roaches. "Albert, this man would like to catch some er them cockroaches yer've got in t' house," says Arthur

Albert scratches his head, clearly puzzled. Then, the penny drops. "Oooh. Tha means t'blackclocks?" I had forgotten that colloquial name for roaches in northern England.

"I've got some reight big uns. Tha can 'ave all tha wants," says Albert. He seems proud of his guests.

Afraid that my natural supplies might be drying up, I started my own roach colony in a big oil drum that I kept under my lab bench. Several of us would amuse ourselves by feeding the critters to a clutch of chickens that one of the students was maintaining. They devoured whatever we supplied with gusto, pecking with amazing accuracy at the roaches as they scurried around frantically within the cage. But, accidents do happen and escapees took up residence in the laboratory. One day, one of the students pulled away a fridge from the wall and a cascade of cockroaches disseminated in all directions. Toward the end of my program, I noticed that some of these fugitives had acquired the ability to fly—a skill which they did not possess when confined to the oil drum. Super cockroaches, they had made the transition from captivity to freewheeling, wild-type living. Research Laboratory 1, as my work place was innocuously entitled, had its own feral colony of the Yorkshire black-clock. Like Kilroy,[31] I had left a memento to denote that I had been there.

As I looked around the lab, I noticed that many of the students were carrying out research that had a more upbeat ring to it than worms up the backsides of cockroaches. Chickens, rabbits, eels, and guinea pigs were being scrutinized with regard to their endocrine systems and molecular biology. Even Dr. Francis' other Ph.D. student was investigating parasites of the laboratory rat, a little closer to human kind than the lowly cockroach. Before my first year of postgrad studies had concluded, I began to question the whole raison d'être of my mission and tried to switch to a medical degree program. I made the mistake of letting Mum know about my plans. She was unsympathetic.

I sit in the back seat of Brian's VW, the second-hand one that he eventually managed to buy to replace the one that had been repossessed. Mum is sitting in the front passenger seat next to Brian, who is driving. We are out for a Sunday drive. Still at this point staying at home, I've invited myself along so that I can break the news to Mum about my proposed change of scholarly intentions. Perhaps something good can transpire from a conversation.

"Mum, I'm thinkin er packing in me Ph.D. studies. They're goin' nowhere. I'm goin' ter see if I can get in ter medical school."

"Bloody 'ell. When are tha goin' to get a job? Spendin' all thee time loafin' around at university. Bloody ridiculous. Don't expect to be sponging anymoore off me. That's all."

"I never expected a reaction like that," I say. Then, unexpectedly, Brian snaps from behind the driving wheel,

"Why the hell did you have to upset your Mum bringing stuff like that up? Just shut up and keep it to yourself."

So much for useful feedback from the home front. When I approached the medical school and found out that if I were to make the switch, I would get no academic credit for my previous years of university study and, more to the point, that I would not qualify for further scholarship support, I decided to throw my lot in with the cockroaches. I reared them, dissected them, infected and injected them, anaesthetized them, even operated on them. I performed brain surgery on those little beasts. I asked questions about the wormy parasites in their hindguts and got some answers. I wrote a thesis, published a scientific paper in an international scientific journal, one of several that I wrote about them. My research was certainly original, but it did not expand the boundaries of scientific knowledge in a memorable way. I did what I had to do to get by.

---

31   The phrase "Kilroy was here" was popular during WW 2. It was used as graffiti in public places to denote an air of mystery—who was here, why, and where might he go next? The origin of the phrase is obscure, but there probably never was a real person called "Kilroy."

# HEARTBREAKS

The nervous breakdown that I suffered at the end of my undergraduate program, along with the physical trauma that accompanied my severe drug allergy, left me emotionally fragile. Against the advice of my friends and with the strong disapproval of my mother, I made a brief but ultimately unsuccessful attempt to re-ignite my relationship with Sandra. When Mum came home one day to find Sandra with me at our home, she pointedly ignored her, then remarked afterwards, "I see tha't wi' that bloody lass who an't got time for thee when tha were sick. Don't bring 'er to this 'ouse any moore." Mum forgot to mention that when I was seriously ill, she herself was "awol," cavorting around the country in a rented caravan with Brian and Lisa. But, in the end, when Sandra told me for the second time that she wanted to broaden her horizons, I realized that she and I were just not meant to be. This time, I was more sanguine about the break-up, though still upset.

For much of my postgraduate years, my social life was on the shallow side of balanced. I spent more than my share of nights drinking with friends, pub-crawling in the city centre.

Whenever opportunity knocked, we would pick up girls. On Saturday nights, I would go to a dance, a university "hop," on the prowl. An endless succession of one-night stands and short but sweet encounters, a fruitless quest to stumble into what was then referred to as a "meaningful relationship."

In any event, I thought I had at last struck gold when midway through my Ph.D. program, in the spring of 1967, I met an attractive, blond-haired undergraduate in the final year of her B.Sc. zoology program. Brenda was in many ways everything that I was not. Self assured, she was an active and respected member of the Student Council. She was so highly motivated and principled that she had applied to the Voluntary Services Overseas organization to carry out a teaching assignment in a third-world country once she graduated. She was sophisticated, she spoke with a soft, south of England accent and she took ballet-dancing classes. She did not smoke, and drank tastefully, in moderation. Quite a contrast from the socially awkward, aimless young man that I had become. A chain smoker, binge drinker with a thick Sheffield accent, to whom the word "culture" meant something growing on an agar plate and whose extracurricular activities included one-night stands, watching Sheffield Wednesday play, and listening to or playing jazz in one of the local pubs. The cliché that opposites attract held true and in the couple of months that we were an item, there was a bond between us that ran deeper than the physical side of things. In truth, we never gave much time to the latter.

The Whitsuntide break came along and Brenda left to go on a field trip to a marine biology research station on the Adriatic coastline of Yugoslavia. While she was away, she sent me a post-card letting me know how much she was enjoying the experience. Then, on an overcast day in early May, students from her class started to drift back into the zoology department. But not Brenda. Little by little, the shocking news began to unfold. Brenda had become seriously sick. She had collapsed and been taken off the train home in Munich. As far as could be determined, she was in hospital suffering from meningitis. I went to speak to Bill Griffiths, President of the Student's Union. Bill knew Brenda well due to her involvement in the student council. That same day, I was on a plane to Munich courtesy of the Student's Union. I had to see Brenda.

When I tracked her down at the hospital, I saw her hooked up to an artificial respirator. She was in a coma. Her mum and dad, whom I had not met before, were there. After a few days, Brenda's sister Anne, a university classmate of mine, joined us. Staying in a hostel near to the hospital, the four of us kept one another's spirits alive when there wasn't very much else around us to feel good about. Brenda's specialist, Dr. Reinmann, told us that her chances of recovery were not good and lessened as each day passed that she was comatose. One evening, as we were strolling in the vicinity of the hostel, Dr. Reinmann pulled up to us in his car, wound down the window, asked us to climb aboard. We all knew what he was about to tell us. Brenda had died. The four of us flew back to resume whatever lives we had left behind. Brenda was in the cargo hold. I was devastated.

My dramatic flight to the bedside of my terminally ill girlfriend was on the front page of the local newspaper, the *Sheffield Star*. Eileen Archer, Sandra's mum, saw it and true to form, bless her heart, she called me to see how I was doing.

"You know Sandra has taken a job in London? Well, I am taking the train to spend a day with her next week. Might do you good to come along for a trip, a day out for you?"

I gladly accepted Eileen's invitation and grasping at straws, entertained the notion of re-kindling the spark that once burned for Sandra and me.

Eileen and I spent an afternoon in London with Sandra, who proudly displayed to us her knowledge of the subway rail system. We all trooped back to her bed-sitter and munched on strawberries and cream. Then, at Charing Cross Station, when it was time to leave, I asked Sandra if she'd like to see me in another week's time. "A friend of a friend is holding a party somewhere in London," I said. That looked like a hollow come-on, but it was true. Predictably, Sandra declined, and then went on to ask me about Brenda and my feelings for her. It was a lovely afternoon. Why did I have to mar it with that shabby pick-up line that had desperation written all over it?

I barely had time to recover from the tragedy of losing Brenda before another person who was dear to me died. At that time, I was ensconced in a bed-sitter close to the university. I was in the habit of dropping up to Herdings View for Sunday dinner. I found it soothing to maintain some semblance of a normal family carry-on even though it did not fit that description. On a crisp December afternoon, Mum was at the door, anticipating my arrival. She had bad news for me. Aunt Ray had died the previous day at the ripe old age of fifty-eight. An asthmatic for as long as I can remember, she had an attack and they were unable to arrive in time with the oxygen cylinder to save her.

I am in Davy's cafe, Aunt Ray's favourite spot. It is the reception after her funeral. I approach my Uncle George, someone whom we had been taught from an early age to shun. I tell him how sorry I am, how much I cared for Aunt Ray. We look at each other with misty eyes, shake hands. In the car on the way back, Mum says thoughtfully, "Our Ray would be so pleased ter see everyone makin' up wi' George." I know what she says is true, but there seems an irony to the fact that my brother and I had no say at the outset in putting Uncle George in no man's land. Aunt Ray was my favourite aunt. She was cut from the same cloth as Granddad Bonsall— understanding, even-tempered, always ready to please, a peacemaker. Quite the opposite of my Aunt Bud and my mother. When Aunt Ray followed my Granddad into the Promised

Land, there was nobody left to hold the family together. So, it fragmented, one piece at a time. What began as the break-up of my parents' marriage evolved into a crumbling of the family at large.

# NERVOUS BREAKDOWNS

During those postgraduate years, my health was in a state of turbulence. The drug reaction that I experienced at the end of my undergraduate studies as collateral damage to my depression triggered a wider sensitivity within my body to a whole swath of medications. As a result of this, I spent almost a week at Lodgemoor Hospital under observation, after I broke out in a rash following one of my nightly roach collection forays. The animal house had been sprayed with a chemical insecticide and I was evidently allergic to it. On another occasion, I experienced vomiting and a fever after taking a sleeping medication prescribed by my doctor. Since no beds were available at the hospitals around town, I was shipped off to a university hall of residence where I spent an entire weekend in bed with no visitors, other than a doctor who dropped by for a single two-minute check up. The residence hall was empty because it was a term break and all the students had gone home.

Perhaps of greater concern than the physical maladies to which I had become prone was the reality that the depression itself did not prove to be a "one off" occurrence. In the spring of 1968, toward the end of the third year of my studies, living alone in a rooming house near the university, my band friends scattered to the winds, my anxiety level became so high that I required hospitalization. Whitely Wood Clinic, where I had been previously accommodated, was full at the time, so I was advised by one of the university's GPs to report to Middlewood Hospital, a place with a dreaded reputation around the city. Known as the lunatic asylum, its fortress-like complex of Victorian-era brick buildings looked more like a prison than a hospital. Patients were known to have entered Middlewood and never come out again. I did not want to go to Middlewood, but I thought that if I went there for a few days, a place might open up at Whitely Wood Clinic. It didn't take me long after entering the ward to which I was assigned to realize that I was about to be incarcerated, not healed. A cavernous, rectangular shaped room containing three long rows of beds, all neatly made like one might find in a military camp. I was shown to my bed, but immediately told that I must not sit on it.

"No sittin' on t'beds allowed," growled the male orderly, who was decked out in his white tunic and slacks. "Ey you, gerroff that bed," he barks to someone who has caught his eye resting his arse on that which is forbidden. So, among the beds, bedraggled specimens of humanity drag themselves around, their faces downcast to the floor, killing time. At the end of this dormitory, there is a small room with a few scattered, dilapidated old chairs that were losing stuffing from their cushioning. There is a snooker table in the middle of the room, but nobody is bothering to use it. The daily drill starts at 6 a.m. as the fluorescent overhead lighting is turned on and one of the orderlies screams "Gerrup. Line up for pills." I have not been prescribed any pills because the medics are afraid that I might prove to be allergic to them. So, I am a patient under detention in the most horrible of surroundings without any drugs to numb the senses or heal the neurones. But I still have to get out of bed. Then make it, stand beside it, and have it checked over by the men in white to make sure every crease is in its proper place. "Tha can do a better job er foldin' that top bedsheet. Do it o'er again." *And Good Morning to you, too,* I think.

We sit down at a long wooden table in the corridor for our meals, which are institutional mush—edible, but barely so. Between meals, I join the rest of the inmates and pace the place like a lost soul, smoking one cigarette after another. It isn't long before a longhaired, twenty-something yob starts to bum cigarettes from me. After a few episodes of this, I realize that I am his nicotine meal ticket and refuse to comply. He grabs hold of me by my collar and thrusts me against the wall of the lavatory, lets me know in no uncertain terms that I don't have any choice about this.

One evening as we were waiting to hear the "all clear" to change into our pyjamas, a fight broke out between two of the patients. The offender was the sleazy cigarette cadger.

His victim was a poor bloke in his mid-thirties who was physically challenged, prone to epileptic seizures, not able to defend himself. A crowd gathered round as cadger landed blows to the nose and eyes of his mismatched victim. It was horrible to watch. As I looked at the circle of people gathered around the affray, I noticed to my amazement a couple of white uniforms among them, arms folded.

"Oh, good. We get ter watch a fight," one of them enthuses.

The victim falls to the floor and starts to seize.

"Everybody disperse. We'll take care er this now," says Whitey. *And Florence Nightingale would be proud of you*, I think, as I walk away disgusted.

After a few days of this torturous environment, I had had enough. In the early hours of the morning, unable to sleep, I called one of the orderlies over to my bed and told him I was going to change into my street clothes and say my goodbyes to the place. "'Ang on, I'll be back in a minute," he says. True to his word, he did come back—with a couple of his bouncer buddies. They held me down while he injected me with something that pacified me. Funny how quickly a drug was administered when it suited their purpose. No fear of allergic reactions there. The following morning, I called Brian and told him of the plan I had in mind. I asked to see the psychiatrist who was supposed to be caring for me. It was the one and only time I was to see the guy.

"I'm feelin' much better now. Think I can go 'ome now," I say to him.

"Are you sure?"

"Oh yes. This place has really helped me appreciate what I have out there," I say to him, tongue planted firmly in cheek.

"Well, if you need any further help, don't hesitate to contact us, will you?"

---

Brian arrived in his VW to pick me up. That ordeal was over. Though there was more to come, it never matched the experience I had acquired at the Lunatic Asylum. Brian drove me to the King residence and I stayed there for the last year of my postgraduate studies and for a few months thereafter. I continued to have psychiatric difficulties well into that last year, 1968, and required a further stint at Whitely Wood Clinic. My nerves were completely shot, my anxiety level extraordinarily high. If I went out anywhere, I started to get restless and panicky, feeling the need to rush back home, yes even the King home, to my bedroom, where I would close the door and fling myself face down on the bed.

I turned to religion for a while, hoping to find a spiritual answer to my inner turbulence. However, my expectations of it were unrealistic and I eventually abandoned this particular quest for the magic elixir. It was during one of the church services that I attended that I met Peggy Hutchen, a middle-aged lady who was a practicing Christian. Peggy was a friend of Eileen Archer, Sandra's mother. Sensing that I was not well, Peggy invited me to visit her at her home. She thought that she might be able to help in some way. So, I caught the bus to Rotherham, a city close to Sheffield, where she lived. After we had eaten lunch, I became agitated and spent the afternoon lying down in one of the upstairs bedrooms. I still find this an odd way for me to have conducted myself in the home of someone who was no more than a passing acquaintance.

No doubt Peggy recounted her impressions of my visit to Sandra's mum, because it wasn't long afterwards that Eileen phoned me to ask if I'd be interested in meeting Sandra, who had taken a few days away from her job in London to visit her. On a bright sunny week day afternoon, Sandra dropped by the house to pick me up in her Mini, a car that the company she worked for had made available to her. We drove around the surrounding countryside, strolled around Clumber Park, stopped by a café for an afternoon tea. Then, the agitation began to kick in and remarkable as it must have seemed, I found myself asking her to take me back home. We had been together no more than a couple of hours. Once home, I rushed upstairs and buried myself in the bed. That was the last time I saw Sandra.

I cannot connect my illnesses with the state of progress of my research program at the university. It was during the final year, when my research had gelled and was nearing fruition, that I hit rock bottom mentally—not when I was banging my head against the proverbial brick wall and getting nowhere with my experiments. Neither can I draw any correlation between my bouts of depression and whether or not I was living at home. I became ill while away from home; I continued along the same vein after I returned home. However, it is probably not coincidental that while I was involved in the band and sharing living quarters with friends, I was depression-free. Left alone to ruminate, it was like pulling a switch. I was later to discover that clinical endogenous depression follows the pulling of switches that differ in their character from one occasion to another.

Sad to say, Dad appears innocuously as a footnote to my university years. Except for the couple of times that he and I encountered one another during the months following the marital break-up in 1961, I only saw him on one other occasion. Like the previous two meetings, underneath the street lamp and at the dance hall, the venue was unconventional. It was during the last year of my Ph.D. studies, sometime during 1968—before I had made plans to immigrate to Canada. He had been missing from my life for at least seven years. On a mid-week early afternoon, I had been to see Grandma, just to have a cup of stewed tea with her, mainly to make sure she was all right. I walked to the end of Talbot Place to catch the bus to Manor Top, from where I would either hop on another bus or walk to the King residence at Gleadless.

Out of the blue, a man in a crumpled beige raincoat approached me.

"'Ello, Roger. 'Ow are yer?"

"Dad. 'Ow did yer know I'd be 'ere?" What a stupid question to ask. Of course he had been following me.

"Would yer like to come for a drink wi' me? Come on. 'Op in t'car. We can go for a drink."

Seeing no harm in it, I got into his car. It was a Mini as I recall. He drove to a pub on City Road, just a short distance of a mile or so, bought me a beer, asked me how I was doing, introduced me to a few people he knew in the tavern. Strange that I don't remember much of what we discussed. The conversation must have been unremarkable. Did I inquire what he was doing, how he was doing, where he was doing whatever he was doing? Why did he want to meet me? There did not seem to be a hidden agenda this time. After about an hour, we parted company without making any arrangements to meet again.

All these years later, it gives me comfort to believe that Dad, the missing parent, did follow me around from time to time—his way of showing that deep down, he really cared. Well aware that my alignment with Mum precluded my taking an objective stance, made any relationship between ourselves impossible, he was the Dad who lurked somewhere in the shadows. His Jack-in-the Box appearance at the bus stop was a step of courage for him. Perhaps he was lonely, in all probability not in the best of mental health. And he wanted to see his son.

What disturbs me the most is the way in which I soon forgot about the encounter, discarded Dad like yesterday's leftovers. Focused entirely on what I perceived he had done in rejecting Mum and his sons, I had progressed little in my thinking since Christmas 1960—the night he showed his hand in wanting out. The hostility had gone. I just had no feelings toward Dad and that's the distressing reality.

# PART IV: CANADA
## (1969–2011)

# Catching a Break

Somehow or other, notwithstanding the difficulties that my personal life had experienced, I managed to carry out a sufficiently extensive barrage of gruesome experiments on my cockroaches for me to write up my thesis. When I finished my program, my work on pinworms of roaches did not set any academic institutions on fire and I was unemployed. The department secretary caught me off guard one day when she called me to the phone.

"A professor from Vancouver wants to speak to you," she said. I picked up the receiver.

"My name is Dr. John Webster. I'm in London right now. Talking to Dr. Donald Lee, who is the examiner for your Ph.D. thesis. He tells me you have been doing some interesting work on parasites of cockroaches."

*Interesting work on parasites of cockroaches? Isn't that an oxymoron*, I thought?

"Like to come up to Sheffield to meet you, see if you'd be interested in coming to Simon Fraser University near Vancouver to work with me as a postdoctoral fellow."

I met Dr. Webster, a well-groomed and immaculately

dressed young man, a day later in the Student's Union. We had lunch together and he asked me to consider moving to Simon Fraser University. After all, he explained, if I can untangle some of the mysteries surrounding the relationship between cockroaches and their benign parasites, I can apply my knowledge to lethal parasites of insect pests and enter the area of biological control—controlling populations of harmful insects by using their naturally occurring parasites against them. Wow. I hadn't thought of that angle.

Part of me really didn't want to move out of my comfort zone of Sheffield, strange as it may seem given that it wasn't very comfortable for me at all. Perhaps the paradox was akin to the Stockholm syndrome in the sense that I had developed reliance upon the confines of my surroundings, lacking the self-confidence to leave them. All the way to Canada? Could I manage that? In any event, my options were limited, so, with much trepidation, I took his offer. But, I still had three or four months to kill before I could defend my Ph.D. thesis and complete the necessary immigration formalities. I had to find work to keep body and soul together and pay my board.

I worked in a small manufacturing firm off the bottom of the Moor in downtown Sheffield. My job was to dip threaded bolts by hand one at a time into a bucket of molten plastic then set them aside for the coating to set. One afternoon, I asked for time off work so that I could defend my thesis. I changed from my grubby work overalls into a shirt and tie and reported to the office of Dr. Ken Highnam, an entomologist who had taken over as my supervisor after Dr. Francis retired. Dr. Donald Lee, my external examiner from Oxford University who had also incurred the misfortune to be assigned pinworms of cockroaches for his Ph.D. topic several years earlier, was sitting next to Dr. Highnam. Just the three of us. After the passing around of cigarettes, sharing of a few off-colour jokes, I was asked a few questions about my thesis. The whole session lasted no more than an hour. As I left the room, I asked how I had done.

"We'll have a word with the Vice Chancellor about you. Enjoy yourself tonight," they chortled. That was it. I had my Ph.D. And I did enjoy myself that night. I was almost arrested for being drunk and disorderly, as I paraded around the streets of Sheffield with a drinking buddy of mine. When told of the circumstances, the constable gave me a warning and I think, used good judgement.

Eventually, it was time for me to leave for Canada. I had said my goodbyes to my friends, to my last girlfriend over on the good old sod, a German lady old enough to be my mother, and to my various relatives. When I left for Canada, the wheels had not fallen off the cart and my Aunt Bud, Grandma, Mum and Brian, Trevor, were all on speaking terms with one other. January 7, 1969, was a dull, dreary, day, the monotony broken only by the occasional downpour of sleet and slushy snow. Brian drove Mum, Lisa and myself in the VW over the Snake

Pass to Manchester Airport. I said my goodbyes to them at the departure gate and boarded the plane with twelve shillings and six pence, all my worldly assets, in my pocket.

"I'll be back in a year or two," I said.

But, I wasn't.

# CARDBOARD BOXES

I sit in the basement of my home in Prince Edward Island, Canada, poring through the contents of two cardboard boxes. Nothing special about the boxes themselves. At one time, they would have contained grocery items—boxes of Kraft® dinner, bags of sugar, or tins of baked beans. But, they've travelled along with me wherever I have relocated during the past forty-three years that I have spent in Canada. One box contains records and paraphernalia pertaining to my academic career—certificates, letters of commendation, a twenty-six page resume, long-service lapel badges, and cards of good wishes from colleagues and friends. I call this the Chalk box. The second box is of a different ilk. It contains letters from Mum, Dad, and a few other relatives that I left behind in Sheffield along with court documents, Dad's old diary, and his work records. To savour the pot, there are numerous well-worn photographs of relatives from days gone by. I call this compilation the Cheese box. The two boxes are as different as Chalk and Cheese both in their contents and in the memories that they evoke.

My emigration to Canada marked a fork in the road, where

I was able to a considerable extent put my troubled past behind me, forge a successful academic career, and, most important, nurture a family life with roots that are firmly anchored. I left behind the road that each of my parents and what was left of my mother's family were travelling. It was a road of strife, bitterness, obsessive personality disorders, and misery. I believe that it would not have been possible for me to step outside of the box and take a dispassionate view of the sorry family scene had I remained in Britain. I would have been forced to continue the practice of taking sides, to become a participant as opposed to a sympathetic listener, and, where possible, a helper. Though I am thankful that I took that fork in the road, I am saddened that the vast majority of my family members did not find other forks leading to the same metaphorical destination that fosters a way of thinking beyond one's self. Given the degree to which my family members' attitudes and behaviours had become entrained, it would have been very difficult for them to change within the confining walls of Sheffield, the only city they had really known. It is not the city itself that is the problem, but the limited view on life that goes hand-in-glove with an inability to see the expressions of the larger world outside of it.

First, the Chalk box. There's a collection of emails that were read out to a large number of faculty and staff members at the University of Prince Edward Island who had gathered in June 2008 to honour my retirement as a faculty member and former Dean. Some emails from former associates at Simon Fraser University are precious to me. After a somewhat turbulent settling-in period in which I played the Friday and Saturday night singles scenes while finding nothing worthwhile to say about Canada, I took a firm grip and started to devote myself to my research project on parasites of locusts. Because the parasites I was studying were lethal to the pests, I was able to see a more practical outcome from my endeavours than had been evident to me from my work on cockroaches. That said, it was not the nature of the research that brought about so sudden a change in my attitude; rather, it was attributable to two of the people around me.

I met Alison a few months after arriving in Vancouver. Born in Glasgow, raised in Ontario, Canada, she was the steadying force that I desperately needed. More than that, she became the true love of my life and we married in June 1970, about a year and a half into my postdoctoral term. The second person who was a major influence in my transformation from an unfocused, philandering nine to fiver to a highly motivated, competent scientist was my supervisor, Dr. John Webster. John never once faltered in his belief in my abilities. He laughed off my indiscretions, respected my opinions on research matters, and treated me as a colleague.

During the two and a half years that I spent at Simon Fraser, I carried out the best research of my career, publishing in scientific journals, teaching, speaking at international conferences, and acquiring recognition as a promising young scholar. In the late sixties and early seventies, Vancouver and the lower mainland of British Columbia was an exciting place to be. A highly cosmopolitan city in a spectacularly scenic setting and with a climate that by North American standards was mild, it attracted young immigrants from all parts of the world. Vancouver was to Canada what San Francisco was to the States. A city on the move. The place to be. Alison and I made many life-long friends there and we hated to leave the place. But, my position there was not permanent, so it was a given that we would have to move on.

More emails—these from former colleagues and students at Memorial University of Newfoundland. In August 1971, Alison and I moved to Newfoundland where I had secured a tenure track position as an Assistant Professor of Biology at Memorial University. Living in what was then a pretty desolate spot, a rocky island off the far-flung eastern coast of Canada, was a culture shock and we suffered separation anxiety from the rest of the world. Newfoundlanders even seemed to speak a different form of the English language and communication proved difficult for a while.

I discovered that anywhere on the mainland of Canada qualified as "upalong," while a "b'y'" was a "boy" or "man," and a "girl" was precisely as stated as well as referring to a "woman." The patriarch of any family was "da skipper," a term that had an affectionate ring to it. Because Newfoundland had only been part of the Canadian confederation for little more than twenty years when we moved there, some of the older generation called Alison and I "Canadians," to denote that we were a breed apart.

We adapted to the vernacular as well as to the rustic, rough and ready, weather-ravaged Newfie lifestyle and settled in there for twenty-six years—half a life time. During that time, our two children were born—David in December 1972 and Christine in January 1979. It was not an idyllic family life that the four of us shared. It had its periods of turbulence, times when the challenges seemed to outweigh our blessings. But we confronted and survived them and we are the stronger for it. Our family can now be described as close-knit, complete with grandchildren and in-laws.

My academic career flourished at Memorial as I rose through the ranks to full Professor, achieved high ratings as a teacher, published and spoke extensively on my research topic of parasites of biting flies, and attracted international recognition as a scholar. I was highly regarded by the students and by the faculty at large and served a term as President of the Faculty Association. As in British Columbia, we developed a circle of friends on what is affectionately known as "The Rock." I took up playing the cornet again, this time in a Salvation Army band, as Alison and I became regular churchgoers. I thoroughly enjoyed the wilderness ambience being so close at hand and developed a keen interest in fly-fishing, a sport that

I mastered reasonably well. Later on, I tried my hand at golf, though my performance at this endeavour had a less promising outcome. The long, harsh winters aside, life in Newfie was complete in most respects.

Toward the end of my time at Memorial, I became disenchanted with the politics of the place. I sought a change from the daily routine of my office and laboratory and wanted to make a contribution as an administrator. The reality was that my persona did not fit in with Memorial's top down, toe the line, chain of command philosophy. Subconsciously, I may have wanted to prove that a working-class kid from a dysfunctional family setting was just as good as my middle-class counterparts from *Leave it to Beaver* homes. A reaction against my past or a proverbial chip on my shoulder? Whatever the reason, I metamorphosed from an introverted supplicant to an outspoken, "tell it like it is" champion of worthy causes. If I disagreed with a policy decision handed down from on high, I would challenge it—frankly, logically, and forcefully. I was not a "yes man" and this put me out of the running for academic leadership positions in the eyes of the administration. My confidence, self-assurance, and outspokenness had become my worst enemies there.

So, in May 1997, I accepted a position as Dean of Science at the University of Prince Edward Island. For me, it was a dream job, a fitting way to end my university career. I spent nine years helping to build programs and pursue opportunities for a promising group of faculty members, many recently appointed. It was a position that was stressful, often frustrating, but overall highly satisfying. I believe I did make a real difference there. I found it to be infinitely more satisfying to give to others than to pursue self-interested goals. That, of course, is a biblical concept, also a truism whatever one's level of faith may be. The emails from folk at UPEI remind me of the large group of people who came that sunny June afternoon to wish me well on my retirement, and of the genuine affection between us. I feel privileged to have been afforded the opportunity to serve such a stellar group of individuals. The happiest and most satisfying years of my career were spent in the beginning at Simon Fraser and at the end at UPEI.

Now retired on Prince Edward Island, I can look back with satisfaction on a career that has been fulfilling, one that has proceeded in an upward direction.

I feel so fortunate to have my family around me—my wife of over forty years, Alison; my grown-up children, David and Christine; their spouses and children, my grandchildren, living nearby. It has not been all plain sailing. There have been difficult times when our marriage has been on an insecure footing. Yet, through perseverance and commitment, Alison and I have outlasted all such setbacks to insure that our Canadian family does not emulate the rancor and destructiveness that characterized the British one that I left behind. Taking the long-term approach, we have followed the advice of renowned twentieth-century Irish poet and playwright, William B. Yeats,[32] who once opined:

*I think a man and woman should choose each other for life, for the simple reason that a long life with all its accidents is barely enough time for a man and a woman to understand each other and in this case to understand is to love.*

Perseverance, understanding, love—an interconnected trio of qualities that have brought happiness and fulfillment to our marriage and in turn, to our family on this side of the pond.

Also challenging has been the fact that the episodes of depression that I suffered back in my university days have resurfaced from time to time and I have required short periods of hospitalization while in Newfoundland and PEI. I have learned to face these setbacks as one would any recurrent medical condition—a strep throat, sinus infection, or a sore bowel. Something that is hard wired into my genome, as the lives of my parents attest to. Definitely not a personality flaw. I am thankful that those around me, my family and colleagues at my places of work, have seen it the same way. I believe that the supportive environment in which I have found myself since those days has helped me enormously in recovering from my infrequent episodes of depression. They have become an interruption in my life, as opposed to a derailment as was formerly the case.

Attitudes about mental illnesses have changed since the 1960s, when the general public looked upon sufferers with puzzlement, even trepidation. Yet, there is still room for improvement, or what, in a different context, used to be called "consciousness raising" by the Women's Liberation movement during the 1970s. Psychiatric illnesses are still viewed by some, even within the health care sector, as being of lesser consequence than physical ailments. Partly because of this prejudice, ongoing professional care for chronic sufferers is not as readily available as it ought to be—both in Canada and, I am given to understand, in the U.K. This unfortunate attitude often leads to a crisis management approach. Would it be alright to adopt the same approach to other illnesses and ignore the early symptoms until someone suffered a heart attack or kidney failure? I think not.

I put the Chalk box away now.

⌒⌣⌣⌒

Next, the Cheese box. While I was making a career and a home life for myself beyond the fray, what was happening on the home front back in Sheffield? This large pile of letters from Dad tells a pretty amazing story. The same Dad who flew the coop while I was still in Grammar School and who was an absent figure from my life for the entire seven-year period that I spent at university—save for two or three spooky, head-scratching appearances on city pavements, under gas lamps, and on street corners. In the first two letters, he scolds me for only visiting my brother Trevor once while Alison and I visited

Sheffield during Christmas 1970. I have vivid recollections of that visit, the first one since my move to Canada and the first one for Alison and me as husband and wife.

We spent New Year, Hogmanay, in Edinburgh visiting Alison's relatives, but the rest of the time we stayed with Mum, Brian, and Lisa. Our time in Scotland was delightful. It was so refreshing to be within a harmonious family setting.

The scene that awaited us as we arrived at the King residence was quite different from the one we had left behind in Scotland. Various members of the family were still on speaking terms with one another, though in most cases relations were strained. Alison and I visited Trevor and his wife. They were living in an old terraced house in a run down area of Sheffield. Trevor was suffering from hepatitis. Dad was right; we only made the one visit. The form of hepatitis that Trevor had was highly infectious and I chose not to make a return visit for fear of contracting the disease, placing my research position in jeopardy, or transmitting the disease to Alison. But, Dad was also right in his observation that I acted out of self-interest. I regret the decision I made. It was not one of the prouder moments of my life. My relationship with my brother, which was never a close one, became more distant, both geographically and metaphorically, after my move to Canada and we did not maintain contact with one another on an ongoing basis. As to whether it was appropriate for Dad, the pop-up figure, to have sent those letters, that's a different story.

It was not long after that visit that Mum severed her ties with Trevor permanently. The situation went from bad to worse for Mum and the Bonsall clan. Another rift in this fractious family opened and was never healed. Following a heated argument, Mum and Aunt Bud never spoke to one another again. Aunt Bud never visited Grandma again, but attended Grandma's funeral, which occurred six or seven years after the spat. She visited a corpse after the flesh and blood version had been left day after day, year after year, to spend her golden years in loneliness in that big, musty, old home on Talbot Place. To give credit where it is due, Mum continued to visit her mother and attend to her needs as best she could.

In March 1975, I received a phone call from Mum to tell me that Brian had died suddenly of a heart attack, leaving Mum to raise Lisa, who was then a pre-teen.

~~~~~~

In April 1976, I made my second visit back to the old sod. I gave a paper at a scientific conference in Swansea, Wales. Alison and three-year-old David came along for a holiday. After sunning it on the beach in Swansea, a welcome respite from the sleet and snow in Newfoundland, we drove up to Sheffield to stay with Mum and Lisa. We were thrust into a situation in which Mum was not on speaking terms with Trevor or Aunt Bud, and certainly not with Dad. Aunt Bud had severed ties with Mum and Grandma, but, we later discovered, had laid out a welcome mat for Dad. Trevor, from what we had heard, was on a friendly basis with Aunt Bud and Dad, while placing Mum and Grandma on his list of adversaries. It was a complicated mess. I decided to play it safe and not fraternize with those on Mum's blacklist, even though I had not formally cut off ties with any of them. Besides, Mum confronted me with a new problem soon after the three of us had walked through the door. Brian had died without having made out a will and his legally recognized wife, whom he never divorced, was in the process of exercising her lawful rights to take possession of the home, Herdings View, in which Mum and Lisa were living. I felt an obligation to help Mum and Lisa out of their predicament. After speaking with Mum's lawyer, it became clear that Brian's wife was on firm legal grounds and that the finale of this drama, had it played out, would have been for Mum and Lisa to be thrown out of their home. I agreed to an out-of-court settlement in which I provided financial assistance to Mum to help meet a payment that was acceptable to Brian's wife in lieu of the house.

While Mum's domestic situation left a lot to be desired, I was heartened to see that her employment was more in keeping with her capabilities. No longer toiling on a factory floor, she had become a fully trained bloodsucker, a phlebotomist, at the Northern General Hospital. Prior to this, in her early fifties, she had attempted to train as a registered nurse. Whether she would have had the bedside manner for that is immaterial. She transferred into a program that was not as heavily dependent on people skills and embodied outcomes that were as straightforward as "roll up your sleeves, let me feel your veins, and won't hurt a bit." Just the job for Mum.

It was during this second visit that I finally decided to make peace with Dad, paradoxically at about the same time that Trevor's relationship with him was nearing its end. On a cloudy morning on April 17, my birthday, I left Alison to wait alone in the rental car in the car park of a block of flats in Gleadless Valley, a neighbourhood that borders the city centre and is not far from Talbot Place where I spent my early childhood. I was not sure what kind of a reception I would get. After trekking up four flights of stairs in the concrete stairwell, I knocked on the door of a unit where, from the addresses on the letters of chastisement he had sent me several years ago, I thought he might be living. A weak voice from the other side of the door answers. "Who is this?"

"It's Roger. From Canada. Your son."

The door opens. It's Dad all right. A bit grey around the temples, a chin with stubble that hadn't yet seen a razor that day, more wrinkles on a worried face, scraggily dressed, he looks like he has seen better days. Then, comes the outstretched hand and I give it a shake.

Inside the flat, we talk, but there's not a lot of warmth between or around us. That's fine because it would have been unreasonable to expect more. Once I realize that there is not going to be an ugly scene, I fetch Alison up to the flat, we talk some more, and I leave behind a photo of David. It would not have been possible to bring David to meet Dad while we stayed at Mum's place because the risk of the little guy letting the cat of the bag and Mum finding out that we had been to see him was too great. So, on the last day of our trip, after bidding Mum and Lisa farewell, the three of us visited Dad in his flat.

During my two visits with him, Dad spent a lot of time talking about his mother, my other Grandma. Dad told me that he was fearful that she was not being well looked after and had been mistreated by her husband, Dad's stepfather, Arnold Lawson. I later discovered that during the preceding year, Dad had been in court on two occasions and at the time of our visit, was serving a suspended sentence for an assault on Mr. Lawson. The official court record describes a scene at the home of Mr. Lawson and my other Grandma in which Dad accused Mr. Lawson of abuse, yelling, "I'll kill you." What happened next is not clear. Mr. Lawson picked up a chair, allegedly to defend himself. Somehow or other he wound up on the floor with a broken rib. While awaiting trial, Dad spent sixteen days in Armley Prison in Leeds. This was only two months prior to our visit, so no wonder he looked haggard.

Less than a month after we had returned to Newfoundland, on May 11, 1976, Dad was arrested again following the most bizarre of incidents. It had come to the knowledge of the police that Dad had constructed a piece of electrical gadgetry that had the potential to cause an explosion. He was threatening to use it maliciously against Mr. Lawson, though he claimed that this was only a cry for help and that he never seriously intended to use it. He was sentenced to three years, eight months hard time in Armley Prison. I kept in touch with him and his probation officer during his incarceration. He was paroled in October 1977 after serving one and a half years. He called me the day after he was freed. He needed a friend and I was the best he had. The flames had gone out on his re-kindled relationship with Trevor—irreconcilable differences. What can I say? Visiting my family in Sheffield became like treading through a minefield.

From the paper trail left behind in the Cheese box, I see that Dad drifted around in a couple of seedy lodging houses after his discharge from prison before eventually finding a council flat in the Norfolk Park estate, a ten-minute walk from Talbot Place where the four of us once lived as a family. He visited his mother, who by then was in a nursing home, every day and he continued to maintain that he had been wrongly convicted of his crime, that he never meant to hurt Mr. Lawson, that Mr. Lawson perjured himself in court, and that his mother had suffered at the hands of the nasty fellow. This is the same other Granddad who had shown kindness to me when I visited his home as a child and whose demeanour appeared to be easy going. When the physical altercation with Dad occurred, Mr. Lawson was a feeble man in his mid-seventies, Dad twenty

368 | ROGER GORDON

years his junior. It's obvious where the sympathies of the court would have laid. Dad's preoccupation with his mother's health came to an end only two months after his release from jail as other Grandma died on December 29, 1977. In recent years, I have come to regret that I did not take the opportunity to visit her as part of my reconciliation initiative with Dad during my 1976 visit. Dad offered to take me to see her and I declined. How could I have done so?

During the winter of 1979, I received a phone call from Mum telling me that Grandma Bonsall had died—alone in her home, discovered when the milkman noticed the bottles piling up at the door. The sad and sordid details of the aftermath of her death are recounted by Mum in one of her letters to me in that Cheese box. The family rift was not buried along with Grandma. As the rag tag bunch of family mourners gathered around the casket in the front room of Talbot Place, Mum and the cleaning lady, Mrs. Paynter, who Granddad 'used to call "Paint Pot," stood apart from Aunt Bud and Uncle Johnny. Mum declined the offer to accompany her sworn enemies, her relatives, and follow the hearse to the City Road cemetery in the funeral car. She and "Paint Pot" went on the bus. My Grandma was buried alongside my Granddad, but it was not possible for the hatchets to be buried as well.

During the summer of 1980, I made my third visit to the UK, this time alone. Again, I combined scholarly and family endeavours as I attended a scientific conference in Cambridge, where I presented a paper describing some of my research. I drove the rental car from Heathrow to the Northern General Hospital in Sheffield to give Mum a ride home from work. She climbed into the car and proceeded to tell me on the way to Herdings View about the new man in her life, a Polish bloke called Gus. Five years had passed since Brian's death, so this in itself was not a problem for me. But, she showed little or no interest in what any of us were doing over in Newfoundland. It was all about her. She sounded like a fifty-seven-year-old teenager. When we got back to the house, I told Mum that Alison and I had started to go to church, thinking this would be viewed as a positive or, at worst, neutral development.

I am standing in the living room, suitcase on the floor, not yet moved up to the bedroom that I had been assigned.

"Goin ter t'church are tha? I've no time for t'church. I went ter one a while back. Nobody bothered ter even speak ter me. Call thersens Christians? Bloody bunch er 'ypocrites if tha asks me." Which I hadn't.

"Sorry you had that experience. Sometimes people just don't realize. I wondered if you'd like to come along with me one Sunday while I'm here."

"And that I won't," she growls. "An' if tha't goin ter go on abart t'church tha can not bother unpackin thee bags. Tha might as well move on thee way. That's all."

*How can "I have started to go to church" degenerate into an eviction notice and a "That's all," I wonder?*

"I can read thee like a book. Tha's said nowt all t'way back in t'car abart Gus. Lookin down thee nose at me again are tha?"

With this piece of irrelevancy and nonsense having been thrown in, I decide against continued rhetoric. I trundle upstairs, suitcase in hand, and sit down on the bed in the tiny spare bedroom. It's the old rejection business all over again, a throwback to my university days. Shall I leave now and abandon any hope of ever being on speaking terms with my mother again? Does she not realize that I had manufactured this trip so that I could see how she was getting on? Can she not see that I have come all the way from Canada to see her? Part of me wants to leave, but I know I'll regret doing it, so eventually I troop downstairs and try to make peace.

"I didn't mean to upset you by telling you I was going to church," I needlessly apologize. "And as for Gus, I haven't met him. He sounds like a decent guy. Can we just keep things on an even keel?" It was really her that needed the even keel, but I didn't mind embracing the "we" in the interests of peacemaking.

"Suppose so," she grunts. "Anyow, Gus is comin' o'er tonight, so tha'll get chance ter meet 'im."

I did meet Gus. Smooth, soft talking Gus. He gave me a cheap tie that he must have bought from Woolworth's as an ice-breaking gift. Gus never said anything disagreeable the entire time I was there. Come to think of it, he never said anything of substance at all. But, he had the personality of a slippery eel. I did not like him and my hunches were proven to be correct. A year or so after that visit, Mum wrote me the most amazing letter. She married Gus, but their marriage was not made in heaven. According to Mum, he underwent a personality transformation. More probably, his real personality came to the forefront. He drank and gambled away most of Mum's savings, leaped out from behind doorways in an attempt to scare her to death, then after being given his walking papers, tried to force Mum to sell the house so he could have his share of it. Then, he started to have an affair with a widow down the street. Yes, good old Mum, she had literally got into bed with a charlatan. To force him off the scene she gave him an out-of-court, lump sum settlement, more than what he had invested in the marriage.

Off to a rip-roaring start in which I was almost thrown out of the home, that trip in 1980 became an exercise in keeping the wheels on the cart. It was the last time that I stayed with Mum. I avoided controversial subjects or disagreeing with her when she sounded forth with one of her opinionated diatribes.

"T'steel workers went on strike for three months. Now t'bloody coal miners are threatenin' ter strike. They want ridiculous wages. Twenty, thirty per cent raises an' moore. Margaret Thatcher won't stand for this. She'll close all t'pits darn an' t'steel works'll be forced ter close. Sheffield'll be a ghost town."

"Shockin' what's 'appenin ter this country. It's not British anymoore. All them Arabs an' Pakistanis comin' in. We're becomin' just like t'Americans. A mongrel race."

I kept my counsel, even took Mum and Gus on rides in the rental car—a trip into Derbyshire and down to Cambridge, where I parted company from them to join the conference. I was relieved when the trip was over and I could leave the confines of that house. It was a throwback to times I had left behind, replete with Saturday morning, out of control cleaning binges and tirades against Lisa, who was now in her late teens.

"Get thee'sen outer bed an' darnstairs. Mornings are for gerrin up. Nights are for sleepin'. That's all."

Poor Lisa came down looking harried, but did not answer back. I know the feeling.

I saw Dad on that trip. He told me all about his experiences in prison, concentrating on how great a miscarriage of justice had been done. He looked worn down and depressed. On the morning I left Herdings View, I told Mum that I had been to see him. I no longer cared if she threw me out. I was going anyway. She told me that it was my decision to have gone to see him, she had nothing but contempt for him, but then she looked at me, a quizzical expression on her face, and told me that she had once undergone hypnosis therapy by a psychiatrist. When the psychiatrist asked her who among the men in her life she really loved, she said it was John Patrick Gordon, my father. That didn't surprise me.

~ ~ ~

It was nine more years before I next visited England—July 1989. This time, all four of us came along. David was fifteen and Christine, nine years old. We split our time between visiting Alison's relatives in Scotland, my bunch in Sheffield, and a proper holiday time together in Torquay. Since my previous visit nine years earlier, I had not maintained contact with my mother. The only letter I had received from her was the one that gave the sordid details of the saga involving Gus. She even found space in that letter to deliver a few blows to me about my judgemental and insensitive attitude during my last visit. I replied to that letter politely, but I had taken enough and decided that she had to assume some ownership of our relationship and take the initiative to maintain contact. Especially troubling to me was the recognition that she had shown precious little interest in David and Christine, her grandchildren. So, the four of us stayed in neutral territory, a farmhouse in the picturesque Cordwell Valley in Derbyshire—a short drive into Sheffield.

Dad received much of our attention this time around. We wandered around the shopping area of downtown Sheffield with him, took him on a day trip to the historic city of York, and visited him at his flat. On the last day that we saw him, he had prepared an afternoon tea complete with canned salmon, Christmas cake, and ice cream. David and Christine were not partial to this very British fare, especially since the Christmas cake was a British version—fruitcake, overlaid with marzipan and icing. But, they gave it a good try and I told them afterwards that I was proud of them. That meal, Dad's treat, meant a lot to him, and our kids were able to see that. We checked in with Aunt Bud. Her husband, Uncle Carl, had died four years previously and she had shut herself away from the world in her flat, mementos of him around her. It was the last time I saw her. She died two years later in April 1991, her hatred of my mother undiminished to the end.

I was having a tough time deciding whether to try to locate Mum. After my last visit and the less than cordial atmosphere that had prevailed since then, all those years of silence, should I leave well enough alone? In the end, I decided to track her down by contacting Lisa, who had given her phone number to my second cousin, Lorna. Lisa was now twenty-seven, a single parent living in a flat in the Gleadless Valley area. I discovered Mum living in a council house on the Base Green estate, a thirty-minute walk away from the home that she once shared with Brian, then Gus, on Herdings View. Predictably, she was living with another man, a gentleman by the name of Ron, though when Mum showed me around her home, she pointed to two upstairs bedrooms and exclaimed, "That one's 'is, this one's mine. And never the twain shall meet. That's the rules I've set."

Mum was now sixty-seven and she might as well have been eighty-seven. Her good looks of former years were gone, she seemed to have become shorter and dumpier, and her grey hair was a lifeless mop. We spent the evening talking about Mum. When I tried to change the subject to myself or to my family, how well we were all doing, she was not much interested.

"Mum, I've now been promoted to a full Professor at the university."

"Hmm." She nods, looking at the floor.

"And David is becoming quite a musician, an accomplished pianist."

"That's nice."

What would the point have been of telling her about Christine's achievements in school or Alison's work helping to run a Home for Battered Women? Pride in her offspring and her offspring's offspring was not her forté. She was totally self-absorbed. We arranged to all go on a family outing to Chatsworth Park. There was quite a gang of us. Alison, David, Christine, and myself in our rental car; Mum, Ron, Lisa, and her little boy, Ben, in the other car. A family divided. We trooped around Chatsworth House with a loose degree of cohesion. Mum stayed within her little family group, we in ours. She paid little attention to her grandchildren from

Canada, one of whom she had not seen for thirteen years, the other she was seeing for the first time. When we arrived back at the farmhouse, Mum never bothered to get out of her car to say goodbye to the kids. I felt disheartened, hurt, and angry at the whole escapade.

"Shall we try an' keep in touch now then?" she asks me.

"Sure," I say. So, she writes down her address on a scrap of paper. I did not try very hard to keep that paper. It soon became lost. I had decided again that it was Mum's turn to try, but as I expected, she never did. That trip to Chatsworth, her last question about keeping in touch, are the last memories I have of her in a cognitively functional state.

Three years after that visit, in December 1992, I received a phone call from my second cousin, Lorna. Dad had suffered a major heart attack and was awaiting open-heart surgery at the Northern General Hospital. I flew over right away, drove up the old A1 from Heathrow, managed somehow or other to get lost, detouring unintentionally en route to Coventry, before rushing to his bedside in the open hospital ward. He was laid out in bed among a tangled array of gadgets, needles, and catheter tubes that were going in and out of his circulatory system. He was expecting me and his face lit up when I arrived. A rare moment that was for Dad, who specialized in worried or impassive countenances. At one point, I walked over to a corner of the ward to ask a doctor about Dad's prognosis. He told me that his chances of survival were forty percent at best. When I walked back to Dad's bedside, he asked me if I had been asking about his chances of recovery. He was not inquisitive about the content of my conversation with the doctor—just pleased that someone cared enough to ask about him. The realization struck me that Dad was unable to show warmth to others because nobody had really shown him how. He was not able to reflect back emotions that he himself had not experienced. So, he had difficulty sustaining relationships and spent a very lonely life. Save for Lorna, who saw him before I arrived, I was his only hospital visitor until the time that he went in for his surgery. I visited him every day for about a week.

On a rainy Saturday morning, I was on my way out of the hospital when I heard the sounds of a Salvation Army band playing Christmas carols in the vestibule. I stood and listened to them. They were playing "It Came Upon a Midnight Clear." A quartet of uniformed Salvationists was singing along with the band.

> *O ye beneath life's crushing load,*
> *Whose forms are bending low,*
> *Who toil along the climbing way*
> *With painful steps and slow;*
> *Look now, for glad and golden hours*
> *Come swiftly on the wing;*

*Oh rest beside the weary road*

*And hear the angels sing.*

The band stopped playing. A uniformed, middle-aged woman, in a voice that was crystal clear, addressed the scattered groups of spectators.

"And everyone here, I want to tell you that though you may right now feel you are beneath a crushing load, you may be bending low and you may indeed be toiling with painful steps, Jesus is here to give you comfort. No matter what your circumstances, however hard, He is your Comforter. May each and every one of you have a very Merry Christmas. God bless you."

I could not contain the tears. She was speaking to Dad up in the ward and to me looking on from the sidelines. The following week, I sought out a Salvation Army chaplain. He prayed by the bedside with Dad and me.

The rain, drizzle, and overcast skies never let up the entire time I was visiting Dad. Football pitches across the city were quagmires, forcing the cancellation of two hundred and fifty fixtures. The city's rivers were dangerously close to overflowing into the streets. Storm drains and their catch basins were overtaxed, roads running in water so pedestrians had to constantly duck the sprays and splashes from passing vehicles. Being inside a building was no shelter from the dampness and the cold, clammy feeling as buildings over there did not have air conditioning, air exchangers, or, in many cases, insulation. Bed sheets and clothing stuck to the skin like the peel around an onion. Everywhere I went people were hacking, coughing, and spitting as the cold and flu viruses had free rein. It was a fitting ambience for the occasion that brought me there.

The news around the city was no better, as it was beset by a spate of muggings, break and entries, and indecent assaults. One schoolteacher lamented that the only pleasures that some of his pupils embrace were "sex and booze." The only light relief from all this despondency was in a couple of news reports. Prince Charles was in town, bringing "winter cheer" by visiting two factories. That must have lifted the workers' spirits. Also, the public toilets in Sheffield's Town Hall were awarded the North East's Loo of the Year after judges toured 1300 entries and carefully deliberated upon their pros and cons. The toilets received a plaque to hang on one of their tiled walls.

On a drizzly Sunday morning, I saw Dad being wheeled from the ward into the operating room. He raised his hand and I squeezed it, wished him good luck, and told him I would be there for him when his operation was over. That evening, I turned up at the hospital to find him still unconscious. The doctor told me that he was being kept in that state because they wanted to give his heart time to recover before exposing him to bothersome stimuli. His vital signs did not improve, but I could stay no longer. My flight home had been booked, the Christmas season was beginning and if I were to linger, I would get caught up in the transatlantic rush. The doctor told me that there was nothing more I could do and that

I had served the most useful role in being with Dad prior to his operation. So, after I had visited and spoken with Trevor, he agreed to set aside his differences and keep an eye on the situation as I headed home. Early the next morning, the phone rang. It was Dad's doctor telling me that he had just died.

~~~

I was told that Dad's funeral in Sheffield was sparsely attended. I held a service of remembrance for him in my home in Canada. A few weeks later, a parcel of some of Dad's paraphernalia arrived in the mail and I stored them in the Cheese box. They tell a story of a deeply troubled and lonely man with obsessive tendencies that surfaced in sometimes ridiculous, often destructive ways. During the early 1970s, a few years after I had moved to Canada, but before I renewed my relationship with him, he sent a letter written on toilet paper to a person whom he claimed owed him thirty-five pounds. He enclosed a baby's dummy[33] with the package. In 1990, only nine months after the four of us came over to the UK and spent quality time with him, he took a woman from Barnsley to small claims court for two hundred and sixty nine pounds, twenty-eight pence. Dad said that he had loaned her the money, while the lady in question claimed it was a gift. According to her version of the story, Dad sought the payment in retribution as he had been loitering around her property and pestering her to go out with him. The fixation that he had about his mother's care (his claim, probably delusional), that his stepfather was mistreating her was consistent with his past history. I am aware that at some point, Dad was committed involuntarily to spend time in a psychiatric institution, though I do not know when this occurred. Dad once told me that he had received lithium, a mood stabilizer used in the treatment of bipolar disorder.

From what I can gather, he left his work with Pyrene in April 1962, a year after his marriage to Mum ended. He worked for a while as a sales representative with a light-manufacturing firm in Doncaster, freelanced as an electrician, then stopped working in his early fifties. Around the time he stopped work he re-married a younger woman, but this did not last long. For the last two decades of his life, Dad spent his days in the reading room of the city library and his nights roaming around the dance halls. He was an accomplished ballroom dancer and did well in local competitions. There is some evidence to suggest that he used the dancing to play the middle age and senior citizen singles scene—like Mum, needing but never finding that ideal partner.

Dad's first signs of psychiatric imbalance may have surfaced during that family holiday in Cornwall back in 1958, two and a half years before the breakdown of his marriage to Mum. That was the time when he collapsed after a long drive to the holiday camp and a doctor was brought in. We'll never know whether that was the case. What is beyond dispute is that after leaving the marriage, his life went steadily down-hill. I never really knew Dad because he was a hard person to get to know, and my interactions with him after he went his own way were spasmodic and separated by long periods of time. This very complex man had many dimensions to his character. He was an introvert who blended into the back-ground—a loner who was lonely. He did not mix well and hence had few, if any, real friends. He came across as emo-tionless, unable to show warmth. Sadness and worry were his hallmarks. He must have harboured intense feelings that he was unable to express constructively, sensitivities that from time to time that flooded to the surface and led to impulsive, irrational, compulsive, and even criminal behaviours.

To say that he had passive-aggressive tendencies would understate the case. His spirit was a damaged one that cried out for what is nowadays called holistic treatment—under-standing, patience, and love from the few who were near to him and proper psychiatric help from the medical profession. I believe he received neither one in anything approaching an adequate measure. When he left the family home he became a pariah to those of us he had left behind and as he drifted around the ballroom scene, he was never able to find emo-tional satisfaction, a partner to absorb some of the strength of his anxieties. As for the psychiatric help that he should have had, when he was most in need of it, the state threw him in jail. Both the verdict and the sentence arising from his court case were abominations. He was clearly mentally incapacitated. Poor Dad. We all should have done more.

~~~~~

After Dad died, I paid a couple more visits to Sheffield. On each occasion, I found myself taking a dart in the rental car over to the Stradbroke estate, parking it outside the old home, sitting, pondering, and reflecting. But, I made no attempt to track down Mum.

August 2009 saw me retired from academia and working on my memoir and family genealogy. Alison and I travelled down from Scotland, where we had attended a wedding of one of Alison's relatives, to spend three weeks in Sheffield. I spent much of my time in the Archives and Local Studies sections of the central library poring through old newspaper records, searching through street directories and electoral registers, and scanning microfiches of ancestors from centuries past. I was immersed in a mission to document my life and the lives of others who had preceded me in my family tree.

It was only during the last few days of our visit that I decided to try to find Mum. Twenty years had passed since that day trip to Chatsworth Park and we had not exchanged a word, written or spoken, since then. I had no idea where she might be living or if she were even alive. To make matters worse, I had few clues to go by. I had long ago lost that piece of paper on which she had scribbled her address on the

Base Green estate. Tracing Mum's whereabouts was not easy after a separation of over twenty years. If she were alive, she would be eighty-six now. I tried using Internet search engines to locate Lisa, but to no avail. I phoned around numerous homes in the city where someone was living with a name that I thought Mum or Lisa might be using, even visited one home where I was told that it was not the right person. But, a few days before we were due to return to Canada, I found Mum. After pouring through year after year of electoral registers at the Local Studies library in Sheffield, I discovered that she had changed her surname, but disappeared from the record four years ago. With the help of the city's Registrar of Births, Deaths, and Marriages and a computer search engine, I discovered that she was in a nursing home. When I telephoned the home, I was told that she had received no visitors since being admitted with dementia six years ago.

On a sunny August afternoon, I find myself at Beech knoll Residential Care Home—a place for the old and infirm, where weary souls and disintegrating bodies are cared for around the clock. In what seems like a cruel reversion to childhood, these once proud citizens of the state receive the most intimate attention from the dedicated staff. Spooning pureed food into sunken mouths, wiping drool from lumpy chins, lathering and oiling folds of skin, and changing diapers are all in a day's work. Where is the dignity? I peer through the glass windows of the day room. Residents, as they are euphemistically called, sit scattered around, hunched over at tables or in wheelchairs, staring into space. Here and there, nursing aides, women in the prime of their lives, stand—keeping watch over their flock. It is a sad but peaceful scene and I am about to enter it. I will be the only man in the room.

"Nellie's over there, 'avin' a nap on t'sofa," says the aide standing beside me.

And so she is. Curled up in the fetal position, her back to me, her head facing the back of the sofa and snuggled into her belly. She looks nothing like the Mum I once knew all those years ago and yet I know it is she. I am her son. I walk over to her and reach down to put my arms around her frail shoulders.

"Mum, it's me. Roger. Your son. From Canada."

She reaches up to hold me, still looking into the sofa.

"I've found you at last," I say.

As I lead her gently away from the sofa, I look up at the staff. They are wiping tears from their faces. I let mine fall.

"She recognized you," says one of the aides excitedly. "You know who this is, don't you Nellie?"

"I made 'im," Mum responds, her limited vocabulary sufficient to convey a message that was infinitely more profound than it sounded.

We walk the corridors hand in hand. We pass through day rooms where worn-out souls stare at television screens, the volume on full blast, blaring out day time soaps and game shows. We brush past one small side table where half a set of false teeth is sitting. *Where's the other half?* I wonder. Mum sits down on a chair next to another table, which displays a half-eaten, decidedly lonely, chocolate biscuit. She picks up the biscuit and begins to eat it. As we continue our walking tour of the premises, I proclaim "she's my Mum" to residents and staff alike.

I leave her for a short while, sitting in a chair, to talk to a staff member about her condition. When I return, the chair is empty. I find Mum sprawled on the floor of a day room. She has fallen down. As a staff member and I help her to her feet, a well-spoken middle-aged lady, one of the residents, touches my arm and asks:

"Is she your Mum?"

"Yes," I reply.

"Oh, because I just wanted to let you know that I think she's getting a bit forgetful."

The staff member and I look at one another. We cannot help but smile.

We return to her small room—a bed, a chest of drawers, and a bedside table. We sit together on the bed holding hands, Mum clutching one of the teddy bears that the staff has supplied to her. The few photographs on display are of people I do not recognize. What has happened to Mum's past? Has someone taken her possessions, her mementos, and replaced them with photos of strangers or at best, distant relatives? I talk to Mum about her dad, her Mum, Talbot Place, carefully navigating around the subject of my Dad. From time to time, she shows faint glimmers of interest, or is it just my imagination? When I ask her if she remembers the carthorses that her dad used to own and she says "yes," is she really just saying what I want to hear? What a cruel irony this is. One of Mum's famous "feel sorry for me" rants used to be that she couldn't wait until the day that she would be in a nursing home with people to look after her.

"Can't think er owt better than ter put me feet up. People cookin' me meals, makin' me bed, cleanin' me room. Smashin', that'll be."

I don't think she had her current predicament in mind.

She continues to look at the floor. The glimmer of light is fading. She is a hollow shell–a bitter irony for this once self-reliant woman to end her days this way. Outspoken, dogmatic, volatile, self important, often uncaring. My mother was all these and more. I have many emotional bruises to bear as witness to the days when our lives were intertwined. For all these years, I have nursed my wounds, unable to forgive her. Our relationship was at best distant, at worst non-existent. But, now I see that forgiveness, not resentment, is the only way toward peace within one's soul. My mother, as she once was, no longer exists. The person whom I have come to visit is a feeble old lady, one who has lived her troubled life, and one who is without the warmth of her family. She needs me.

After returning to Canada, I received an email from a friend of mine back in Sheffield alerting me to the fact that Ben King, Lisa's son and my nephew, had posted a message on a Sheffield Forum website. He had recognized me from my user name and postings as his uncle. After a sequence of emails and telephone calls, I was reunited with my sister, Lisa. It was time for me to pay another visit to Sheffield. So, in the summer of 2010, Alison and I made another trip to the Steel City. This was a visit that called for a family reunion, so I made the necessary arrangements. What a remarkable scene that was on a partly sunny August evening in 2010 on the steps of the Town Hall in Sheffield. My sister, brother, and myself, Mum's three off-spring, each estranged from her and from one another for varying periods of time, gathered together. We all had a meal at a downtown pub. I wish that I could report that the camarade-rie that was so evident on that occasion was of the permanent variety. However, I have learned that nothing is permanent in the Bonsall/Gordon clan. Alas, my relationship with my brother has since taken another nosedive.

During the 2010 trip, I visited Mum at the nursing home. Her condition was much the same. Since then, Lisa, who like myself was unaware of her whereabouts, visited Mum—along with her two sons, Ben and Sam.

Like Dad, Mum was plagued with psychiatric illness. In her case, like myself, she suffered from depression and spent

STARTING TO FRAME | 389

time at Whitely Wood Clinic. The day after Alison and I were married in June 1970, I phoned Mum at the King residence, as arranged, from the Sunshine Coast in British Columbia, where we were spending part of our honeymoon. A weak voice answered the phone.

"I din't want ter tell yer. Wudda spoiled yer weddin'. I've been let out for t'weekend so's I can speak ter yer. I'm in Whiteley Woods. I lit a candle for yer yesterday..." and so the cheerful patter went on.

That put a bit of a damper on proceedings. It wouldn't have been so bad if I had known the situation, but she thought she was protecting me from the harsh realities of life. Didn't I already know a bit about depression and Whitely Wood Clinic?

I cannot comment knowledgeably about the quality of psychiatric care that she received, but I was not impressed when Mum told me one day that she felt vindicated about her choice to sever all ties with several of her family members because the psychiatrist had told her to remember that "God gave us our relatives; thank God we can choose our friends."

Oh, dear. That old Ethel Watts Mumford[34] chestnut. Just what Mum needed to hear.

So, I look at Mum as I look at Dad, as someone who has a damaged spirit, psychiatrically impaired. In her case, her preoccupation was mostly for herself, but like Dad, she yearned for true affection from the opposite sex and she never found it.

The exact opposite to Dad, her extrovert personality was accompanied by a good dose of tempestuousness, anger, and bitterness. But, like Dad, her fortunes progressively declined after the break up of their marriage. I have regrets about the way I treated Mum, as I know that I played my part in the family shenanigans. But, I believe that she received a better deal from others around her and from me than Dad did.

Until my retirement in January 2008, my two foci had been my Canadian family and my academic career. I was a hard worker who set his hand firmly to the plough. True, I paid sporadic visits to the city where I had spent the first twenty-six years of my life and I corresponded with family members who still lived there. But in reality, I had kept the place and the memories that it harboured at arms' length from my deepest thoughts. I had every intention of continuing in the same vein in my retirement years—acting as a scientific consultant, writing a biology text book, using the skills that I had honed over my career as a scientist and academic. Then one day, I was sharing my feelings about my Sheffield family with a friend of mine, when he suggested that I write about it. It was at that moment that I realized that I wanted my retirement to be spent in a quite different fashion than doing "more of the same." I needed to bring those arms in closer to my body and try to come to terms with a past that is part of who I am. Emily Dickinson[35] once said: *The past is not a package one can lay away.* To a great extent, I did lay it away for four decades. I kept it in two cardboard boxes.

Time to pack away the boxes now.

---

32     William Butler Yeats (1865–1939); Source of quotation unknown.

33     North American: a "pacifier."

34     Ethel Watts Mumford (1876–1940) was a U.S. novelist and playwright, best known for some of her memorable quotations.

35     Emily Dickinson (1830-1886), renowned 19th century American poet.

# EPILOGUE

Through emails and phone calls to the Beechy Knoll staff, I kept abreast of Mum's condition as best as I could. I spoke with Mum on a couple of occasions, but there was no meaningful comprehension. Mum spoke in gibberish, while I am sure that I came across in the same way to her. Did she or could she have wondered who I was? The phrase "nobody at home" accurately, though unkindly, characterizes who Mum had become. I did keep a promise that I had made to myself and insured that she received cards, flowers, and whatever else seemed fitting on her birthdays, Christmas, and Mother's Day as per the British calendar. Was there a tinge of remorse embedded in these gestures— ones that had passed their "due by" dates? Maybe, but I am satisfied that my feelings and motives were rooted in genuine compassion.

At 3 a.m. Atlantic Standard Time on December 20, 2011, the ringing of the phone woke me. I knew what it was.

"She went very peacefully," said the caregiver.

It was a cold and blustery Friday afternoon at the City Road crematorium in Sheffield on January 6, 2012. A small group of family members sat on one side of the sanctuary, a larger one from the nursing home on the other side. The family contingent comprised ten in all, including Alison and myself, and Alison's two cousins and their spouses who had never seen Mum but nonetheless, made the trip down from Scotland to offer their support. Mum's casket was surrounded by photographs of her in her younger days. She deserved to be remembered as someone more than her years at Beechy Knoll would have signified. I spoke selectively about the fond memories that I have of her, mostly in my early childhood, before she became the kind of person who would have been difficult to eulogize. Lisa read a poem. The Catholic sister who led the service, but who had never met Mum, did her best to generalize and fill in airtime. Mum, the staunch anti-Catholic in her heyday, must have been tossing and turning inside the casket. When there was nothing more to be said or recorded songs to be heard, we all marched out to the strains of Vera Lynne singing, "We'll Meet Again." Then, Lisa, her sons Ben and Sam, along with Alison and myself placed roses on Grandma and Granddad Bonsall's grave, which was nearby.

It was an inauspicious end to an often troubled and turbulent life. I like to think that in amongst it all, Mum found some measure of contentment. She was the last of her generation as far as my particular branch of the Bonsall family tree goes. Her life now spent, she leaves me with more questions than answers. But, I shall not ponder either of them any longer.

Now that both of my parents have died, there is little reason

394 | Roger Gordon

for me to visit Sheffield. Yet, I still maintain an interest in past and current events there. Digital technology is a great enabler. As well as participating in a Sheffield Forum website, I listen to live broadcasts of every Sheffield Wednesday game, cheering every time they score a goal. Alas, this has not been very often lately. I even join in the camaraderie of a Sheffield Wednesday fans' on-line forum. The fact that I am triple the age of most of the fans on that web site is appreciated by one and all.

Since immigrating to Canada all those years ago, I have left my past locked away in cardboard boxes and within the recesses of my mind. After retiring from academia, I decided to pause and take a peek. But, now I can hear that sixties group, The Byrds, singing, "Turn, Turn, Turn."[36] Yes, to everything there is a season. For me, it is a time to move on, untrammelled by the past, and with hope and optimism for the future. For both my parents, my wish is that it is indeed "a time of peace."

---

36   A hit song by The Byrds in 1965. Pete Seeger composed the music. The words of the song were adapted from the book of Ecclesiastes (3:1) in The Bible.

# GLOSSARY

**Note to readers:** The Sheffield vernacular is best appreciated by reading it at normal speed and grasping the meaning as one goes along. Although some of the vocabulary may be unfamiliar, the meaning can usually be discerned without referring to a word-by-word translation. Saying that, I can give you two helpful tips.

First, the letter "h" is rarely used to begin a word; if a word beginning with a vowel does not make sense, the reader can try placing a letter "h" in front of the vowel (e.g., "'ouse" = "house").

Second, in spoken Sheffield dialect, the definite article is not used. Instead, a consonant sound known as a *glottal stop*, which is a strange combination of a pause and a grunt, is used. In written form, this glottal stop is denoted by a t' (for "the") preceding the next noun (e.g., "I've taken t'dogs for a walk" = "I've taken the dogs for a walk").

A list of Sheffield (many of them Northern England) expressions is presented below for anyone finding mastery of this dialect challenging. For readability, I have attempted to simplify it throughout.

**Abart**: About

**Allus:** Always

**Ampt:** Haven't

**An't:** Hasn't

**An all:** As well

**Blinder:** Great performance

**Chuff:** A derogatory term applied to someone who is offensive; milder than some other nouns such as bastard, bugger, or varmint

**Chuffed:** To feel pleased

**Chuffin:** A milder and less crude form of the British swear word "bloody," used pejoratively as an adjective in every day speech (e.g. That chuffin kid from next door is throwin rocks at t'street lamps again.")

**Chuff off:** Take off

**'Cus:** Because

**Darn:** Down

**Dinnit:** Didn't it

**Din't:** Didn't

**Dun't:** Doesn't

**Er:** Her or of

**Eyup:** See here

**Fag:** Cigarette, or a first-year student at High Storrs

**Gander:** Look

**Gerrin:** Getting or Get in

**Gerroff:** Get off

**Gerron:** Get on

**Gerrout:** Get out.

**Gerrup:** Get up

**Gio'er:** Give over!

**Innit:** Isn't it

**In't:** Isn't

**Inter:** Into

**Lerrit:** Let it

**Mardy:** Grumpy, sulking

**Mek(kin):** Make(ing)

**Misen:** Myself

**Moore:** More

**Nowt:** Nothing

**O'er:** Over

**Outter:** Out of

**Oreight:** Alright

**Owt:** Anything

**Puff:** Derogatory slang for male homosexual.

**Reight:** Right

**Shun't:** Shouldn't

**Sithee:** Imagine that!

**Slash:** Defaecation

**Smashin:** Great, delightful

**Summat:** Something

**Sods:** Similar to chuffs, a derogatory term applied to someone

**Soddin:** Similar to chuffin; Adjective intensifier

**Summat:** Something

**Tek(kin):** Take (ing)

**Tekin:** Taking

**Ter:** To

**Thee'sen:** Your self

**Thersens:** Themselves

**T'owdlad**: "the old lad," an affectionate term for a male, usually senior, person

**Turrah:** Good bye

**Wi:** With

**Yer:** You or Your

# Acknowledgements

This book has been the result of approximately six years research, contemplation, and writing. It has brought a spectrum of feelings to the surface of my mind, ranging from agony and dejection to celebration and satisfaction. It has not been an easy task. It could not have been completed without the support and assistance of a number of people who have played key roles in its development. First and foremost, I wish to thank my wife, Alison Gordon, for all the encouragement she has given me throughout this endeavour. I could not have embarked upon such a project as this without her tremendous support. I am grateful also to three people who played a key role in the polishing of the text. Prince Edward Island author Jane Ledwell conducted an insightful critique of my first draft, while my daughter, Christine Gordon Manley of Manley Mann Media, did a first-rate job of editing the script for publication. Jaime Lee Mann of Manley Mann Media also reviewed my first draft and provided welcome encouragement. Members of my writing group have played a valuable role in maintaining my interest in creative writing and on occasion, offering comments of snippets of the early narrative of this book. I am grateful to PEI authors Libby Oughton and Dianne Morrow, whose courses on creative and life writing acted as a catalyst for my creative juices.

I am greatly indebted to Prince Edward Island author Patti Larsen who graciously and expertly guided me through the self-publishing process—a task that appeared at first daunting, but which I managed to navigate with her invaluable mentoring. In this regard, I also appreciate the helpfulness of Valerie Bellamy of Dog-ear Book Design, Nova Scotia, who masterfully provided the expertise needed for the cover and interior designs of this book.

I spent two summers poring over old editions of the *Sheffield Star* and *Sheffield Telegraph* at the Local Studies Library on Surrey Street in Sheffield. I appreciate the help that the staff there provided in enabling me to use the microfiche machines and card index system efficiently. A special thanks is extended to Gillian Richards, Registrar of Births, Marriages and Deaths for Sheffield, who provided valuable assistance in tracking down my mother's status and whereabouts. I am indebted to a host of posters on the internet site Sheffield Forum (**www.sheffieldforum.co.uk**), especially those who have posted on the History and Expats section of the site. Reflections and memories of days gone by have been helpful in enabling me to recreate the past.

Aside from the *Sheffield Star* and *Sheffield Telegram* newspapers, and of course my own memory, I found a publication by the *Star* helpful in reconstructing life in the 1960s: *Sheffield in the Sixties* by Peter Goodman (Breedon Books, 2001). The web site by Sheffield historian, Chris Hobbs, contained useful information about the Sheffield Gale of 1962. As well, the online BBC archives (**www.bbc.co.uk/archive**) were consulted from time to time, as were several other web sites, too numerous to mention.

Without the collection of old letters and memorabilia that I have safeguarded over several decades, it would have been difficult to have reconstructed events in Sheffield that occurred after I relocated to Canada.

# ABOUT THE AUTHOR

 Roger Gordon was born in 1943 in Sheffield, England, where he spent the first 26 years of his life. After obtaining his B.Sc. and Ph.D in Zoology from Sheffield University, he immigrated to Canada in 1969. He pursued a successful career as a scientist and faculty member at three Canadian universities and served as Dean of Science at the University of Prince Edward Island from 1997–2006. Author of approximately 60 scientific publications, Roger has also received awards in three annual competitions sponsored by the Prince Edward Island Writers' Guild for his literary compositions. He is now retired from academia and lives with his wife, Alison, and his family on Prince Edward Island.

Made in the USA
Charleston, SC
12 April 2015